पुरातत्त्व

PURĀTATTVA

Bulletin of the Indian Archaeological Society

No. 26 1995-96

Editors

K. N. Dikshit & K.S. Ramachandran

Assisted by

S. Ganesh Rao and Ashwani Asthana

D.K. Printworld (P) Ltd.

New Delhi

Cataloging in Publication Data — DK
[Courtesy : D.K. Agencies (P) Ltd. <docinfo@dkagencies.com>]

Purātattva : bulletin of the Indian Archaeological Society, no. 26, 1995-96 / editor, K.N. Dikshit & K.S. Ramachandran.
p. cm.
Includes bibliographical references.
ISBN 8124603014

1. Archaeology — India — Periodicals. 2. India — Antiquities — Periodicals. 3. India — Civilization — Periodicals. I. Dikshit, K.N. II. Ramachandran, K.S. (Kattalai Sivasubramanium), 1939- III. Indian Archaeological Society.

First Published in 1996
First Reprinted in 2005
ISBN 81-246-0301-4
Price for volume 26 (1995-96): Rs. 800 US $ 40

Reprint authorised by
Indian Archaeological Society
New Delhi - 110 016

Purātattva is published annually.

Manuscripts (whether in the form of articles or notes or book reviews) offered for publication should be sent to the Editor, Purātattva, Indian Archaeological Society, B-17, Qutab Institutional Area, New Delhi - 110 016.

Published and printed by:
D.K. Printworld (P) Ltd.
'Srikunj,' F-52, Bali Nagar
New Delhi – 110015
Phone : (011) 2545 3975, 2546 6019 Fax : (011) 2546 5926
E-mail : dkprintworld@vsnl.net
www. dkprintworld.com

PURĀTATTVA

CONTENTS

Obituaris

Professor B.N. Puri
(1916-1996)

Born on 25 January, 1916, Dr. Baij Nath Puri passed his M.A. and LL.B. from Lucknow University in 1937 and 1939, respectively. He took in 1944 training in Field Archaeology under Sir Mortimer Wheeler from Archaeological Training School at Taxila. He joined as Lecturer in Ancient Indian History and rose to the position of Professor and Head of the Department in Lucknow University. From 1961 to 1971, he was Professor in the National Academy of Administration and used his time at the Academy to add to his publications. His first book in Hindi - *Puratattva Vijnana* was published in 1952 and in English - *India in the times of Patanjali* in 1957. He has to his credit 32 books and numerous articles in different journals of the country and abroad. His *History of Gurjara Pratiharas* with a foreward by T. Burrow, *India as described by Early Greek Writers*, *India under the Kushanas*, *Secularism in Indian Ethos*, etc. are a few outstanding publications. His last contribution was *Ancient Indian Historiography - A Bicentenary* in 1994.

Dr. Puri loved to read biographies and autobiographies, music and poetry and also religious texts. In his own words 'Both God and religion are firmly integrated in my life. I have derived great solace from both. My religion is universal in the sense that I have always welcomed anything and everything from any quarter which I find interesting and helpful'.

Dr. Puri is no more with us but his image with three piece suit, a bag, astylistic felt hat, and an umbrella will always haunt all his admirers, students, friends and colleagues for all time to come.

Shantaram Bhalchandra Deo
(1923-1996)

Born on 9th June 1923 at Talegaon Dhandhere, Dist. Pune, Prof. Deo had his early education at Pune and graduated from Fergusson College and took his M.A., in Pali and Ardhamagadi from Bombay University in 1947. He received his Ph.D. on Jain in Monachism from Inscriptions and Literature from Bombay University in 1952.

Beginning his career in the Deccan college as a Lecturer, he rose to the highest position of Director of the organization which he held till his retirement in 1985. In between he had been out of the Deccan College to become the Professor of Ancient Indian History and Culture at the Tribhuvan University, Kathmandu, and Professor and Head of the Department, Ancient Indian History, Culture and Archaeology, Nagpur University, Nagpur.

After his retirement in July, 1985, he served as Director B.L. Institute of Indology, Delhi for a year and later worked on ICHR Projects under Senior Fellowship scheme.

In his long academic career, Deo had visited many foreign countries such as USA, U.K., USSR and continental Europe for delivering lectures and participating in seminars and conferences. Prof. Deo has more than 35 books (some jointly written) and excavation Reports and hundreds of research articles to his credit in the fields of Archaeology, Indology and Indian Culture.

The death of Prof. Deo leaves a great void in the field of Archaeology and Culture which will be difficult to fill for years to come.

Prof. Lakshmi Kant Tripathi
(1952-1995)

Born and brought up at Unnao, a small district of Uttar Pradesh, Prof. Tripathi remained close to his roots all his life. He was a bright student earning his Bachelor's degree from Agra University in Ist division, Banaras Hindu University drew his attention as a centre of Sanskrit learning which he wished to take up for higher studies. Instead, he became a student of Ancient Indian History, Culture and Archaeology earning a degree with high marks and a prestigious rank in his batch. Almost immediately after, he started his career with a service in the Archaeological Survey of India, New Delhi. But later joined the Banaras Hindu University as a Lecturer. He continued to serve this Institute till his last days. He appeared to possess grit and perseverence of purpose right from his early days of his career. This manifested itself throughout his life, paving a way upto the high post of Readership of Banaras Hindu University, the very institution where he was once a student. He had also held other administrative positions like the Headship of the Department of AIHC & Archaeology and Deanship of the Faculty of Arts of Banaras Hindu University.

He had organised a number of national and international seminars, conferences and workshops. Between 1985 and 1992, he had organised about nine academic meets of various dimensions. His international seminar on the Buddhist *Stupa* in India and South-East Asia at B.H.U. had attracted scholars of Art and Architecture from different parts of the world.

The field of AIHC & Archaeology will miss his thundering invocations, refutations and assertions in course of discussions during the seminars and conferences. He generated heated debates, inspired enthusiastic participation into otherwise dull academic discussions..

Sita Ram Tripathi
(1907-1996)

Pt. Sita Ram Tripathi was an apostle of Sanskrit learning and an embodiment of Indian culture. He was a true scholar pursuing knowledge for the sake of knowledge, dedicating himself to ancient Sanskrit texts without the slightest expectations of returns of any kind. There would scarcely be a text or commentary in Sanskrit or regional language on Mahabharata, Gita and Bhagvata Mahapurana which he has not gone through with a thoroughness of dedicated scholar. In the line of the older generations of scholars of Varanasi, he was known to be an authority on Sanskrit grammar and perhaps the most profound scholar on Bhagvata Mahapurana and the Bhagwat Gita. He virtually knew these texts by heart and a deep understanding of the meaning and implications of the complex verses.

His exclusive qualities caught the attention of Pt. Madan Mohan Malaviyaji, the founder of Banaras Hindu University. He groomed him for imparting moral-spiritual training to the young students. Sita Ram Tripathi was entrusted with the job of teaching this subject to the aspiring graduates of B.H.U. for decades. The number of students whom he taught was so large wherever he went he was recognised by his old students. His kindly and inspiring personality of a true teacher had won him affectionate regards from this large population of students.

His passing away has left a void in Sanskrit learning.

PURĀTATTVA

Number 26 **1995-96**

Editorial

Puratattva No.26 is placed here. We have tried to accommodate as many articles as we could; we wish we had more financial support to include more pages in the present issue. We hope to able to do it from the next number.

The Board of Management of the Society has selected Dr. Y.D. Sharma, former Deputy Director General, Archaeological Survey of India, for the 'V.S. Wakankar Award for Excellence in Field Archaeology' for the block year 1995-1996. We take this opportunity of felicitating him. The award will be conferred on him on the 24th of Nov. 1996 at the inaugural function of the forthcoming Annual Conference of the Society.

This year we are holding the XXX Annual Conference of the Indian Archaeological Society in the premises of the Society; we are thus 30 years old as of now. ; the Society was founded in 1967 at the Banaras Hindu University by Prof. A.K. Narain and his colleagues. The conference is being held for the first time in the premises of the Society which should give a great sense of satisfaction and achievement to all of us. This became possible, as we all know, solely due to the generous gesture of making the land available to us by the late Dr. Devahuti, and the Late Prof. D.P. Singhal, her husband.

During these three decades what we have achieved is common knowledge; the achievements have been very modest indeed, mainly due to the lack of adequate finances to support the publication and training programmes. There has been a suggestion to get the publications made by private publishers. We have been doing it, more than a dozen titles have appeared by this system, but it has not brought either any credit to the Society or any notable financial earnings. To put our publication programme on a viable footing we need a sum of five to ten lakhs rupees as revolving fund so that the programme of our publications does not feel any financial crunch. To begin with, we are planning a series of books of about 100 pages each.

From 1997 onwards we are also planning to start a few teaching and training programmes on archaeology, art and other cognate subjects, of course, depending upon the availability of funds and the human resource.

Unfortunately, we could not start our major building in spite of our best efforts; may be 1997 turns out to be the lucky year in this regard. We are trying our best to enlist the support of our well-wishers.

In the publication of this number many people have helped us in many ways. We are extremely thankful to our Assistant Editors for their untiring efforts in finalising the manuscript for the press. Shri Ashwani Asthana has further helped us in formatting the entire manuscript in Society's own computer along with Shri Rakesh, our office in-charge. But, for these two present issue could not have been printed.

We thank the Director General, Archaeological Survey of India, and the Chairman, ICHR, for the financial assistance they gave to us for the publication of this number.

Finally, we thank Dr. S.P. Gupta our Chairman, who has, during the last two decades, done more than anyone else in the country to serve the cause of Indian archaeology through non-governmental agencies.

– Editors

Faunal Quantification : Review of New Trends

P.P. JOGLEKAR*

Archaeozoology, like other sister disciplines such as palaeontology, palaeobotany and palynology, is in the process of using postulates or axioms based on mathematical foundations and thus is increasingly depending on numerical methods leading to quantification (use of numbers).

It is necessary to follow changes in the faunal quantification by looking at two allied disciplines — palaeontology and archaeozoology — which work on animal remains yet which have their roots in different disciplines - biology and social science- respectively. A complete review of the trends in quantification is required since the available commentaries/parts of reviews are isolated, inadequate and not comprehensive. Quantification is not just the use of numbers or percentages. Neither is it restricted to the measurements of taxonomic abundance nor to bones. Quantification is an application of statistical tools along with the associated theories and logical constructs.

The aim of this paper is to provide a review of the general trends in faunal quantification, with an emphasis on recent developments in the techniques and concepts in archaeozoology as well as review the position of Indian archaeozoology in these recent developments.

Development in Palaeontology

Since the early work of Romer and Prince (1940), many palaeontologists have attempted the use of statistical techniques. An important methodological problem in palaeontology is, how to compare the faunal list from two or more sites. Many indices of faunal similarity are available and they are used routinely in palaeontology e.g. Jacquard coefficient and Dice coefficient (Fallow 1979)

Many mathematical techniques have been used with remarkable success in order to compare measurements taken on fossils. A review of palaeontological literature reveals that palaeontologists have gone beyond the initial phase of "just application" and are now fully furnished with the necessary mathematical models to interpret the outcome of mathematical techniques.

Developments in Archaeozoology

During the early days of archaeozoological work, often the material was discarded without realising its scientific potential. Many times, the study was confined only to the best preserved specimens. Obviously, the role of quantification was yet to be perceived.

The general pattern of archaeozoological research in the direction of quantification has always been to resolve the following problems: (a) represent taxonomic richness of various species, (b) ageing and sexing, and (c) estimation of the body-size using the bones from archaeological contexts.

Measures of Taxonomic Abundance

Quantification of faunal remains-describing animal bones using numbers is widely used in archaeozoology. Several methods of counting bones are available, like

*Deccan College, Pune

simple number of the Identifiable specimens (NISP); calculations of Minimum Number of Individuals (MNI) or its variants such as the Minimum Number of Animal Units (MAU) and the Modified general Utility Index (MGU); and the weight method.

All these methods have inherent advantages as well as disadvantages. None of the above methods is 'error proof' and thus use of either of them or a combination has became indispensable in modern faunal studies, because they provide the necessary objective frame of reference to compare faunal assemblages from different sites.

Serious objections are being raised against all these methods based on the study of taphonomy and human behaviour. Several behavioural and taphonomic factors such as the post-depositional preservation conditions are likely to affect the survival probability of a bone. This is obvious because the sample passes through a variety of stages before it reaches the archaeozoologist for identification and subsequent statistical treatment.

As early as the 1970s Clason (1972) and Uerpmann (1973) pointed out the importance of not only the identifiable material, but also the unidentifiable fragments. These fragments if quantified can tell us about the representatives of the identified material. A rather different approach has been taken by During (1985, 1986) to solve the problem of bone material that cannot be assigned to species level. An elaborately discussed method of 'Q-score' has been proposed which is based on principles of statistical sampling theory.

It is necessary to recognise that there cannot be any ultimate solution to the problems of deposition and the interference of taphonomic factors. The situation does not call for acute pacifism.

Perusal of the available literature on faunal reports in the Indian context reveals that firstly, in many of the publications there is no mention of the animal remains found at the site e.g. Prakash - a Chalcolithic site in Maharashtra. It is obviously unlikely that no bones were encountered during the excavation at Prakash. In many cases we have nothing to work on and thus the question of quantification does not arise.

Secondly, several excavation reports deal with selective collections. These type are of reports just lists of the animal species found at the site e.g. George (1955) who studied the animal remains at Nasik and Jorwe, has not mentioned about the quantity of bones recovered and analysed. Rao (1968) has studied exactly 100 bone fragments (out of what total quantity is not mentioned), Shah (1968) in her study of bones from Kaundinyapura provided the trench-wise distribution of species encountered. This was a significant feature of her study.

The reports of animal remains from Rangapur (Nath 1963) and those from Ahar (Shah 1969) are also important because the authors had given a detailed distribution of bones in such a manner that it could be re-analysed and quantified. The animal remains at Kayatha studied by Alur (1975) indicate a new way of interpretation of faunal data. Thomas (1977) started a detailed study of osteometric as also the quantitative methods in the faunal studies. His thesis on the Mesolithic sites of Bagor and Tilwara and the Chalcolithic sites of Prabhas Patan and Khanpur show several quantitative techniques used for drawing conclusions about the ancient food economy.

A review of faunal reports published since 1980 show an increasing tendency to apply quantitative methods. The study of faunal remains at Inamgaon by Thomas (1988) deserves special mention because of three reasons. Firstly, the report has dealt with faunal quantification methods like MNI, NISP, Meat weight of animals, etc. Secondly, the publication has given detailed spatial and temporal distribution of bones. Thirdly, the report has discussed the methods in detail ; the report is a comprehensive study of Chalcolithic fauna at Inamgaon.

Aging-Sexing and Species Identification from Animal Bones

Aging and sexing of bones unearthed at archaeological sites are two basic problems in archaeozoological research. Using biometric methods, the first phalanges of cattle (of unknown breeds) were examined in order to distinguish males from females.

Bones of American bison (Bison bison) were examined statistically by Skinner and Kaisen (1947) which revealed that sexes can be separated on the basis of metapodial measurements. A simple index of breadth divided by length enable to separate males from females into two clear zones. In this case, the separation of the sexes was due to the nature of the sample itself. Since American bison was in the wild form, there was no interference of castrated animals. However, this success encouraged other workers to look for such measurements that can achieve sex separation in the archaeological sample.

Zalkin (1960) used bone measurements to separate the sexes in sheep and goats. He used metapodia of sheep and goat to identify sexes using metrical attributes.

Higham (1969) clearly demonstrated that metrical indices can be used for ageing and sexing of ancient populations even if the sample size is around 15-20. This is an important contribution, since it established that a sample as small as 15-20 is adequate.

A major stride towards applications of metrical methods in archaeozoology was taken by von den Driesch (1976), when she published *A Guide to the Measurement of Animal Bones from Archaeological Sites.* This was indeed of immense importance because it achieved standardisation in measurement procedures as can be seen from archaeozoological literature of the post-1976 period.

The most critical issues in archaeozoology are, and have been, the problem of separating loosely related species as well as the separation of domestic/wild forms. A large number of publications are available in which bones measurements have been used with considerable success. The corpus of literature on animal remains from Indian archaeological sites is largely devoid of such efforts except a few.

Morphometry and Estimation of Body Size

The estimation of the body-size or the stature of ancient animals, has assumed importance over the past few years. Estimating stature of ancient domestic animals is especially important from the point of ancient animal husbandry and the domestication process The unit of body size is called Osteometric Linear Unit (OLU). This unit was used for the separation of closely related species, but its use has been restricted to only non-mammalian vertebrate fauna. For unknown reasons, both archaeozoologists and palaeontologits have not followed the method further.

Height at Withers

Metapodial measurements were used for estimation of the height at Withers in cattle by Boessneck (1956) and Zalkin (1960). These two methods are called 'B' and 'Z' methods, respectively.

The estimated height at Withers in cattle has an error range of 1.05 to 2.75 cm and thus can be said to be fairly accurate. A large number of scholars have worked out the factors to obtain the height at Withers for animals other than cattle, e.g. dog, pig, sheep, goat, and sheep /goat.

The very idea of measuring bones emerged rather late in Indian archaeozoology, i.e. 1965 onwards. Thomas (1977) gave a detailed account of the measurements of modern bones and their comparison with archaeological samples. This approach on faunal quantification by Thomas (1977) and Clason (1979) are consequential milestones in morphometry in Indian context.

Live-Weight Estimates

One of the important uses of the measurements is to estimate live weight of the domestic animals and further the usable meat weight. Equations based on a few bones are available which were essentially derived from the data for modern animals. It is notable that there is not much work being done in the direction to establish useful equations for obtaining live-weight estimates in other domestic animals.

Advanced Statistical Methods

An advance in computer technlogy has opened up diverse channels to archaeologists to apply complex and sophisticated multivariate methods. Multivariate methods can be employed effectively during the final stages of exploratory data analysis.

A large number of statistical techniques involving complex numerical operations, and based on advanced theoretical models, are available in literature. These methods include principal component analysis (PCA), riminant functions, cluster diagrams, factor analysis, etc. Essentially, physical anthropologists have actively used such methods to resolve the issues in cranimetry and somatometry. Archaeozoologists too have ventured into the field of multivariate analysis as evidenced from a large number of works.

Specialized Techniques

Several works can be cited in the archaeozoological literature where an attempt has been made to deviate from established procedures and to develop newer tools tc analyze bone material. Some of the noteworthy among these is by Meadow (1984). Meadow has suggested a method of transforming the bone measurements to the log scale and has effectively demonstrated its use to compare relative animal sizes.

Conclusion

A general review of the literature on studies of faunal remains in archaeology (although the literature is simply too vast to be reviewed from all possible angles), established that like the parental branch-archaeology-archaeozoology too has not shied away from asking questions and seeking answers through numerical procedures.

A large number of archaeologists and archaeo-zoologists alike are still reluctant to use statistics on a routine basis, perhaps because they are unaware of the virtually unlimited capabilities of mathematical theory and methods to resolve problems in interpreting the past. Yet another concern, may be of primary nature, is that the application of techniques foreign to the educational background seem to be highly technical and thus hard to comprehend.

Acknowledgements

I am grateful to Prof. A.T. Clason and Dr. W.Prummel (Groningen, The Netherlands) and my teacher Dr. P.K. Thomas for allowing me to use their large collection of archaeozoological articles.

This is a modified version of the paper presented at the Third World Archaeological Congress (WAC-3) held during 4-11 December 1994 at New Delhi.

REFERENCES

Alur, K.R. 1980. Faunal Remains from Vindhyas and the Ganga Valley, in G.R. Sharma, V.D. Misra and J.N. Pal, (eds.) *Excavations at Mahadaha*-1977-78, pp. 89-115, Allahabad: University of Allahabad.

Badam, G.L. 1982 Faunal Remains from Naikund with special reference to Domestication in S.B. Deo and A.P. Jamkhedkar (eds). *Naikund Excavations*, pp,1-22. Pune: Deccan College.

Badam, G.L. 1986. Preliminary Report on the Faunal Remains from Chalcolithic Daimabad, Maharashtra, *Archaeological Studies*, pp. 93-100. Varanasi: Bharat Kala Bhavan.

Becker, C.and F.Johannson 1981. *Saugetiera, in Die Neolithischen Ufersiedlung von Twann*, pp. 35-77. Bern:Zweiter Bericht.

Boessneck, J. 1956. Ein Beitrag zur Errechnung der Widerristhoha nach metapodienmassen bei Rindern, *Zeits-chrift fur Tieezuchtg and Zuchtgsbiol* 68; pp 75-90.

Boessneck, J. and A. von den Driesch 1978. The Significance of Measuring Animal Bones from Archaeological Sites, in R. H. Meadow and M. Zeder (eds.) Archaeological sites, in *Approaches to Faunal Analysis in the Middle East,* pp 2539. Cambridge, Mass, : Peabody Museum.

Brothwell, D.R., A.Malaga and R.Burleigh 1979. Studies on Amerindian dogs, 2: Variation in early Peruvian Dogs, *Journal of Archaeological Science* 6: 139-161.

Chaplin, R.E, 1971. *The Study of Animal Bones from Archaeological Sites,* London and New York: Seminar Press.

Christopher, R.A.. and J.A. Waters 1974. Shape Analysis using fourier transforms, *Journal of Paleontology* 48(4) : 697 - 709.

Clason, A.T. 1972. Some Remarks on the Use and Presentation

of Archaeozoological Data, *Helinium* 12 ; pp 139 - 153.

Driesch, von den A. 1976. *A Guide to the Measurement of Animal bones from Archaeological Sites,* Cambridge, Massachusetts; Harird University Press.

During, E. 1985. On Relative Quantification of Faunal Remains from Archaeological sites, *ISKOS* 5 pp.227-231.

_______, 1986. The Fauna of Alvastra, *OSSA* 12; pp 1-210.

Durr, G. 191. Neue Funde des Rindes aus dem Kelischen Oppidum von Manching, *Studien an vorund frugeschichtlichen Tierrsten Bayerns,* 12, Munich, Kiefhaber and Kiefhaber.

Eisenmann, Vera 1986. Comparative Osteology of Modern and Fossil Horses Half-asses and Asses, in R.H. Meadow and H.P. Uerpmann (eds) *Equids in the Ancient World,* Vol.I, pp. 67-116. Wiesbaden : Dr. Ludwig Reichert Verlag.

Fallow, W.C. 1979. A Test of Simpson Coefficient and Other Binary Coefficients of Faunal Similarity, *Journal of Palaeontology,* 53 pp. 1029-1034.

Fock, J. 1966. *Metrische Untersuchungen an metapodien einiger Europaischer Rinderrassen,* Dissertation, University of Munich.

George, J.C. 1955. Identification of bones in H.D. Sankalia and S.B. Deo (eds). *Report on the Excavations at Nasik and Jorwe* 1950-51, pp. 142-146. Pune : Deccan College Postgraduate and Research Institute.

Higham, C.F.W. 1969. The Metrical Attributes of Two Samples of Bovine Limb Bones, *Journal of Zoology,* London 157, pp. 63-74.

Howard M.M. 1931. The Metrical Determination of the Metapodials and Skulls of Cattle,in Mourant ad Levner (eds). *Man and Cattle,* pp. 91-100. Royal Anthropological Occassional Paper.

Ingren, E. and S.G Stenflo 1982. An Osteological and Statistical Attempt to Interpret Seasonal Occupation of Dwelling Sites in Northern Sweden by Studyng the Beaver *(Castor fiber L.), PACT* 7 : 225-234.

Klein, R.G. and K.Cruz-Uribe 1984: *The Analysis of Animal Bones from Archaeological sites,* University of Chicago Press. Chicago and London.

Kratochvil, Z. 1985. Tierknochenfunde aus der Siedlung Mikulcice (I), *Acta Societatis Scientiarum Naturalium, Brno* 19(8). pp. 1-40.

Kratochvil, Z. 1987a. Tierknochenfunde aus der Siedlung Mikulcice (II), *Acta Societatis Scientiarum Naturalium, Brno* 21(8-9), pp. 1-62.

_______ 1987b. Tierknochenfunde aus der Siedlung Mikulcice (III), *Acta Societatis Scientiarum Naturalium, Brno* 21(11), pp. 1-50.

Lasota-Moskalewska, A. 1984. The Skeleton of a Prehistoric Cow with Characteristics of Both Primigenious and Brachycerous Cattle, *OSSA* 9,pp. 53-72.

Macarthur, R.H. 1971. Bird Species Diversity, *Ecology* 42(3), pp. 594-598.

Meadow, R.H. 1984. Notes on Faunal Remains from Mehrgarh. With a Focus on cattle in B.Allchin (ed.) *South Asian Archaeology,* 1981, pp. 34-40, Cambridge, Cambridge University Press.

Nath, B. 1963. Animal Remains from Rangpur, *Ancient India,* pp.18-19: 153-160.

Prummel, W. 1988. Excavations at Dorestad 2, Nederlandse Oudheden 11, *ROB* : Amersfoort.

Rao, V.V. 1968. Animal Remains from Paunar, in S.B. Deo and M.K.Dhvalikar (eds). *Paunar Excavations,* pp. 117-127, Nagpur : University of Nagpur.

Romer, A.S. and L.T.Prince 1940. Review of the Polycosduriais, *Geological Society of America* 28, pp. 1-538

Sahu, B.P. 1988. *From Hunters to Breeders.* New Delhi: Anamika Prakashan.

Shah, D.R. 1968. Animal Remains from *Excavations at Kaudinyapura,* in M.G. Dikshit (eds). Excavations at Kaudinyapura . pp. 148-157.

Sheldon, A.L. 969. Equitability Indices and Species Counts, *Ecology* 50;pp. 466-467.

Simpson, G.G., A.Rowe and R.Lewonton 1960. *Quantitative Zoology,* New York : McGraw Hill.

Skinner, M.F. and .C. Kaisen 1947. The Fossil Bison of Alaska and a Preliminary Revision of the Genus, *Bulletin of the Americal Museum of Natural History* 89, pp. 127-256.

Thomas, P.K. 1974. Zoological Evidence from Prehistoric India with Special Reference to Domestiction, A Review, *Bulletin of the Deccan College Research Institute,* XXXIV (1-4), pp.

195-210.

________, 1975. Role of animal in the Food Economy of the Mesolithic culture of Western and Central India, in A.T. Clason (ed). *Archaeozoological Studies*, pp. 322-328. Amsterdam : North Holland.

________. 1988. Faunal Assemblage, in *Excavation at Inamgaon*, Vol.I, Part ii (in M.K.Dhavalikar, H.D. Sankalia and Z.D. Ansari(eds.). pp. 822-961. Pune, Deccan College.

Uerpman, H.P. 1973 Animal Bone Finds and Economics, Archaeological, A Critical Study of Osteo- Archaeological Methods, *World Archaeology* 4;pp.307-322

Zalkin, V.I. 1960. Metapodial Variation and Its Significance for the Study of Ancient Cattle, *Bull. Moskova Obshch. Ispit . Pri. Biol.* n.s. 65(1),pp.109-126.

Sothi Pottery at Kalibangan: A Reappraisal

J.S. Nigam*

Kalibangan (29° 29' N; 74° 08' E), Distt. Hanumangarh, (formerly Ganganagar) with its triple mounds is situated on the left bank of the now dried up Sarasvati river. The largest mound lies in the middle, on the west is the 'citadel' mound, and on the east a small low mound believed to be a ritual centre. These are known as KLB-2, KLB-1 and KLB-3 respectively. Here a large-scale excavation was planned and commenced by B.B Lal in 1960 on behalf of the Archaeological Survey of India. Later, it was excavated jointly by others and carried out till 1969. But for the summary of each season's findings and stray writings, details of the excavated remains and materials are generally unknown.

The author was associated with these excavations for several seasons, and besides actual digging had the responsibility to study the excavated objects, especially the pottery. During the first season of the excavation the discovery of a new type of pottery had been reported. "From their co-occurrence with the typical Harappan pottery on the one hand and the level of their occurrence on the other, it appears that they formed part and parcel of the Harappan complex in its earlier stages but went out of vogue in the later" (*IAR* 60-61:32). The picture became clear from the second season's work and the author's association began henceforth.

The extensive excavation at the site were preceded by exploration in the region by Ghosh (1951). He had visited Sothi and Nohar as well as Kalibangan. He also had excavated at Sothi (1952). The relationship between the two types of pottery, nonetheless, remained unsolved.

However, the excavations at Kalibangan revealed the stratigraphic position of the non-Harappa and Mature Harappan pottery. Ghosh (1965) had rightly christened this non-Harappan pottery as 'Sothi Ware'. While discussing the non-Harappan pottery from Kalibangan here, the same will be called Sothi Ware belonging to the Sothi Culture. However, in India the term 'pre-Harappan' and in Pakistan 'Early Harappan' are in usage for this assemblage.

The exciting discovery of the vestiges of the Sothi culture, in the lowest levels of the citadel mound, hereafter referred to as KLB-1, perched right on the natural soil with a habitation deposit of 1.60 m yielded remains of this complex. The pottery during the field study with a view to distinguishing the same from the well known Mature Harappan ceramics, was tentatively classified, based on the individualistic features, into six fabrics, named from A to F. Since no attempt has been made to give a proper name to the Sothi pottery from Kalibangan, the author is venturing his own assessment of the pottery from Period I and also to restate the chronology of the site based on the evidence, particularly of pottery basically the Sothi Ware can be broadly grouped into three categories on the basis of surface colour-red, including its different shades, buff and grey. These have paintings in black pigment, but very often as an auxiliary, white pigment has also been employed, which at first glance distinguishes it from the Mature Harappan pottery. The prevalent classification alphabetically into six fabrics is briefly mentioned below.

Fabric A: "The vessels of this fabric, although made on wheel, were carelessly potted, betraying unskilled

*2, Nigambagh, Kundri, Rakabgunj, Lucknow

handling with tell tale traces of irregular striations. Comparatively light and thin in section and red to pinkish in colour, most of the vessels were painted in black, combined at times with white, over a dull red surface, the field of decoration being confined to the portion above girth".

Fabric B: "Distinguished primarily by its paste-texture and surface treatment. The vessels of this fabric were carefully potted on the wheel and were treated with a red slip upto the shoulder, the slipped area being further diversified by black-painted horizontal bands of varying thickness. The remaining surface of the vessels (excepting perhaps the base) was covered with a thin clayey solution, often mixed with sand, and while wet, roughened by horizontal or wavy combings or by tortoise shell (?) or dendritic impressions. Over this rusticated surface naturalistic designs........ were painted in black, combined at times with the ancillary white".

Fabric C: "Marked by a finer-textured paste and all over smooth-slipped surface in shades of red and plum or purple-red, the repertory of painted designs, which are essentially in black, included the recurrent carefully-ruled horizontal bands or loops or latticed loops or pendant triangles. Of special interest, however, are the panelling of palm-tree with a bird....... and a butterfly or a double-axe motif, wavy verticals and the Indus *scales*".

Fabric D: " Characterised by vessels with thick sturdy section and slipped red surface. The common shapes included heavy jars including the one with an accentuated flange round the neck; bowls and basins or troughs. The last-named, however, was the most characteristic of this fabric. The basins with a ring-base was decorated internally on the sides with sharp ridged incisions of varying patterns often bordered by wavy lines and on outside with single or multiple rows of cord impressions. The incised patterns were executed by a reed-fragment when the paste was plastic or yielding as evidenced by the raised or burred edges along the incised lines. The decoration on bowls and the flat-bottomed basins, however, consisted of grouped wavy lines, doubtlessly produced by the employment of multiple-pronged tool held with a pencil grasp. Besides, black painted horizontal bands and loops were not infrequent in this fabric".

Fabric E: "Comprised vessels with a buff or reddish buff slip.Common shapes include:large and medium-sized jars including those with a hole-mouth or a flange round the rim; lids; bowls; and offering-stands and dishes including a small chalice. The painted decoration (in black sometimes tending to purplish and occasionally white pigment) consisted of the ubiquitous horizontal bands; oblique line with fronds; sigmas in horizontal sequences above joined semicircles with fillers and borders of scales and latticed or plain scallops or loops; and such individualistic motifs as multi-petalled flowers, fish, cock (?) and stylized butterfly or double-axe within wavy verticals".

Fabric F: "The grey coloured pottery was represented in forms commonly met with in other fabrics, viz., dish-on-stand, basins, bowls and vases. For decoration, the use of both black and white pigment was current" (*IAR*, 62-63: pp 20-30).

The observations of the author are expressed below. As mentioned before, the entire ceramic industry of the Sothi culture at Kalibangan is broadly divisible into three major wares, viz. red, buff and grey. In each of these wares there is a pottery technically sharing the mode of manufacturing, decoration and some popular shapes, but for the difference of the surface colour. The same will be demonstrated as we proceed. This class of pottery is made of a clay, not well levigated, in which sand was used as a *degraissant*; potted on a slow wheel or turn-table resulting in irregular striations. It is self-slipped which having been obtained in the process of potting by application of wet hands on the pot. Thus the clay sticking to the potter's hand gave a smoothing effect and obscuring the striations on the exterior. The other distinguishing feature being that the rims have been shaped separately and luted to the body of the pot, inwardly showing an overlapping of two edges by way of thickening at the junction. Sometimes due to not being careful enough, a void inadvertently escaped the luting. Further evidence of luting is provided by finger impressions in some cases. The rim part after luting was given a finish and most likely a piece of coarse cloth was used for this purpose. This resulted in unsteady and at times broken striations. The author has observed a potter from Tripura giving finish to the pottery by a piece of canvas. The ring or pedestal bases which also had been made separately and wherever, necessary, luted later.

This class of pottery is generally bichrome employing black or purplish colour in case of buff ware and white pigments. The pottery quantitatively is more thin and uncommonly medium in case of bowls, vases and jars, depending on the size of the vessels. Numerically, the red or pinkish pottery was more in demand, the buff ware having second preference and the grey ware was seemingly less preferred. There is a generic relationship between all these three wares. The limited similitude in the shapes of the vessels, including the painted designs, is evident. This entire gamut of pottery may be termed 'ill-bred' or 'ill-textured'.

Now we come to the shape in each of these wares, followed by the painted design *repertoire*. The shapes met in the red ware are with bowls with vertical, internally bevelled, everted, out-turned or out curved, thickened rims and convex or tapering profiles, often with ring or pedestal base (Figs. 1, 1-9) and vases of various sizes with out-turned or out-curved rims, also providing ring or high and low pedestal bases (Fig.1, 10-20). It is an unusual feature to have pedestal base in the vases. A bowl (Figs. 1,7) has a ridge on the body below the waist. Amongst the vases a new type occurs, having a hole-mouth (Figs 1, 21). It was achieved by blocking the neck by a clay disc luted to it ; the disc was perforated prior to luting. It may be pointed out that the dish-on-stand is conspicuous by its absence in this ware. The pained designs are executed in bichrome (in the drawings the white pigment has been shown by way of hatchings), at times only black paint has been used. The rendering appears to be free hand; clearly there is a predilection for geometry, and rarely the plant or insect is also represented. The linear depiction's are made by way of horizontal lines, bands, blocks, wavy lines, vertical or oblique or criss-cross, scales or chain, triangles or squares, semi-circles, single or multiple and or in combination with others appear. Naturalistic elements such as leaves, flowers, eye-design, 'cacti-like plants' and a spider are met with. Most of these were used as fillers (Fig. 2).

The buff ware has very limited shapes confined to a chalice (Figs. 3, 1) and a few vases (Fig.3, 2-3) including one with a hole-mouth (Figs. 3,4). The linear designs include horizontal, wavy lines, loops in multiples. The paintings are rendered in black, occasionally using white pigment also (hatchings in the drawings).

The grey ware was rare and the shapes met with are bowls with vertical rim (Figs. 3,5) and vases with flaring mouth (Figs. 3, 6). The painted pottery is much less. However, horizontal lines and criss-cross are common and white pigment has been used (shown in hatchings in the drawings) along with black paint (Figs. 3,7).

The other class of pottery occurring along with the one described above may be termed 'better-textured'. It is made of well levigated clay and fired to maturity, sharing all the qualities of the later Mature Harappan pottery. The similitude is so much that isolation of one from the other, if not impossible,is certainly difficult to a greater extent when both are recovered from the same level. Here, however, an attempt is made to explicate the same. This category of pottery is also divisible into three groups based on the body colour-red , buff and grey wares. All these are made of fine paste, thrown on a fast spinning wheel as indicated by hair-thin regular striations and except the grey ware fired to the maturity. Perhaps sand was mixed in the clay as seen in the thicker variety of the pottery. With the exception of the dish-cup-on-stand which were potted in pieces, the rest of the pottery was thrown in one piece. Each ware with its individuality is discussed below, including the shapes and painted designs.

The red ware here includes all the three currently known Fabrics, B, C and D as they fall in the category of red ware on the dictum of surface colour They are divisible into two groups, i.e. medium or thick corresponding to the size of the pot. The vessels of medium thickness were exteriorly treated with a slip all over 'in shades of red and plum or purple-red'. In case where the profile of the jar was to be rusticated the area of the slip was confined to nearly down the shoulder. The method for obtaining the rustications was of two kinds. A clay solution, often mixed with sand, was applied on the body of the pot when it was dry and before firing. Thus the applied solution while wet was removed gently creating a series of horizontal or wavy horizontal bands or their combination or dendritic look (Figs. 4,3-5). The flaking of rustication indicates that it was done even. after firing. To what use these pots ware put is difficult to imagin. these, surely, not all of them were kept buried as rustications in some cases bear paintings. The only form recovered is represented by globular jars. These are painted with horizontal lines or bands on the rim, neck or shoulder (Fig. 4, 1-3) in black pigment. However, the rusticated zone is painted, in black using white as an additional colour, with naturalistic patterns, including various flowers, animals like bull and ibex, scorpion and duck, etc. (Fig. 4, 6-16).

The other forms in this category of red ware are straight sided bowls (Fig. 5, 1), dishes with flaring sides thickened and externally bevelled rim (Fig. 5,2), dish-on-stand with flaring sides and short splayed out rim (Fig. 5, 3), cup-on-stand with concave sides and horizontally splayed out lip (Fig. 5,5), bases of the stands (Fig. 5, 5-7), vases with ovoid or globular profile, constricted or high neck, at times with a ledge on the shoulder, globular jar with externally beaked rim (Fig. 5, 8-17) and a lid (Fig.5, 18). The painted designs as reported are in monochrome black and share the horizontal, wavy horizontal lines or blocks, criss-cross, loops, triangles and scales with the 'ill-bred' or 'ill-textured' pottery dealt with above. Special mention may be made of bipinnates, metopas, butterfly or double-axe and a banana-plant with a peahen (?) (Fig. 5, 19-28). It may not be out of place to mention here that the author who was associated during all the three seasons of excavations at Rupar (now Rupnagar, Panjab), while re-examining the excavated pottery fom the lowest levels of the trench RPR-1 at Ropar, was thrilled to identify a few shards of the 'ill-bred' or 'ill-texture' red ware (currently known as Fabric A) and a red-slipped fragment of a jar of 'better-texture '. Unfortunately, it is broken in such a way that no idea of the complete painted design can be had. What remains appears to be a long drawn loop with double base lines. The lower line has tassels. On the left and right upwards are two rayed circles. Below on the right are two sets of lines meeting separately at two points making the design of a star or multi- petaled flower. The entire design is in black pigment but both the rayed circles and the star or the flower are filled with white pigment (Fig 3,8). This indicates that the 'better-textured' red ware of Sothi complex is also bichrome (Nigam, 1971). It may be emphasis here,as also can be diserned from the foregoing description, that the currently known two Fabrics B and C are in fact one ceramic industry.

The thick variety of red ware (currently known as Fabric D) has sturdy vessels, made of compratively not very well levigated clay as those of the medium thickness discussed above. Besides the other most conspicuous identifying feature is mentioned below. Author's experience is that when two pot sherds of the same size, i.e. one of the Sothi culture and the other from the Mature Harappan culture are put together they can be identified on the basis of their comparative weight. The Sothi sherd weighs lesser than that of the Mature Harappan. The other corresponding feature that was noticed was the difference in the density of the core. The Sothi Ware core was not so dense when compared with the Mature Harappa pottery which has a very compact core. The shapes in this thick sturdy ware are the bowls with flaring sides and generally an everted rim (Fig. 6, 1-3), basins with flaring sides and externally thickened rim (Fig. 6, 4-6), troughs with vertical or flaring sides and collared rim (Fig. 6, 7-9), base of the dish-on-stand (Fig. 7,8) jars with ledge on the shoulder (Fig. 7, 6-7) and storage jars (Fig. 7, 2-5). A cylindrical vessel with an opening at the bottom (Fig.7, 1) appears to be the forerunner of the perforated jar type of the Mature Harappan Culture. This range of pottery is generally plain, but painted examples have horizontal lines, bands, blocks and at times in combination with wavy lines (Fig. 6,4) rendered in black paint only. The most eye-catching mode of decorations confined to bowls, basins and troughs, are the incised patterns met with inside these vessels. They consist of lines, horizontal or wavy, in groups, oblique lines and floral motif obtained by employing a multi-pronged fork like instrument or a single point as per requirement, perhaps made of bamboo (?). The process would have been completed before the dehydration of the pots began. Single or multiple rows of cord impressions was another means of decoration on the exterior of the storage jars and troughs, etc. some of the troughs were provided with a ring base and at times with an open bottom. To what use such vessels were put leaves all of us guessing.

The other congruent pottery of the Sothi culture is the buff or reddish buff-slipped ware. It shares the properties of the red-slipped ware. The shapes are bowls with collared rim or internally thickened and externally bevelled rim, flaring sides with a ridge on the exerior (Fig. 8, 1-3), dish and dish-on-stand (Fig. 8, 4-8), cup-on-stand (Fig.

8,9), lids (Fig. 8,10,11) vases with everted rim (Fig. 8,12), and jars of medium to large size with flanged rim and ledge at the shoulder or below the rim (Fig. 8, 13-17). The repertory of painted designs, which are rendered in black or purplish pigment, consist of ubiquitous linear or curvilinear bands, scales, loops sometimes hatched, butterfly or double axe, monopenates, flowers, fish and chicken (?) (Fig. 8, 18-27). It may be mentioned that the use of white pigment has not come to notice in this ware. Likewise the rustications on the buff ware are not reported. The author can vouch the presence of rusticated pottery in this ware which consists of horizontals.

The better-textured variety too has a grey ware (currently known as Fabric F). It shares all the characteristics of the corresponding red and buff wares of the Sothi complex. The pottery shapes and painted designs are also common. The forms represented are basins with collared rim and ring base (Fig. 7, 9-10), dish and dish-on-stand (Fig. 7, 11-13) and medium to large size jars (Fig 7, 14-15). The painted designs are simple, linear and curvilinear rendered in black paint (Fig. 7, 13).

The foregoing explication of the Sothi pottery at Kalibangan clearly demonstrates that there are two dinstinct strains, one represented by the 'ill bred' or 'ill-textured' and the other with better texture. It is an established fact that both these ceramic traditions occur together in the same levels. Do they have different origins? It is difficult to answer precisely at our present stage of knowledge. A comparative study of the pre/ Early Harappan materials obtained from various excavated sites now in Pakistan does help to correlate the Sothi pottery. The interaction may not, however, be direct. Gumla in Gomal basin yielded in Period II 'a few jars similar to Kot Dijian style pottery in shape and decoration and a few examples of Quetta Wet type pottery' (Dani, 1971). The pottery of Period III has similitude with that from Kot Diji and Amri (Shaffer, 1979). Rehman Dheri in Gomal plain, Period II; represents typical Kot Dijian specimens with some motifs, such as pipal-leaf, peacock, etc.' (Durrani, 1984). Lewan in Bannu basin yielded pottery of Kot Diji and Rehman Dheri complex. A dish-on-stand in dark red is painted with black bands, a row of fish motifs in black outline with white fillings is of significance. A similar fish design painted in black outline with white filling is reported from early levels at Rehman Dheri (Durrani, 1981). Sarai Khola is located on the Potwar plateau. Here the Period II pottery is wheel-thrown and treated with a red slip/wash, with wide band decoration on the neck. Pipal leaf is also painted. Many of the jars have fluted/grooved exterior. The pot forms include bowls, dishes, lids and dishes-on-stand. The pottery of this period has similarity with the Kot Diji (Halim, 1972a and b; Mughal, 1972a). Jalilpur is situated on the left bank of the River Ravi, about 65 km south-east of Harappa. The pottery from Period II is bichrome, including black and white on red. A few specimens of Quetta Wet ware were also recovered, 'vessels forms included a globular jar with a short neck which was often decorated with a black/ brown band, and had the exterior surface fluted or grooved. Other forms identified were: globular jars with flanged rims, carinated bowls, lids and dishes-on-stand' (Mughal, 1972b, 1974a; Durrani, 1984). Kot Diji, located in the ancient flood-plain of the Indus, is towards north-east of Mohenjo-daro. The pottery bears bichrome paintings and some pots have their exterior roughened. Both these have parallels in Mundigak III-5 and IV, Anjira III-IV and Damb Sadaat II-III (Allchins, 1982). The early pottery from the defence at Harappa, suggests that there existed a phase of Early Harappa habitation. This however, can be confirmed only after further excavation at the site. The pottery has striking similarity not only in forms but also, linear paintings which are black-on-red, including neck bands and grooves on the exterior too (Wheeler, 1947). This pottery has many parallels in the Sothi ceramic 'better-textured' complex at Kalibangan. The excavation at Sandhanwala yielded Sothi pottery in Period I (Dalal, 1980). Durrani has claimed many parallels in the pottery between Jalilpur II, Kot Diji I, Sarai Khola, Gumla II-III and Sothi pottery from Kalibangan.

In India, as stated above, Sothi and Nohar were excavated before Kalibangan. Later, several sites containing Sothi culture have been explored and excavated (Joshi and others, 1984; Suraj Bhan, 1975 and Bisht, 1986-87, 1987-88). At the present state of our knowledge it may be surmised that the Sothi culture with its 'ill-bred' or a 'ill-textured' pottery originated in the Ghaggar/ Sarasvati/ Hakra valley in the desert region of Cholistan and northern Rajasthan. It was locked up with the people manufacturing 'better textured' pottery sometime in their initial stage and the result was a conglomerate ceramic industry during the Sothi/ Early Harappa phase. This hypothesis has to be confirmed by further field work in Sind, Rajasthan and Haryana. Leaving aside the 'ill-bred' 'ill-textured' pottery, minus the use of white pigment and internally incised treatment of the vessels, the manufacturing of the pottery, both in technique and painted designs - most of the pot-forms, such as bowls, dishes, dish-cup-on-stand, basins, vases, medium size jars and lids - have intruded into the succeeding Mature Harappa-culture (Nigam, 1979) and was very popular.

Now we discuss the chronology of the mounds at Kalibangan in view of the occurrence of pottery, the most valuable record for the archaeological studies. As expressed earlier there are two habitational mound viz., KLB-1 and KLB -2. The Sothians settled on the virgin soil and constructed a defence wall around their habitation. The locale is now known as KLB-1. They lived there quite peacefully for about two hundred years. The corrected ^{14}C date for Sothi culture here is 2900-2700 B.C. They had to leave the site perhaps owing to a natural calamity, most probably an earthquake. Evidence of such an eventuality is afforded by the 'cleavage-cum-displacement of the strata and walls'. Where did these people take shelter after the earthquake? It is a natural instinct, even followed these days, that when such a tremor is felt people run out in the open for safety. The Sothians did the same at Kalibangan. Whatever the reason, they did not rebuild their houses on the debris, but chose to settle on the open land which is now known as KLB-2. In this mound the excavation on the northern side much within the fortified area, revealed that the first settlers were the Sothians. The lowest level yielded purely Sothi pottery. After more or less two decades they were joined by a people who do not appear to be aliens. There is no sign of violence or destruction. The newcomers were technologically more advanced with Harappan traits. Both the people lived in harmony. The pottery study indicated that with the passing of time, the Sothi influence was fading and the Harappan dominance was progressively increasing. A time reached when the Sothi culture was diluted and crystalized into the Mature Harappan culture. Thus it would seem that there was a transition phase/period between the Sothi culture, i.e., Period I and the Mature Harappan Period III, the beginning of which must have syncronised with the occupation of the mound KLB-1 by the Mature Harappan people who raised platforms and the defences to make a citadel over the debris of the Sothi settlement there. It may be pointed out that Sothi pottery has not ben found in the citadel. The intervening transitional phase between the Sothi culture and the Mature Harappan culture should be discerned as a separate phase as Period II.

A transitional phase between the Early Harappan and the Mature Harappan has been defined at several sites. For example at Amri, the material of Amri culture (Period I) continued with the Harappan material in the succeeding Period II, whereas, the Mature Harappan took over the next Period III. At Kot Diji the same phenomenon is noticed. The Mounds A and B were initially occupied by the Kot Dijians. After two massive conflagrations the Kot Diji settlement came to an end on Mound A. But on Mound B both the Kot Dijians and the Harappans came to live together till the Mature Harappans settled on the citadel Mound A. Some more evidence about the overlapping/transitional phase between the Sothi and the Mature Harapa culture has come to light. Such a phenomenon has been observed at Banawali and Siswal (District Hissar); Mitathal (District) and Balu (District Jind) in Haryana and Ropar (District Rupnagar) in the Punjab.

The excavations at Banawali have established beyond doubt a transitional phase between the pre-Harappan (Sothi/ Kalibangan I) settlement (Period I) and introducton of certain new traits recognised as Mature Harappan elements. The ceramic tradition of the Sothians though continued, gradually shrinking with a progressive increase of the Mature Harappa wares. The architecture, planning and antiquities conform to the Harappa Cuture *(IAR, 86-87; 87-88).*

Trial excavtion at Siswal, a village settlement throughout revealed that the site was originally occupied by the people who lived in Sothi (Kalibangan I) tradition. "The bulk of the ceramic shapes and design elements have broad Kalibangan affinities, but there are noticed individualistic or regional features both in shapes and design patterns". Due to these variations this culture has been named Siswal A culture. The next phase is marked by the arrival of the Mature Harappa at the site and recorded at Siswal B. The characteritic Sothi/Kalibangan I/ Siswal A pottery survives in this phase. However, at this stage a group of new comers joined who brought Mature Harappa traditions as represented by their pottery. Thus, Siswal B signifies the overlap/ transitional phase of the two traditions when the Sothians/ Kalibanganians I/ SiswalA people and the Harappans lived together till the site was deserted by them (Suraj Bhan, 1972).

Mithathal excavations laid bare a pre-Harappan (Sothi/ Kalibangan/ Sisawal A) settlement recorded as Period I, consisting of the ceramic repertory associated with this known culture. However, sprinkling of the Harappan pottery has also been noticed in this deposit. The succeeding period (Period II) in its earlier 'Phase A' has evidence of a full-fledged Mature Harappa repertoire with doubtless continuence of the pre-Harappan (Sothi/ Kalibangan I/ Siswal A) traditions at least in the ceramic industry. This confirms the co-existence of both the people and represents that phase in the life history of the Sothians when they were joined by the Harappans with their urbanised refinement, indicating thereby an overlapping of the two cultures (Suraj Bhan, 1975).

At Balu, the overlapping between the pre-Harappan (Sothi/ Kalibangan I/Late Siswal) and Harappa culture had been noticed in the excavation. Here the Phase A is characterised by the ceramic repertoire of the pre-Harappan tradition. Whereas, in the succeeding Phase B the Mature Harappan pottery appears in conjunction with the pre-Harappan pot-forms. Consequently, the Phase B represents the co-existence of the two groups of people and an overlapping period in the admixed culture (*IAR*, 78-79).

The chronology of Ropar Period I has been recomputed into three phases A, B and C, after the excavations at Kalibangan. The present writer had identified the presence of Sothi/ Kalibangan I pottery occurring in the lowest levels of the trench RPR-1 together with the Mature Harappan pottery. Later Sharma has pointed out the parallels in pot-forms between Ropar and the pottery from pre-Defence Harappan, Kot Diji, Sothi, Kalibangan I and Siswal B (Sharma, 976). Thus Ropar has also recorded that phase of settlement when both the Sothians and the Mature Harappa people lived together. This demonstrates co-existence of these two settlers.

In the light of the above facts the existing chronology at Kalibangan needs to be revised as Sothi culture-Period I, overlapping or intermediate phase - Period II and the Mature Harappan culture - Period III.

REFERENCES

Allchin B and Allchin F.R 1982, *The Rise of Civilization in India and Pakistan.* Cambridge, p. 102 ff.

Cassal, J.M.1964, *Fouiles D'Amri,* 2 Vols. Paris.

Dalal, K.F.1980, A Short History of Archaeological Explorations in Bikaner and Bahawalpur along the 'Lost Saraswati' River, Indica, 17, No.1, pp.4-40.

Dani, A.H.1971, Excavations in the Gomal Valley, *Ancient Pakistan,* vol.V, pp. 1-177.

Durrani, F.A.1981, Indus Civilization: Evidence east of Indus, in Dani, A.H. (ed) *Indus Civilization: New Perspectives,* p.135.

———,1984, Some Early Harappan sites in Gomal and Bannu Valleys, Gupta S.P. and Lal, B.B.(eds.), *Frontiers of the Indus Civilization,* New Delhi, pp.505-510.

Ghosh, A.1952, The Rajputana Desert - Its Archaeological aspects, *Bulletin of the National Institute of sciences of India*, No.1, pp. 37-42. A. Ghosh 1965, The Indus Civilization: Its origin, authors, extent and chronology, in M.S. Mate and V.N. Misra (eds.) *Indian Prehistory:* 1964, Pune, pp. 113-156.

Halim, A.1972 a, Excavation at Sarai Khola (Part I), *Pakistan Archaeology,* V, VII, pp. 23-89.

———,1972 b, Excavations at Sarai Khola (Part II), *Pakistan Archaeology,* V, VIII pp. 1-159.8.

I.A.R. 1960-61 pp. 31-32; *1961-62,* pp. 39-44; *1962-63,* pp. 20-30; *1978-79,* pp. 69; *1986-87,* pp.33-34 *1987-88,* pp.21-27

Joshi, J.P. et al 1984, The Indus Civilization: A Reconsideration on the Basis of Distribution Maps, in Gupta, S.P. and Lal, B.B. (eds.), *Frontiers of the Indus Civilization,* pp. 511 ff.

Mughal, R.1972 a, Introduction to the pottery of Periods I and II of Sarai Khola, *Pakistan Archaeology,* V, pp. 34-76.

_______,1972 b, Summary of Excavations and Explorations in Pakistan (1971-72), *Pakistan Archaeology,* V, pp. 114-158.

Mughal, R. 1974 a, New Evidence of the Early Harappan cuture from Jalilpur, *Pakistan Archaeology,* V, pp. 106-113.

Nigam, J.S.1971, Unique Potsherd from Rupar, *Journal of the Oriental Institute,* Vol. XX, No.4, Baroda, pp.370-371.

_______,1979, Harappan Pottery, in D.P.Agrawal and Dilip K. Chakrabarti (eds.), *Essays in Indian Protohistory,*New Delhi, pp. 135-161.

Shaffer, J.G.1979, The Indus Civilization: New Evidence from Pakistan in D.P. Agrawal and Dilip K. Chakrabarti (eds.) 1979, *Esssays in Indian Protohistory,*(D.K. Publishers and Distributors, New Delhi.)

Sharma,Y.D.1976, Transformation of the Harappa Culture in the Punjab ,in U.V. Singh (ed.) Archaeological Congress and Seminar: 1972, pp 9.

Suraj Bhan. 1975. Excavation at Mitathal (1968) and other Explorations in the Sutlej-Yamuna Divide, *Kurukshetra,* pp. 13-17.

________,1976, Transormation of the Harappa Culture in Haryana,in U.V. Singh (ed.) Archaeological Congress and Seminar: 1972, pp. 24-27.

Wheeler, R.E.M. 1947, Harappa 1946, The Defences and Cemetery R 37, *Ancient India,* No.3, pp. 58-130.

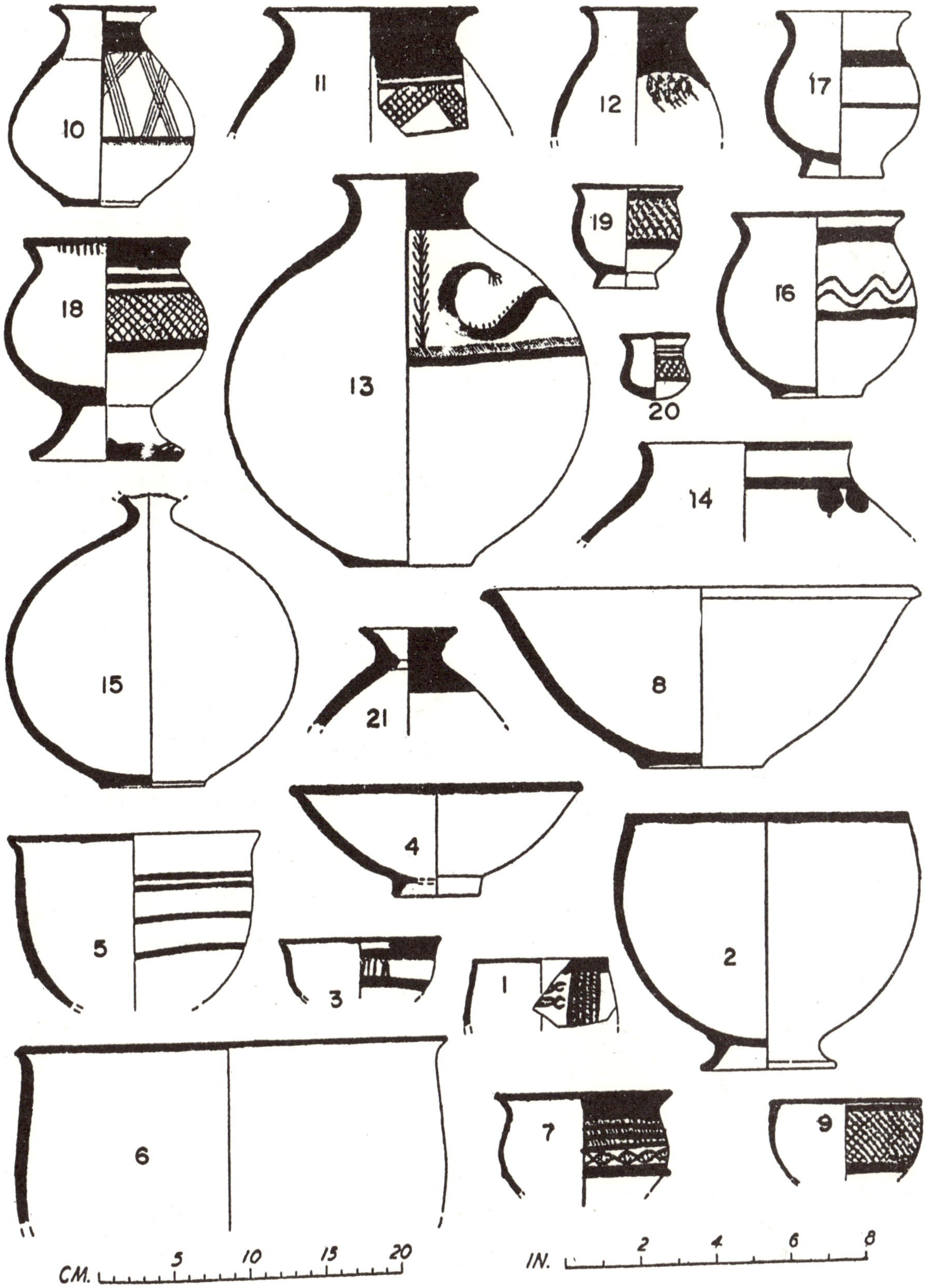

Fig. 1

Fig. 2

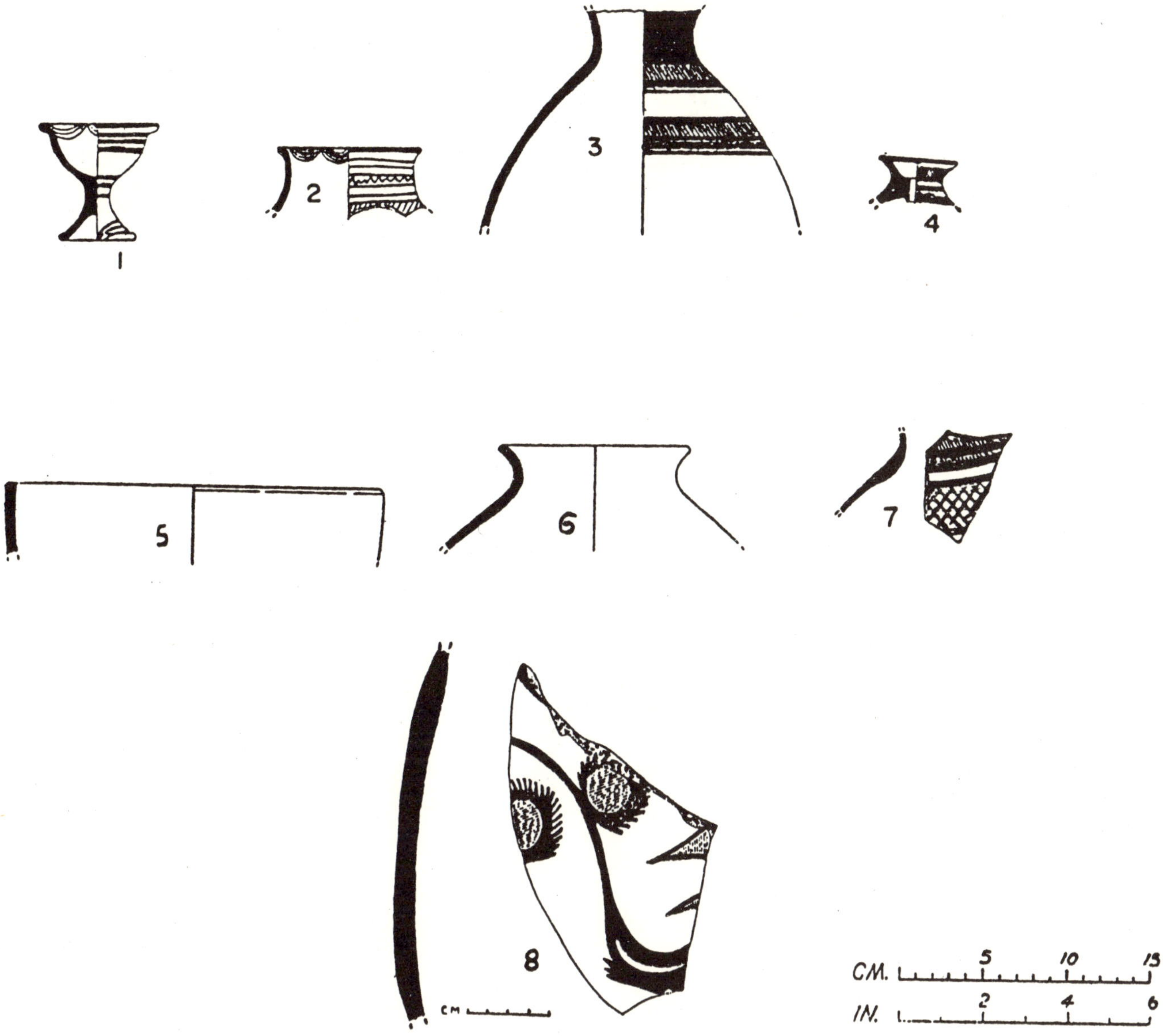

Fig. 3

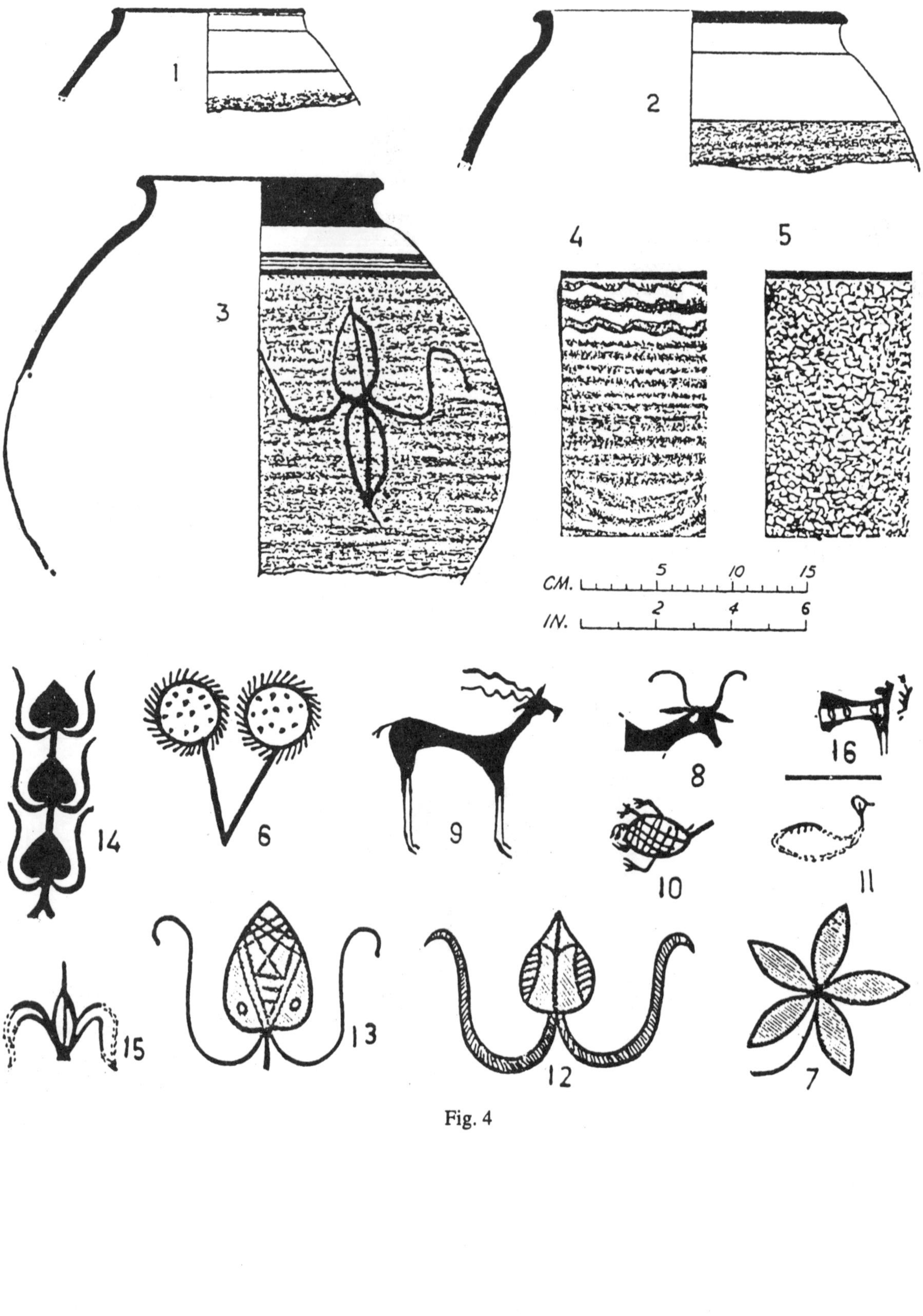

Fig. 4

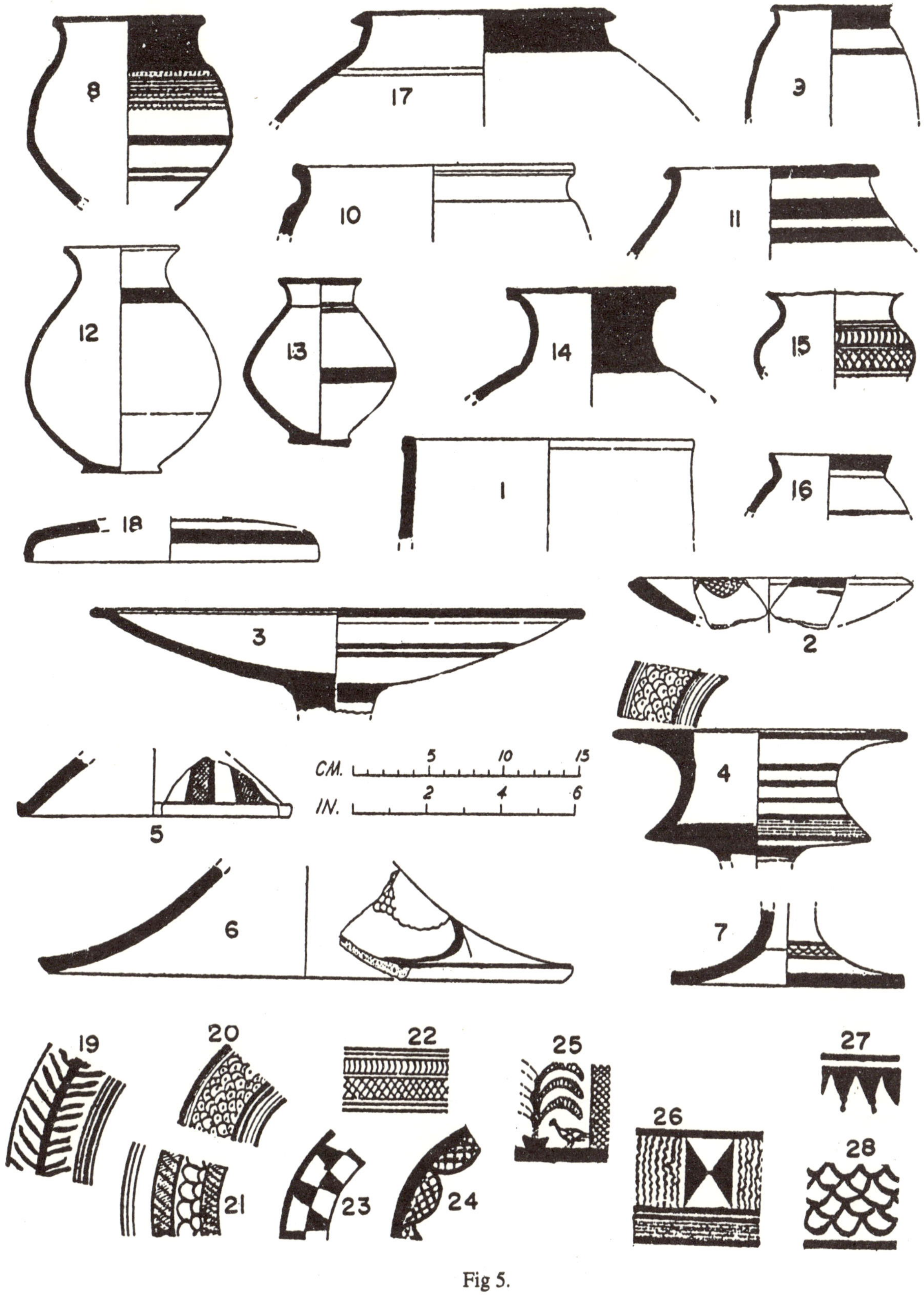

Fig 5.

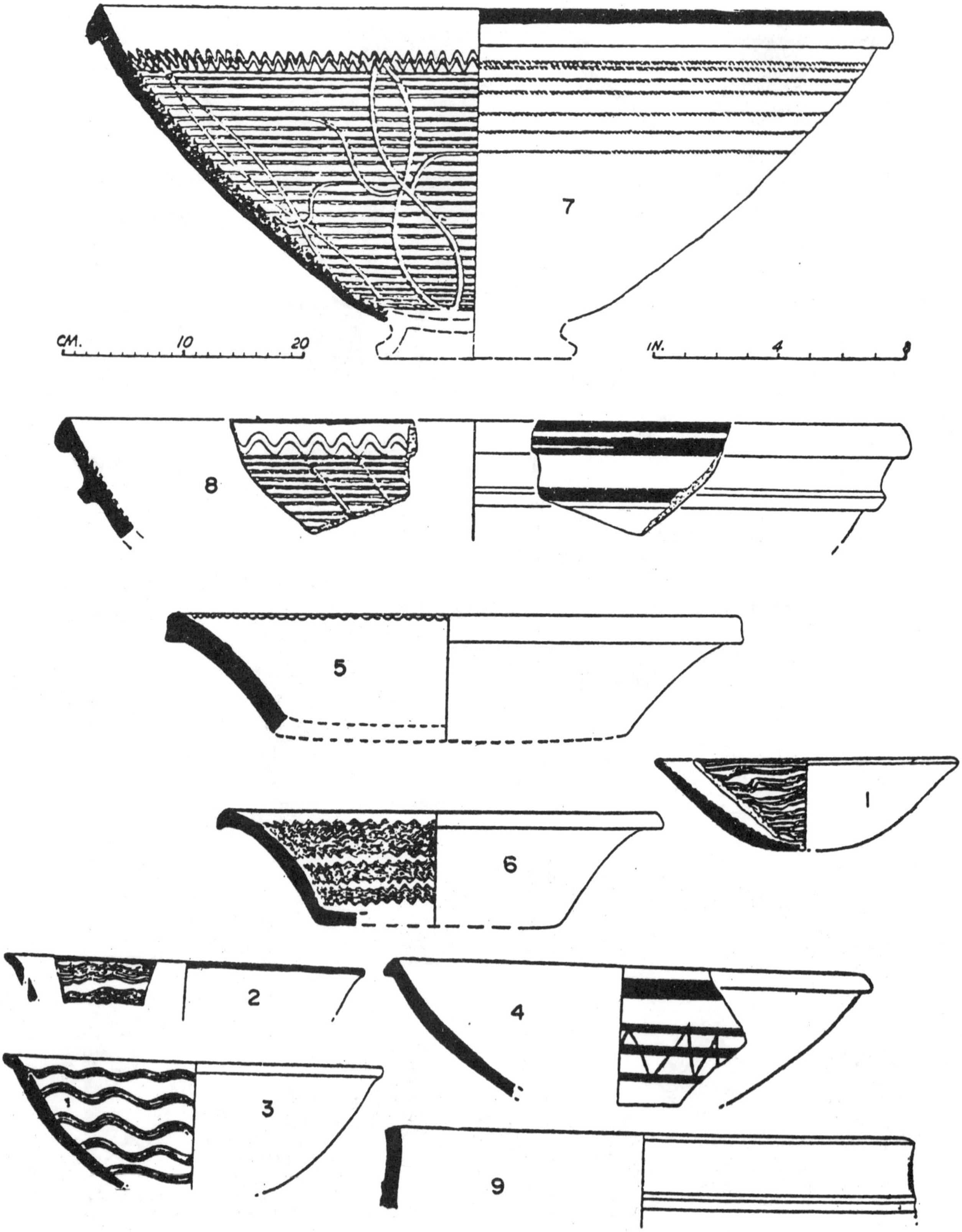

Fig. 6

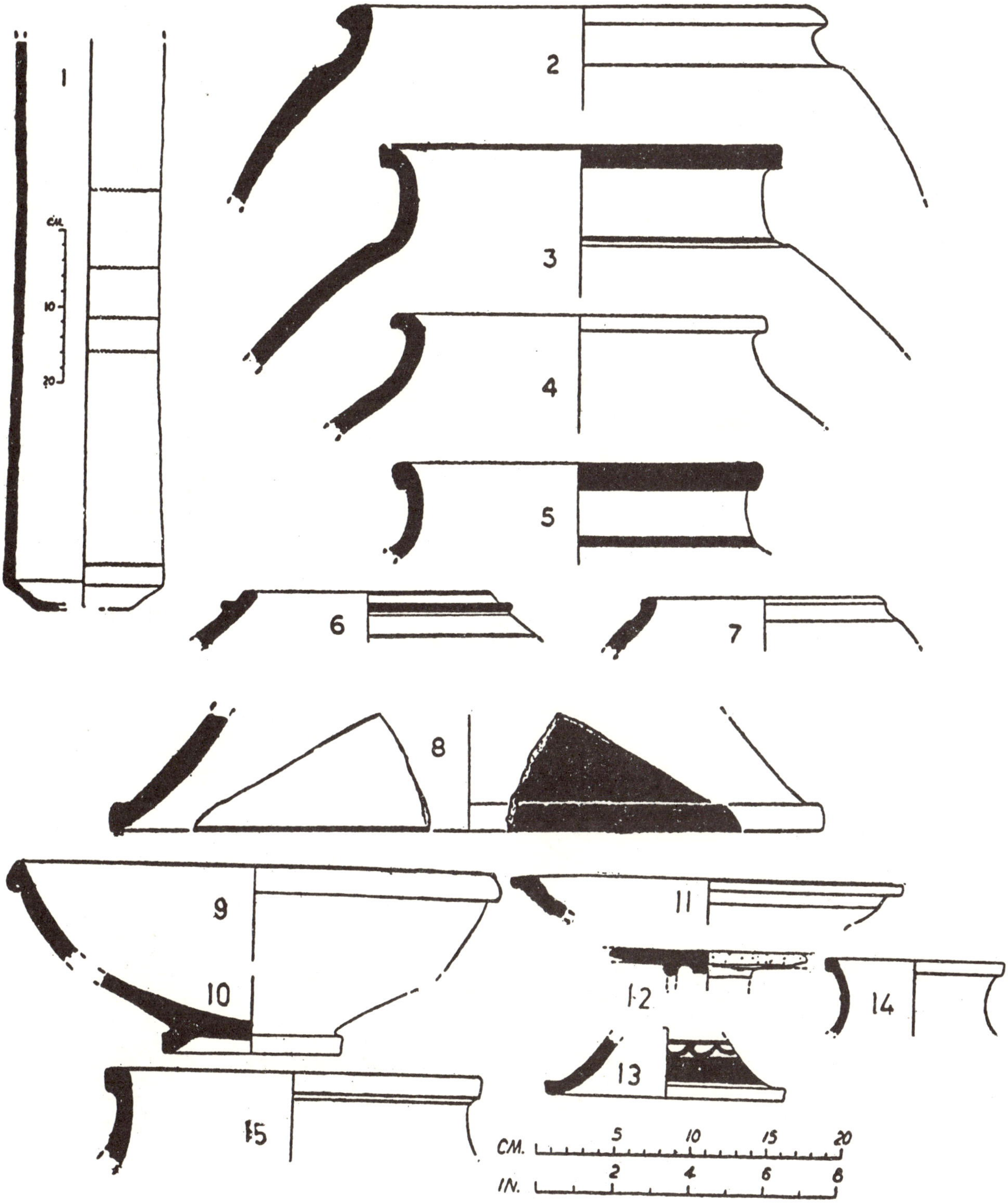

Fig. 7

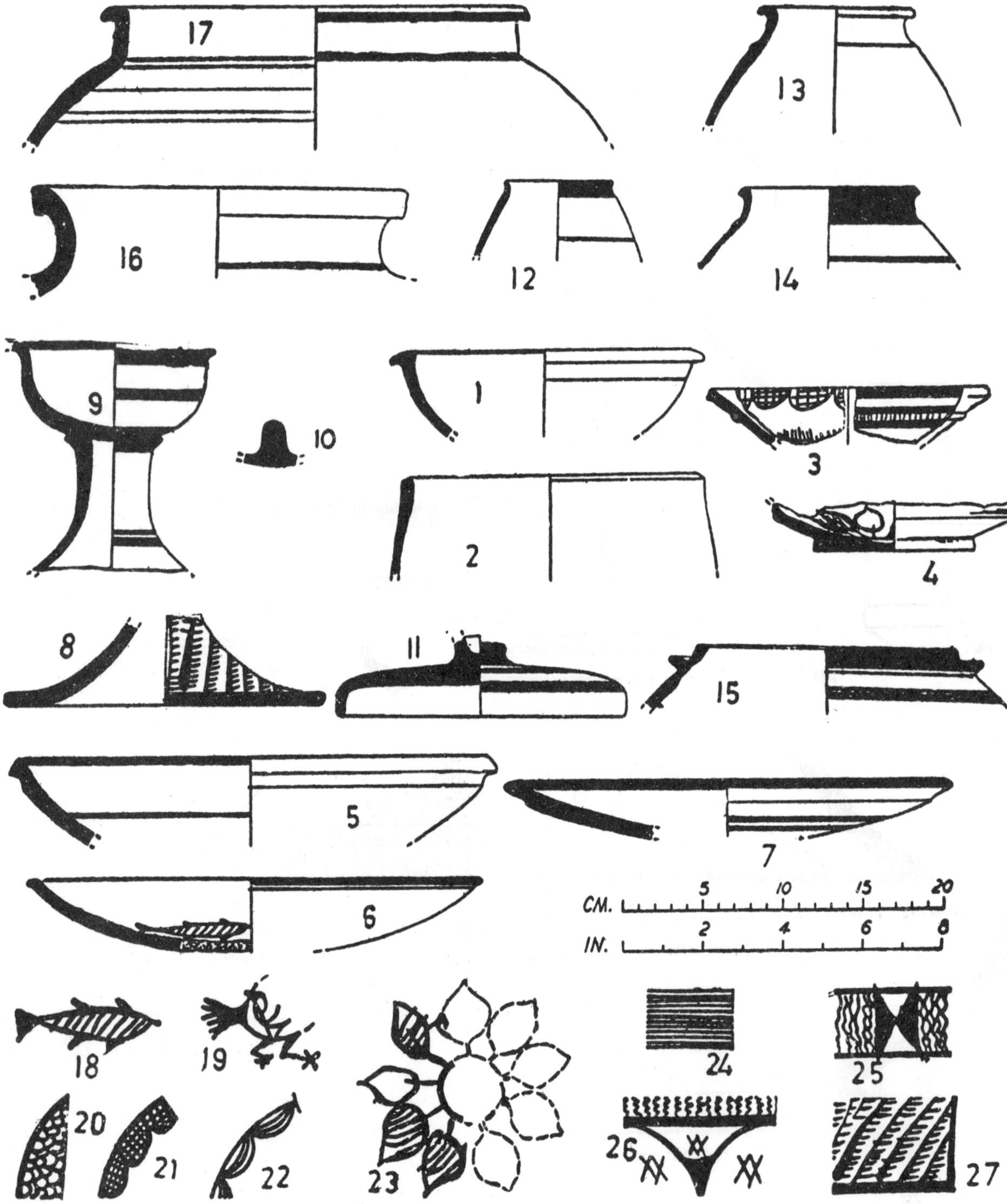
17
13
16
12
14
9
10
1
3
2
4
8
11
15
5
7
6
CM. 5 10 15 20
IN. 2 4 6 8
18
19
24
25
20
21
22
23
26
27

Fig. 8

The Anthropomorphs in the Copper Hoard Culture of the Ganga Valley

MAHESHWAR P. JOSHI*

Discoveries of copper objects — often in caches — have been reported from time to time from different parts of India. However, the Ganga Valley copper objects have a significant place in Indian archaeology.

Among various artefacts of the Ganga Valley Copper Hoards, the anthropomorphic figure is singularly unique in that it has no parallel in the entire Copper - Bronze Age world archaeology. Yet, this significant aspect of the copper anthropomorph has not been assessed adequately by scholars. While earlier writers like Smith (1905; 1907), Shastri (1915), Heine-Geldern (1936; 1956) and Piggott (1944; 1950) made almost no comments on the Anthropomorphs, later writers like Gordon (1958: 137), Gupta (1963; 1965), Dikshit (1968), The Allchins (1968; 1983), D.P. Agrawal (1971), Shukla (1980), M. Lal (1981), Jayakar (1982), R.C. Agrawal (1984), Pant (1989), Sharma (1993) and the author himself (Joshi 1990a). sought to explain the functional significance and probable identification of the anthropomorphis. Consequently, one of the major issues concerning identification of the anthropomorphic figure in the Copper Hoards has escaped the attention of scholars. In the present paper this particular issue is stressed.

Among the earlier scholars Smith (1905) was the first to attempt at a comprehensive study of the" Copper Age" objects, including the Copper Hoards, found in India. While Smith discussed the probable origin of different copper artefacts as well as their functional utility, he remained silent on the copper anthropomorph, though as a "class" he called it "human figure" (Smith 1905: 236). Smith's silence may be understood in his own words: "extraordinary ... I presume that the figure was used as a religious symbol or image" (Smith. 1905: 238). It may be noted here that while studying these objects Smith had neither any knowledge of the Harappans nor was he obsessed with the idea of the archaeology of the Aryan migration.

In the 1930s when Childe's migration and diffusion hypothesis was gaining ground, Heine-Geldern (1936; 1956) pleaded that the Copper Hoard artefacts were the traces of the Aryan migration in India. Piggott (1944: 181-82) also held the same. However, subsequently he changed his views and attributed the Ganga Valley Copper Hoards to the Harappan refugees (Piggott 1950: 238). It may be noted that while both Heine-Geldern and Piggott discussed at length the probable origin and diffusion of the forms of some of the artefacts, notably, celts, bar-celts, harpoons, and antennae swords, none of those discussed the anthropomorphic figure. Obviously, owing to its distinctive form which had no parallel outside the Ganga Valley, the anthropomorph did not suit their theories .

Lal's (1951) attempt to study the Ganga Valley Copper Hoards typologically within a contextual framework gave a new dimension to the Copper Hoard archaeology. He suggested that 'bar celts' were developed from the prototype of stone celts found in the "hilly tracts of southern Bihar, western West Bengal and northern Orissa", and 'the harpoons' from "long harpoon headed poles"

*Deptt. of A. H. & Archaeology, Kumaon University, Nainital

such as depicted in the archaic paintings of Central Indian plateau, notably, Ghormangpur and Likhunia caves (Mirzapur District, U.P.). On the basis of circumstantial evidence Lal postulated that the authors of the Copper Hoards and Ochre Coloured Pottery were interrelated. Lal (1972a) sought to prove his hypothesis by his subsequent archaeological excavations at Saipai (District Etawah, Uttar Pradesh). He suggested that the authors of the Copper Hoards could be identified with the tribal folks mentioned in the Vedic literature as Nishadas whose descendants are represented by the modern tribes of Mundas, Santhals, and others belonging to the Proto-Australoid group of Indian people (Lal 1951). Though Lal did not say anything about the origin and functional significance of the anthropomorphs, but still he realized their individuality when he said "... as far as the author is aware, their occurrence has not been reported from anywhere else in the world" (Lal 1951: 35). Thus, Lal is the first archaeologist to suggest an independent indigenous origin of the Ganga Valley Copper Hoards.

Gupta (1963; 1965) has also studied the problem of Copper Hoards at length. On the basis of typology and technology as well as distribution of different copper and low grade bronze artefacts in different parts of India, he suggested that all are interrelated. He says: Because of its all India character in distribution, instead of 'Gangetic basin Copper Hoards' 'Indian Copper Hoards' has been preferred as this common heading (Gupta 1963: 150).

Gupta agrees with Lal in that the origin of the Copper Hoard folks lies in eastern India (Bihar, Bengal, Orissa, and adjoining parts of Madhya Pradesh), among the ancestors of the present day Mundas etc., whence they migrated to west (Gupta 1963: 157-60). He believes that a branch of the chalcolithic cultures of Malwa-Rajasthan moved northwards and eastwards. "There is, therefore, every possibility that these two cultures moving within the same area in opposite directions somewhere met each other. The traces of influences in the chalcolithic cultures are due to this possible contact" (Gupta 1963: 165). However, tracing the development of the Copper Hoard artefacts he says that simple forms like celts, shouldered celts, and bar-celts originated in zone "A" i.e., eastern India. From zone "A" the Copper Hoard folks migrated to zone "B", i.e., Ganga-Yamuna *doab* where they developed complex forms like harpoons, spear-heads, swords and anthropomorphs. Gupta believes that the harpoon was developed as a weapon of chase " such as hunting rhinoceros and fishing heavy variety of fish in two big *doab* rivers", the sword as a weapon of war "against the westerners" — the Aryans who pressed them, and the spear-head was used for both chase and war. The anthropomorph may have had magico-religious purpose, or else, it was used as a "hurling weapon of war" (Gupta 1963).

It may be noted that Gupta is the only scholar to have attempted at a thematic study of the Indian Copper Hoards covering, as the very title of his paper reads, "their homogeneity, stages of development, origin, authorship, and dating" (Gupta 1963). In connection mention may be made of Yule's this recent work (Yule 1985) which catalogues nearly all published and unpublished non Harappan copper and bronze objects known upto 1983. This stupendous work has facilitated morphological study of the Copper Hoard artefacts considerably. There are many archaeologists who have written on the Copper Hoards but their treatment of the problem does not add to the basic issues taken up by Lal (Lal 1951; 1972b), and Gupta (Gupta 1963; 1965). Since the scope of Indian Copper Hoards is very wide, I have confined this paper to the genesis of the form of the anthropomorph which happen to be an exclusive diagnostic artefact of the Ganga Valley Copper Hoards.

The Anthropomorphic figure

The anthropomorphs are so named because they look like stylized human figures. If the Patna Museum (P.K. Agrawal 1967-68: pl. XI) specimen is to be included in this category, as indeed Agrawal does (Agrawal: 96), these objects represent male anthropomorphic figures. The Patna Museum specimen shows a prominent male genital organ. From the published accounts as well as personal physical examination of some of these objects, it becomes clear to me that these figures were first cast in a mould and then beaten with a chisel-like instrument so as to look like an anthropomorphic figure. However, it passed through various stages before it evolved as an articulate, complex anthropomorphic figure. In the discussion that follows an attempt is being made at tracing these evolutionary stages as observed from the available archaeological records. Before discussing the various stages of its evolution, it would be pertinent to give a brief description of the various known anthropomorphic figures. In order to make my argument meaningful propose to classify these figures morphologically into four basic and three miscellaneous types as follows.

Type I: Bankot (fig. 7) and Kiratpur (fig. 8) figures.

The Bankot anthropomorphic figures were discovered by the author at Bankot (District Pithoragarh, U.P. Hills) in March 1989 *(IAR 1988-89: 87-88).* Eight in number, two of which in fragments, these artefacts were picked up by local labourers from a rocky mountain slope at Bankot where copper ore is also found.

These anthropomorphic figures are cast in a tray-like single, open mould as is evident from the flat surface on one face which in some examples has wrinkled skin due to atmospheric cooling. No "beating" has been done after casting as a result of which the entire body, including the core, of the artefacts is porous. These figures weigh between 2.5 (fragmentary ones) and 3.5 kg., and measure approximately 22 cm in height/length, 29 cm in breadth/ width (including arms), and 1.5 to 2 cm in thickness (Joshi 1990a).

These have an elliptical "head-like" upper portion with straight out-stretched semi-cylinidrical "arm-like" projections. The lower part has a slightly concave abase with two cone-like "feet" projected in very low profile. It looks like a fish-tail. the elliptical "head" portion appears to have been provided with a cutting edge.

The Kiratpur (District Bulandshahar, U.P.) figure appears to be a smaller and lighter version of the Bankot figures and is 11.0 cm high, 15.5 cm abroad, and 0.4 cm thick, its weight being 161.1 gm. has an elliptical "head", straight out-stretched "arms", and a fishtail-like base. It may be noted that the "arms" and "feet" of the Kiratpur figure are longer than those of the Bankot figures.

Type II: Bisauli "A" (fig. 9), Saipai (fig. 10), and Brooklyn Museum (fig. 11) figures.

Three anthropomorphs have been reported from Bisauli (District Badaun, U.P.) which I call "A", "B", and "C". all of them are cast in mould and subsequently obtain into required shape. However, morphologically Bisauli "A" is different from Bisauli "B" and "C", and falls in type II of my classification. It has an elliptical "head", its out-stretched straight "arms" are incurred at the far ends (i.e., "hand" apportion), and the base, somewhat concave, is provided with two prominent "feet-like" projections. However, in this case too "feet" are made to look alike a fishtail.

The Saipai (District Etawah, U.P.) and the Brooklyn museum figures are similar to Bisauli "A" with the following differences:

a. Their arms are slightly slanted and curved, and

b. The lower portion is no more concave, instead it is provided with two cone-like "feet" giving a chevron-like appearance.

A noteworthy feature in all these figures is that the outer curved portions of the "arms" as well head" are thinned out so as to provide a "cutting edge".

Type III: Basil "B" (fig. 12) and Fatehgarh (fig. 13) figures.

Basil "B" and Fatehgarh (District Farrukhabad, U.P.) figures are morphologically different from type II, although there is a general resemblance among all of them. The characteristic features of Type III figures are as follows:

a. These are elongated figures, i.e., their height/ length is more than their width/breadth.

b. The "head" is blunted and resembles nail head. This feature is unique.

c. They have pronounced feet. In fact the Fatehgarh figure has the most prominent feet.

Type IV: Basil "C" (fig. 14), Sheorajpur (figs. 15, 16, and 17), Chandausi (fig. 18), and Almora-Haldwani (fig. 19) figures.

All of these figures are cast in mould and subsequently beaten into required shapes like Types II and III. in general appearance these figures are almost similar to type III, but there are certain notable points of departure They are:

a. These are massive in size and weight as compared to the rest.
b. Their "arms" are coiled and the length of the elongated feet" is almost equal to that of the upper body.
c. The outstanding feature is the "head" which is provided with a canopy-like projection having a "prominent ridge" on both sides outlining the "head".

Though emissive in appearance, these figures have a slander look are of high quality metalwork.

Miscellaneous Types

Type V: Patna-Manbhum (fig. 20) figure.

So far it is the only example of its kind which looks like a male anthropomorphic figure. Its head" is somewhat rectangular in shape, the bent "arms" hang down and the "abdomen" is bulged. in between two wide-stretched "feet" there is a protuberance indicative of male genital.

Type VI: Lothal (fig. 21), and Ambala (fig. 22) figures.

The Lothal (District Ahmedabad, Gujarat), and Ambala (District Ambala, Haryana) figures are fragmentary. The Lothal figure survives only in its the elliptical "head"Yet, it bears prominent"chisel marks", the characteristic feature of the anthropomorphic figures. Therefore, on the basis of its module and fabric it can be assigned to Type II, as its "head" does not bear any ridge. In fact Rao (1985: 530) calls it a "crescent sleeved axe". of the Ambala figure only a fragment of "arm" has survived. it also bears "chisel marks". Yule (1985: 7, 52) places it in his Type II which falls in Type IV of this paper.

Type VII: Chokhopani (fig. 23) figures.

Two copper sheets with chisel marks, characteristic of anthropomorphic figures, have been reported from Chokhopani (District Mustang, Nepal). Their association with high mountain ancient cave system is doubtful (Simons *et al* 1994). Each of these sheets has four prominent projections indicative of "arms" and "feet" (?). However, the "head" portion is missing (Simons *et al* 1994: fig. 10). Mishra (Mishra 1994) associates them with the Gang Valley Copper Hoards. It is likely that these objects represent "headless" anthropomorphs.

Identification of the Anthropomorph

Majority of scholars hold that the anthropomorphic figures are religious in nature. Thus, Smith (Smith 1995: 238) suggests that the Anthropomorphs have religious significance. Yule (1985: 105) suggests a "cultic interpretation for them". Lal (Lal 1951: 24), however, is not sure about their exact use which, according to him, could have been "religious or utilitarian". Dikshit (Dikshit 1968: 43-50), Shukla (Shukla 1980), and R.C. Agrawal (R.C. Agrawal 1984) identify it with a proto-type of Sani devata of Hindu mythology. P.K. Agrawal (1967-68) seeks to affiliate it with what he calls it "the babe of the mother-goddess Sri (*Sri-vatsa*)". According to Jayakar (Jayakar 1982: 88-89) it is a symbol of fertility. Sharma identifies it as a *nandipada* symbol. Deshpande (Deshpande 1969) suggests that it might represent a *vajra.* According to Das Gupta (Das Gupta 1975) the anthropomorph represents Vedic-*vajra*—a weapon which was fitted with a handle and thrown.

Gordon (Gordon 1958: 137) and Pant (Pant 1989) a multipurpose weapon having hammering and cutting properties.

Gupta (Gupta 1963) draws our attention to a type of "anthropomorphic figure" found in Southeast Asia which symbolises "the ancestors of the people", and the defender of the race. He suggests (Gupta 1963: 151):Though the similar magico-religious interpretation can be attached to these figures, their utility as hurling weapon of war cannot be ruled out. Allchins (1968:204; 1983: 256) take these figures for a type of *parasu* (axe) and add (Allchins 1983: 256) that "They bear some resemblance to 'anthropomorphic' sacrificial axe of iron or steel used by the

Santals and other tribal people of Chota Nagpur, but their actual function was more probably as some kind of ritual figure. D.P. Agrawal has given an altogether different interpretation which is based on his own experiments. He made "an imitation-model" of the Anthropomorph and "tried it as a missile". He says (D.P. Agrawal 1971: 200): It goes in a whirling fashion. It is forged in such a way that if it is thrown at, say, a flying bird it can bring down the bird in any of the three ways: the sharp forearms will produce cut; the heavy head will stun the prey; and if the prey is caught in the curved arm the whirling motion will entangle it and bring it down with the missile. I think the thickening of the head (manipulation of the centre of gravity) helps its whirling motion, and may impart some boomerang like property.

Sankalia (Sankalia 1974: 48) has questioned Agrawal's interpretation on the grounds that "such a heavy and complicated weapon for bringing down birds is in every way uneconomical, and not expected from such unsophisticated folk. All over the world, and throughout the ages, much more simple methods have been employed which are still in use". In connection with this it may also be noted that Agrawal's suggestion loses ground if applied to type I (Bankot and Kiratpur) figures. Furthermore, it is also doubtful if I and II types of figures would produce the same results as types III and IV, since the first two have cutting edge "head", while the last two have a ridge on both sides of the elliptical "head". Yule (Yule 1985: 105) believes that the anthropomorphs are "poorly suited as weapons". Refuting Agrawal he says: "suffice it to say that any flattish objects when thrown can travel in a whirling fashion".

I have, elsewhere, suggested (Joshi 1990a) that the anthropomorph is a ritual axe and represents one of the earliest examples of a personified axe (*parasu purusha*). Although this suggestion is similar to that of Allchins, yet the conclusion has been arrived independently relying on diffferent material and ideas. This is elaborated in the discussion.

Genesis

The most common artefact among the Copper Hoards, found in exceedingly large number, is the axe/celt. It has many varieties, such as simple flat celts, shouldered celts, bar-celts, barbed celts, double axes, etc. Yule (Yule1985: 53-79) has listed 418 celts/axes which he classifies into seven types. In addition, he has listed further 171 axes/ celts which he calls axe-ingots. Interestingly, these axe-ingots are also classified into seven types. Thus he has listed 589 axes/celts of various types and sub-types in his monumental work. To this 589 we can add 251 more axes/ celts which Yule (Yule 1985: 107-11) notes in the Appendix of his work as "non evaluatable, unpublished finds".

The cutting edge of all types of celts/axes is always broader than the butt-end. It is either straight or convex, but its functional utility for cutting/digging/chopping, etc., is beyond doubt. However, it is the "barbed celt" (fig. 1) which is of central interest to us. There are not many examples of this variety unique feature is its elliptical protruding edge (figs. 2 & 3) which in some examples is so made as to look like two barbs joined the convex edge at each flank (fig. 1). These protruding barbs have practically no functional utility as it would bend or break if pressed against a solid mass. Why then extra metal was used for a nonutilitarian purpose, especially when metal was a scarce commodity during those days ? Of the various possibilities for providing these barbs or protruding ends, ornamental aspect is one, and magico-religious is another. It is also likely that originally addition of protuberances may have been aimed at proividing "these special" features to a simple celt so as to distinguish it from the rest.

With these distinguishing features, the "barbed celt", in the apprises of evolution, branched off into a "lugged celt" — the "barbs" being changed into "lugs" (fig. 4). The Mohammadabad figure (near Sitapur, U.P.) (Gupta 1987: 46, pl. 10. IX), and the Kathmandu (Nepal) figure (Yule 1985: 16, 72, fig. 798) are two complete examples of this kind. The broken anthropomorph from Lothal which is described as crescentic sleeved axe by Rao (Rao 1985: 530) might represent this variety, when intact. It is to be noted that while the Mohammadabad figure (fig. 5) has a flat base, the Kathmandu figure (fig. 6) has a slightly concave base. Although small in size (11.8 x 14.2 x 0.4 cm) this figure has a close morphological relation with the Bankot specimens. It is to be noted that whereas Mohammadabad is situated in the plains of U.P.,

Kathmandu and Bankot are in the Himalayan region. However, there is no direct link between Kathmandu and Bankot, as each of them is situated in a certain geographically circumscribed area. we know that in the historical times these geographical barriers were broken. How far it was true in the protohistorical times is a of guess. The Chokhopani copper sheets might give us a clue (?).

The Bankot object (fig. 7) revealed the next step in the process of evolution of the anthropomorph. In this connection the following are noteworthy:

a. The Bankot specimens have a slightly convex "head"/ cutting edge which terminates at the point where it joins the straight out-stretched "arms". On the other hand, the upper part of the "head" portion of the "lugged axe" is convex and terminates abruptly while the lower part, which is joined to upper part having the "lugged portion", is concave (looking like a carrinated pot).

b. The Bankot figures have relatively longer "arms", somewhat semi-cylindrical in shape. The "lugged axe" has flat "lugs".

Here we see that an attempt is made at providing some sort of "human" organs to a particular celt/axe had already taken off. Thus, the "lugs" seem to have been intended for the "arms". Its base is broader/wider than the middle portion. Apparently, it gives impression of a narrow "waist" and a wider "loin", somewhat like a human body (example: Mohammadabad figure - fig. 5). In Kathmandu figure a further development is noticeable in the concave base — looking like a fishtail. The sunk portion in the middle and low projections on the sides of the base of this "lugged axe" gives impression of "feet". In this connection Guppy's comments on Mohammadabad anthropomorph are worth quoting:

"The elliptical end, it is significant to note, resembles, to a great extent, the elliptical end of an anthropomorphic figure. However, instead of 'hands' of the usual anthropomorphic figure, it has two rectangular lugs. Similarly, instead of 'legs' of the usual anthropomorphic figure,it has straight base ... Typologically and functionally the tool was thus meant to be an axe and not an anthropomorphic figure" (Gupta 1987:46).

It may be noted that Gupta narrowly missed the evolutionary features from the axe to the anthropomorph. The link between the "lugged celt" and the evolved anthropomorphic figure may be seen in the Bankot and Kiratpur figures which are conceived in terms of "human" figure, as can be observed in the highly elliptical "head", relatively longer "arms" and cone-like "feet". It is yet to be determined whether the Bankot figures were beaten by a chisel-like instrument so as to give shape to figures like type II (i.e., Bisauli "A", Saipai, and Brooklyn Museum figures). But one can figure out the various successive stages of gradual evolution in these anthropomorphs.

Thus, in Type II figures (figs. 9, 10, & 11) the process of giving a particular celt "human" shape continues, as is apparent from the execution of " arms" and "feet". Here instead of semi-cylindrical "arms", and cone-like "feet" having low profile (such as of Bankot figures), we notice flattened, elongated and hook-like incurved "forearms", and relatively prominent and well shaped "feet". However, the cutting edge of the "head" portion is continued. Apparently, though conceived in "human" form, the original functional significance of this "special axe" was not forgotten. since the act of "cutting" is done by the "hands" and not the "head", the special feature provided in type II figures was the additional "cutting edge" worked on the outer edge of the curved "forearms". In type III figures (figs. 12 & 13) the "head" portion lost its "cutting edge". Instead, it was blunted and provided with a "nail-head" in low relief. Thus, the elliptical axe got transformed into a "human" figure with "hands" discharging the "cutting function". The final stage of the complex anthropomorphic figure is to be seen in type IV figures (figs. 14, 15, 16, 17, 18, & 19). In these examples we notice a massive stylised human form with a canopy-like ridge provided on both sides of the flat surface of the "head" portion. There is a rhythm in these figures. Their contour gives an optical illusion of a standing, mighty human figure. Thus, a "weapon" gets metamorphosed into a "human" figure. I must hasten to add here that this hypothesis rests on the assumption that the evolution took place in the order described but cannot be proved stratigraphically/chronologically in the present state of our knowledge as the Copper Hoard artefacts are found in caches.

Discussion

In ancient Indian literature axe/celt is termed *parasu*. Therefore, I propose to identify this figure as *parasu-purusha* (axe personified). I further venture to add here the mythology of Parasurama (Rama — the wielder of *parasu*) who in pursuit of vanquishing Kshatriyas was humbled by Dhanurdhara Rama (Rama — the archer) (Pargiter 1922: 199-200). In this connection to this it is significant to note that the implements found in the Copper Hoards of the Gang Valley do not include arrow-heads. Does it suggest that the weapon of war of the Copper Hoard folks was predominantly axe? Did the axe wielders encounter the bow wielders who extended their domains in the Ganga-Valley (cf. Gupta's " westerners the Aryans", 1963: 165)? If so, in the mythology of Parasurama-Dhanurdhara Rama encounter we can find echo of a tradition relating to confrontation and ultimately reconciliation of two warring groups representing two different types of technology.

In the present essay I am concerned with the genesis of the anthropomorphic figure rather than applying theoretical models to the Copper Hoard archaeology which I have discussed elsewhere (Joshi 1994a). However, here I touch upon two approaches, namely, "structuralist" (cf. Hodder 1982), and " innovation" (cf. van der Leeuw and Torrence 1989). To me the anthropomorphic figure represents some sort of structural formation, that is, its presence suggesting "leadership" (be it political, economic or religious). Furthermore, I view it as a "symbol" of that leadership". I understand that in the apprises of evolution, the functional significance of the axe was "transformed" into "symbolic" one. It is at this stage that the concept of "innovation" comes to my mind. Here I view the process of "innovation" working not only in the technological plane (i.e., casting and shaping the anthropomorphic figure), but also in cultural configuration. Here we can identify the "active individual" (cf. Hodder 1986: in *passim*) in the act of innovating a "distinct *parasu*" as a symbol of "leadership" (Parasurama ?).

While closing this discussion, it would be appropriate to add here that in the present state of our knowledge it is an open issue as to the identification of the authors of the Copper Hoard Culture of the Ganga -Valley. There is no doubt that they are associated with the authors of the Ochre Coloured Pottery (OCP) as evidenced at Saipai. However, it is also true that there are many places, for example, Kumaon and Nepal, where anthropomorphs have been found, but not the OCP. Discovery of the anthropomorphs in Kumaon and Nepal leaves no room for doubt that these two Himalayan regions also contributed to the cultural and material make up of the Copper Hoard society. Significantly, in Kumaon-Garhwal and nepal there is a community of the coppersmiths called *Tamtas*. They are traditional coppersmiths. Evidence of large scale local copper, brass, and bronze-works in Kumaon-Garhwal during the early mediaeval period (*circa* seventh-tenth centuries) may be seen in the metal sculptures (M.C. Joshi 1970), colossal tridents, finials of temples, etc. (Joshi 1990b: 51-52). Hieun Tsang records presence of copper mines in Kumaon-Garhwal (Beal 1884: I, 198). In the revenue records of the Chandras (who ruled Kumaon from *circa* 1250 to 1790), the coppersmiths are referred to as *Agaris* and *Tamatas*. They had to supply copper ingots as well as copper utensils as items of tax in kind (Joshi 1994b). These evidences show that from at least seventh century AD the coppersmiths formed a class by themselves. The same may hold true during the earlier times also. On these grounds I have, elsewhere, suggested that these coppersmiths might represent the ethnic survivors of the authors of the copper Hoard culture (Joshi 1996). Sadly, scholars working on the central Himalayan region have ignored this important aspect (Nautiyal et al 1991 and Agrawal et al 1995, who are concerned with iron metallurgy *vis-a-vis* Painted Grey Ware culture without any substantial ground).

Acknowledgement

The project on which the present study is based has been partly financed by the University Grants Commission (UGC). The UGC, however, is not responsible for the facts and conclusions stated in this study.

Mr. Silke Fuger, Cultural Attache kindly provided me with Yule's book (1985). Most of the line drawings reproduced in this paper are after Yule. For this I am obliged to him.

BIBLIOGRAPHY

Allchin, Bridget and F.R. Raymond. 1968. The *Birth of Indian Civilization: India and Pakistan before 500 B.C.* Penguin Books, Harmondsworth.

_____.1983. *The Rise of Civilization in India and Pakistan.* Cambridge World Archaeology, Select Book Service Syndicate, New Delhi.

Agrawal, D.P.1971. *The Copper Bronze Age in India.* Munshiram Manoharlal, New Delhi.

Agrawal, D.P. *et al* 1995. "Cist burials of the Kumaun Himalayas". *Antiquity,* 69: pp 550-54.

Agrawal, P.K.1968. "A prehistoric bronze anthropomorph in the Patna Museum and its identification". Puratattva,1:pp 96-98.

Agrawal, R.C.1984. "A unique copper anthropomorph from Sheorajpur, Kanpur". *Bulletin of Museums and Archaeology in U.P.,* 33-34: pp 9-10.

Beal, Samuel.1884. *Si-Yu-Ki: Buddhist Records of the Western World.* Trubner and Company, London. Reprinted, Oriental Books Reprint Corporation, Delhi 1969.

Das Gupta, Tapan Kumar. 1975. "Der Vajra, eine vedische Waffe". Alt- und Neu-Indische studien ... Seminar fur Kultur und Geschichte Indiens an der Universitat Hamburg, 16 (vide Yule 1985: 118).

Deshpande, M.N.1969. Comments on Krishna Deva's paper, in B.P. Sinha (ed.) *Potteries in Ancient India:* p 81. Department of Ancient Indian History and Archaeology, Patna University, Patna.

Dikshit, K.N.1968. "The Copper-Hoards in the light of recent discoveries". *Bulletin of Ancient Indian History and Archaeology,* II: pp 43-50.

Gordon, D.H.1958. *Prehistoric Background of Indian Culture.* Bhulabhai Memorial Institute, Bombay.

Gupta, S.P.1963. "Indian Copper Hoards: the problems of homogeneity, stages of development, origin, authorship and dating". *Journal of the Bihar Research Society,* XLIX (i-iv): p 147-66.

_____.1965. "Further Copper Hoards: a reassessment in the light of new evidence". *Journal of the Bihar Research Society,* LI (i-iv): pp 1-7.

_____1987. 'Copper hoard' implements in the National Museum Collection: 1986". *Puratattva,*16: pp 45-46.

Heine-Geldern, P.1936. "Archaeological traces of the Vedic Aryans". *Journal of the Indian Society of Oriental Art,* IV: pp 87-115.

_____1956. "The coming of the Aryans and the end of the Harappa Civilization". *Man,* LVI: pp 136-40.

Hodder, Ian (ed.).1982. *Symbolic and Structural Archaeology,* Cambridge University Press, Cambridge.

_____1986. *Readings the Past: Current Approaches to Interpretation in Archaeology.* Reprinted 1989 Cambridge University Press, Cambridge.

Indian Archaeology 1988-89 — A Review: pp 87-88.

Jayakar, Pupul.1982. *Aditi,* Exhibition Catalogue. The Handicrafts and Handlooms Exports Corporation of India Ltd. New Delhi.

Joshi, Maheshwar P.1990a. "New horizon of the GangaValley Copper hoard Archaeology". *Bulletin of Museums and Archaeology in U.P.,* pp 45-46: 1-6.

_____ 1994a. "Symbols and structures: new perspective in the Copper Age archaeology of North India". Paper presented to The World Archaeological Congress - 3, New Delhi.

_____.1994b. "The Silpakaras (artisans) of Central Himalaya: a diachronic study".In: Maheshwar P. Joshi, Allan C. Fanger and Charles W. Brown (eds.), *Himalaya: Past and Present,* III (1992- 93):pp 300-33. Shree Almora Book Depot, Almora.

_____.1996. "Tamtas (coppersmiths) of Central Himalaya: a diachronic study". *Journal of Human Ecology* (Special Issue on Himalaya). In press.

Joshi, M.C.1970. "Metal sculptures in the Kumaun Hills and the tradition about Pona Raja". *Journal of the Oriental Institute,* XIX (4): pp 433-39.

Lal. B.B.1951. " Further Copper Hoards from the Gangetic Basin and a review of the problem". *Ancient India,* 7: pp 20-39.

_____.1972a. "A note on the excavation at Saipai" *Puratattva,* 5: pp 46-49.

_____.1972b. "The Copper Hoard culture of the Ganga Valley". *Antiquity,* XLVI:pp282-87.

Lal, M.1981. "Copper Hoard culture of India: a Reassessment". *Puratattva,* 12:pp 65-77.

Nautiyal, Vinod et al.1991. "Beginning of Iron Age in Garhwal, Mid-Central Himalaya: an ecological overview". *Puratattva,* 21: pp 29-35.

Pant, G.N.1989. "Copper Hoards".in: A. Ghosh (ed.) *An Encyclopaedia of Indian Archaeology,* I: pp 350-52 (Subjects). Munshiram Manoharlal, New Delhi.

Pargiter,F.E.1922. *Ancient Indian Historical Tradition.* Reprinted Motilal Banarsidass, Delhi 1972.

Piggott, S.1944. "Prehistoric Copper Hoards in the Ganges Basin". *Antiquity,* XVIII: pp 173-82.

_____.1950. *Prehistoric India.* Penguin Books.

Rao, S.R.1985. *Lothal: A Harappan Port Town 1955-62,* Vol. II. Archaeological Survey of India, New Delhi.

Sankalia, H.D.1974. "Functional significance of the O.C.P. and P.G.W. shapes and associated objects". *Puratattva,* 7: pp 47-52.

Sharma, D.P.1993. "New Light on anthropomorphic figure". *National Museum Bulletin,* 7-8: pp 43-51.

Shastri, H.N.1915. "Recent additions to our knowledge of the Copper Age antiquities of the Indian Empire". *Journal of the Asiatic Society of Bengal,* XI: pp 1-6.

Shukla, S.P.1980. "Copper Anthropomorphs: Some observations". Paper presented to Silver Jubilee Year Seminar, Department of Ancient Indian History, Culture and Archaeology, Allahabad University, Allahabad.

Smith, Vincent A.1905. "The Copper Age and Prehistoric bronze implements of India". *Indian Antiquary,* XXXIV: pp 53-57.

_____.1907. "The Copper Age and Prehistoric bronze implements of India 6 Supplement". Indian *Antiquary,* XXXVI: pp53-57.

Van der Leeuw, S.E. and R. Torrence (eds.)1989. *What's New? A Closer Look at the Process of Innovation.* Unwin Hyman, London.

Yule, P.1985. *Metalwork of the Bronze Age in India.* Becksche Verlagsbuchhandlung, Munchen.

Rock Engravings in The Rock Shelters Of Upland Orissa

S. PRADHAN*

It was in the early thirties that K.P. Jayaswal(1933) reported one of the earliest evidence of rock engravings in India from the rock shelter of Vikramkhol in Sambalpur district of Orissa. But unfortunately such an early and sensational discovery of Jayaswal could not arouse much attention for further investigation of rock-art sites and its research in Orissa. The works of N.P. Chakravorti (1936), S.N. Rajguru (1950), J.P. Singh Deo (1976), G.C. Mohapatra (1982) and the reports of the District Gazetteers give a sketchy picture about only a few rock shelters; viz., Gudahandi and Yogimath (now in Nuwapara district) in Kalahandi district, Manikmoda and Ushakothi in Sundargarh district, Ulap and Vikramkhol in erstwhile Sambalpur district and now in Jharsuguda district and Pakhna Pathar in Mayurbhanj district. Behera (1992) and Neumayer (1992 and 1993) have added five more rock shelters to the list of the rock-art sites. But the recent discovery of sixteen new rock-art sites by the author has given a new dimension to the rock-art research in Orissa.

The rock-art sites of Orissa are found from the Western highlands (17°15'–22°34'N and 82°27'—86°25'E) i.e. from the districts of Mayurbhanj, Sundargarh, Jharsuguda and Kalahandi with its richest repository in Sundargarh, which alone accounts for more than three-fourth of the rock-art sites of Orissa (Map-1) i.e. 23 out of the total of 28 rock- art sites (82%) discovered so far.

The obvious reason for such a distribution is because of its most favourable geomorphological situation. Since this part of Orissa is an extension of the Chhotanagpur plateau and the Chhatisgarh basin, the geomorphologial set-up of this area is comparable to the rock-art sites of Central India which records more than two third of the country's rock-art heritage. Here the rock system is represented by the sedimentaries of fossiliferous, purple ferrugineous sandstone, silt-stone, shells and grits. The rocks are soft, medium grained sand stone and red shale of Cuddapah group which weathers easily. Sandstone hills topped by extensive plateaus with a dense vegetation are dissected by several seasonal and perennial nallahs and streams. It is at the fringes and cliff of these sand stone hills that nature has made cavities of varying dimensions. Such naturally formed rock-cavities and rock-shelters hidden under a dwindling foliage, having a strategic location as good look-outs for the movement of wild animals and game, in an ideal eco-system, attracted Prehistoric men to livein them. They in course of their stay have left behind their signatures in the form of paintings and engravings on the walls and roofs of these rock-shelters along with other artifacts lying embedded in and around the shelters. Although there exists a large numbe of rock-shelters in this geological formation, paintings and engravings are encountered in a few of them. And out of the twentyeight painted rock-shelters discovered so far, rock engravings have been documented from the following thirteen (46% of sites) shelters. They are Vikramkhol and Ulap (Ushakothi III) in Jharsuguda district, Lekhamoda III, Lekhamoda VI, Ushakothi-I, Tongo, Bauri Kupa, Chormoda, Jhinkamoda, Imlimoa I, Imlimoda II, Jodabilmoda, and Manikmoda in Sundargarh district. As many as 748 specimen of engravings have been recorded

*Deptt. of History, Sambalpur University, Joti Vihar, Orissa

from these thirteen rock shelters, which constitutes more than 1/3 of the total rock pictures of Orissa, a rare phenomenon, not found elsewhere in India. Situated within a radius of 10 km all these rock shelters can be approached from the village Kanika in Hemgir Tahsil of Sundargarh district. Kanika is connected by the Howrah-Bombay trunk line of the South-Eastern Railway where the name of the Railway station is Hemgir Road (295.5 m MSL) at a distance of about 34 k.m. from the railway junctions of Jharsuguda (Orissa) and Raigarh (M.P.)

Lekhamoda III

Fig. 1 LEKHAMODA III ———— 60 cm.

Lekhamoda III, situated in the reserve forest of Sukha-Mankar, is an extensive rock shelter measuring 67 m. In length, 5m in width and 6.70m in height. The rock shelter oriented Southwest - Northeast and facing to the North-west, preserves twentytwo specimen of paintings in monochrome of dark red and engravings of two animal forms (deer?) with a post (?) between them (Fig.1). The animals are executed in bold outlines facing to the Northwest. While the small animal is standing erect with its two legs, the bigger one behind it is executed upside down. The total engraving measures 2.49m in length and 0.67m. in breadth whereas the individual forms measures 0.56m x 0.30m and 1.57m x 0.66m. respectively. The traces of dark red pigment in the grooves of the engravings suggest that originally the engravings were filled in with a paste of dark red pigment. Two more specimen of engravings of circles with a diameter of 0.70m. and 0.08m. are also found in the rock shelter along with a Roman 'V' shape.

Lokhamoda VI

Lokhamoda VI measuring 13.35 m in length, 5.45 m. in breadth and about 11m. in height is situated in Tentlikhol (Chichirakhol). Oriented east-West and facing to the South, the highlights of the rock-shelter are a host of engravings randomly executed all over the back wall. As many as 41 shapes could be identified out of 61 specimens,

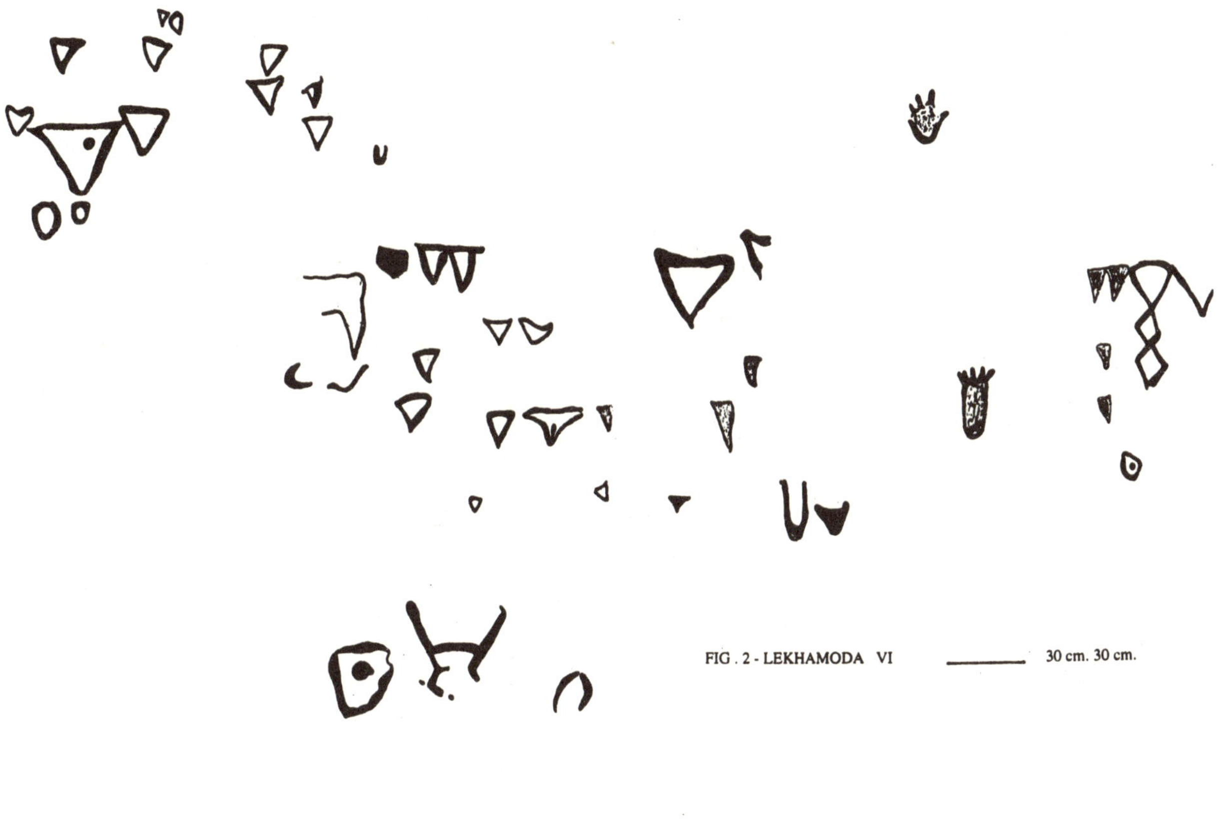

FIG. 2 - LEKHAMODA VI ———— 30 cm. 30 cm.

which include 13 triangular, 3 oval, 2 circular, 2 entwined lines, a palm, a pair of foot prints and 19 other miscellaneous shapes (Fig. 2). All these engravings were originally filled in with a paste of red ochre. Though red ochre has been profusely used for filling the engraving, this is the only rock shelter in the group without any painting in red. On stylistic ground, colour composition and superimposition the white painting of human figures armed with sword, stick and musical drums found in this rock-shelter belong to a much later peiod than the engravings (Fig. 2). The presence of a central hole with or without a slit and sometimes with a central line in the triangle suggest that they were nothing but a host of female genitals (Fig. 2).

Manikmoda

By far the largest rock-shelter discovered so far, the

FIG . 3 - MANIKMODA

rock shelter of Manikmoda oriented East-West and facing to the south measures 89.50m. in length, 11.50m. in breadth and 7.32m. in height. Gifted with a perennial water source oozing from its deep recesses the rock-shelter is adorned with fifty six specimen of paintings in monochrome of dark red, orange red, white and yellow and the lone specimen of an engraving of a serpentine shape measuring 2.50m. (Fig. 3). This deeply incisd serpentine shape just above the water pool baffle all interpretations.

Tongo

The rock-shelter of Tongo near the village Giripur is oriented East-West and facing to the south. It measures 50m. in length, 6.10m in breadth and about 11m. in height. The rock shelter has got 190 specimen of engravings randomly executed on its bacck wall in an area of 35m Triangular shapes resembling female genitals predominate the engraved forms. The other forms are palm and foot prints, rhombic patterns (honey-comb), serpentine and a host of forms resembling Roman characters like X, Y, T and H. The rhombic pattern is a marked decorative motif of Tongo. Serpentine at places it takes the shape of a female genital (Fig. 4). All these carvings were originally filled in with a paste of ochre in their grooves. Though there is nodiscernible ochre in their grooves though there is no discernible painting at Tongo, in one

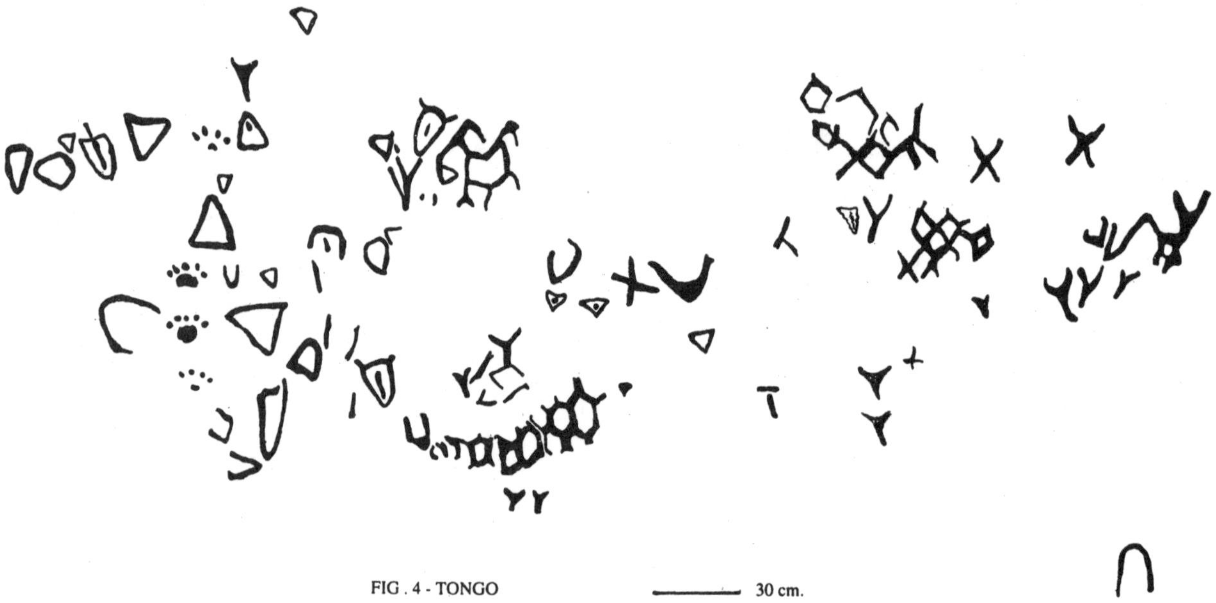

FIG . 4 - TONGO —— 30 cm.

case the shape of a scooped out female genital has been exquisitely is embroidered in yellow over red. The decorative pattern has been achieved through an urge for sophistication in simplicity.

Ushakothi III

The rock-shelter at Usakothi III perching at the summit of a hill near the village Ulap is locally more known for the ramparts of a late medieval fortification on its top. A prickly path leading to the rock shelter negotiates the stiff gradient. While Lekhamoda VI and Tongo are for their engravings, Ushakothi III exhibits a happy blending of engravings and polychromatic as well as monochromatic paintings. The engraved forms (985 specimen) found in the midst of paintings are palm and foot prints, female genitals, zig zag lines, circles, brackets, dots, loops, hoops, cobra-hood-marks and many other forms that defy any geometric pattern or interpretation. However, a large canine animal is conspicuous in the midst of these engravings (Fig. 5). It is significant to note here that the engravings have mostly been executed at the bottom of the rock shelter.

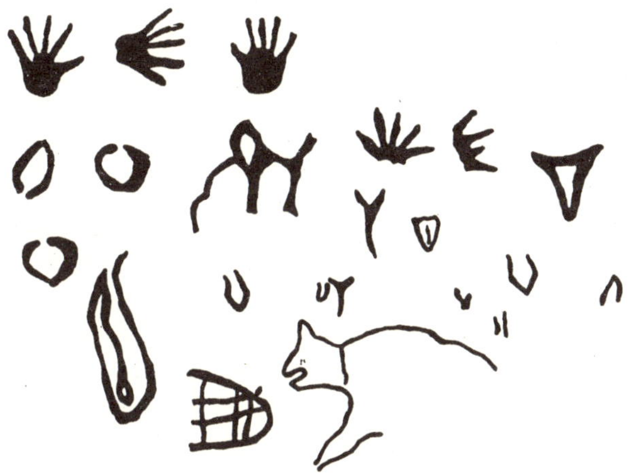

FIG . 5 - USHAKOTHI III

Vikramkhol

The overhanging rock-shelter of Vikramkhol facing North-east measures 37 m. in length, 5.65 m in breadth and 8 m in height. It bears the illegible signature of the time past in the form of engravings (68 specimen) and paintings in an area of 11 m x 2.10 m K.P. Jayaswal (1933), the first palaeographist to study these engravings, was of the opinion that the engravings of Vikramkhol is a pictographic inscription, partially incised and partially painted in two lines. He further said that the writing was from right to left and "the characters in Vikramkhol inscription belong to a period intermediary between the script of Mohenjodaro and Brahmi. Some letters still retain their original or proto-Brahmi forms. This proves the origin of Brahmi to be Indian and throws a flood of light on the history of writing, as from Brahmi the Phoenician and European scripts are derived".

While N.P. Chakrabarti (1936: 229) and Charles Fabri (1936 :230) have supported Jayaswal's theory that Vikramkhol engravings have the salient features of an early writing, scholars like Gordon (1960 : 133) have raised serious objections and commented, "the left hand portion of this mass engravings is by far the clearest, but even here it is difficult to believe that what we see is writing, although a certain number of rings have some what alphabetical-form in appearance". G.C. Mohapatra (1982 : 99) is of the opinion that "frequent repetition of some symbols, their interwined character, linear arrangement along with use of dots, loops and dashes leave little doubt that these are writings. They strongly recall the style of early rock inscriptions of India". However, it is worthwhile to give a description of the depictions before jumping into any definite conclusion on the controversy. Barring the lone specimen of a honeycomb painting in dark red, what we see at Vikramkhol are a host of engravings (68 speccimens) of the usual triangular female genitals, foot prints, obliterated portions of rhombic patterns, double triangles, cobra hood marks, brackets with dots and identifiable geometric and floral patterns which are also noticed elsewhere at Leekhamoda VI, Tongo and Ushakothi III (Fig. 6). The conspicuous depiction of an animal standing with two disproportionate legs and with a small tail and a pointed mouth (poited dog?), just below an oval shape being filled in with vertical lines next to a female genital is not only interesting but also intriguing (Fig. 6B). Since a major portion of the engraving has already been eroded by the rain water streaming on the rock surface from the top, it is dificult to identify or describe the surviving incisions which look more like a host of strokes, lines, dots, loops and Roman X and Y. It seems that all these engravings were originally filled with a paste of red ochre whose traces are still available in their grooves. Besides engravings the remaining surface of the rock-shelter appears to have been originally painted with different figures and patterns, as evident from a still surviving design of a honey comb pattern in dark red at the right end of the engravings.

FIG . 6 - VIKRAMKHOL

Ushakothi I

At Uṣhakothi paintings are found in three rock shelters namely Rishikund, Sitakund and Sarpa Gumpha whereas engravings (67 specimen) are found in Rishikund and Sitakund. At Rishikund engraving is found executed in a well prepared rubbed surface of 8.57 m x 0.73 m. the engraving is in one line and the characters are smeared with a layer of ochre. Though it is difficult to identify the forms/patterns, its style of execution may well be compared with the engravings of Vikramkhol. The local tribals believe that it is a writing of seven and half alphabets. G.C. Mohapatra thinks that although there are many features common between the writings of Vikramkhol and Ushakothi in their techniques of engravings, style of symbols,use of red ochre paint, selection of identical type of rock shelters and surroundings, each of them separately is not devoid of their distinctive individuality. At Ushakothi the writings are small in size, irregular in arrangement and somewhat more geometric in shape than those at Vikramkhol. On the other hand straight linear arrangement, bold intertwined appearance, systematic disposisition in rows one below the other give the Vikramkhol writing an individuality which is distinct from that of Ushakothi. Mohapatra further brings the gap of a generation or two between them and concludes by saying that they could be ritualistic in their purpose. However, a wide exposure to all the engraved rock-shelters does not confirm the hypothesis of an antique script in all these engravings. In fact what we see at Ushakothi is a host of palm and foot prints, triangles resembling female genitals, sometimes in pairs and many other geometric and non-geometric patterns and symbols as found elsewhere.

Baurikupa

The rock-shelter of Baurikupa is situated in Bhauripahar in the deep Reserve Forest of Jangir, at a distance of about 6 km from the village Girsima in Hemgir Tahsil of Sundargarh district. Oriented North-South and facing to the North-East the rock shelter measures 22 m. in length, 8 m. in width and about 9 m. in height. The highlights of the rock shelter is a host of engravings executed on the back wall over an area of 14 m x 4 m. Though the engravings have largely been eroded and disfigured by natural weathering agencies, as many as 96 specimen have been documented, which include specimen like palm, rhombic patterns, triangular female genital shapes,heart pattern and a host of abstract zoomorphic, and anthropomorphic forms. The grooves of these engravings has traces of dark ochre and yellow pigments.

Chormoda

The rockshelter of Chormoda in Bagh-chagha-kendu reserve forest can be approached from the border village of Chanarpur (6 km). Facing to the south, the rockshelter measures 12.40 m. in length, 13.05 m. in depth and 5m in height and the shelter is so named becuse during the British Raj it was a hideout of the thieves on the highway from Raigarh to Sundargarh. The rock shelter is featured by a host of cup-marks randomly executed all over the shelter walls along with a lone specimen of an engraving. There are as many as 826 specimen of cup-marks executed on the walls extending over an area, above 0.70 m. from the present ground level to approachable heights. Though they are unevenly distributed, their concentration is more in the Western wall (Fig. 7). The cup marks vary in their size and spacing; with an average of 2.5 cm radius, the largest one being 6.5m and the smallest being 5 mm. in radius. They are distributed in a number of clusters with higher sparse concentration mostly without any identifiable forms.

FIG . 7 - CHORMODA ——— 30 cm.

On the basis of their distribution they may be classified as; (a) linear forms of straight or parallel lines (b) some what circular/apsidal/triangular forms (c) and independent marks being isolated from each other, without forming any pattern, which constitutes the majority of cup-marks. In linear form is an interesting specimen of 190 cup marks arranged in two parallel lines of 95 cup-marks in each line running North-South in the western wall to a length of 4 m. (Fig. 7). In the same wall there are cup-marks in small alignment of single line, double lines and lines of three. In one case there are 15 cup-marks arranged in 5 rows with 3 marks in each row and in another case there is the vertical alignment of 40 cup-marks arranged in two parallel lines of 20 marks in each line just above a horizontal line of 11 marks in the eastern wall. An apsidal/triangular pattern made of 17 marks with a central bigger cup mark in the eastern wall is no less intriguing. A closer scrutiny reveals that originally these cup-marks were filled in with a paste of ochre. From the distribution of the cup-marks it appears as if there is an attempt to depict the sky at night with the stars and planets in constellations and in isolated occurrences, because the whole representation is as enigmatic as the sky itself. Whatever the purpose might be the recent discovery of this rock shelter is an important addition in the rock-art heritage of India.

The lone specimen of the engraved pattern on the western wall just above the longest parallel alignment of cupmarks is also intriguing. The rock shelter has a thick occupational deposit yielding microliths from the surface collection.

Jhinkamoda

Situated at a distance of about 1/4 km from Chormoda on the right bank of Ranidarha nallah, Jhinkamoda measures 28 m. in length, 7 m. in breadth and 6m. in height. Facing to the North-east the rock shelter exhibits the engraving of seven traingular female genital patterns along with a few eroded and unidentifiable specimens. As usual the groves of these engravings originally had ochre filling.

Jodabil

Jodabil rock-shelter locally so known for the two large sub-terranian pits, is situated right on the left bank of the perennial Bhalu-juria nallah, a tributary of Sapne nallah in Diagarh reserve forest of Hemgir range in Sundargarh district. Oriented East-West and facing to the North the rock shelter measures 26 m. in length, 10 m. in breadth and 6.55 m. in height. The rock-shelter is featured by hundreds of mud-dubber nests (a kind of wasp that makes small mud-nests on house walls), which have largely disfigured and concealed the paintings and engravings executed therein. Traces of paintings are noticed at places along with 21 specimen of engravings featured mainly by triangular female genital patterns. (Fig.8). The grooves of these genital forms, as usual elsewhere, were rubbed with moistened haematite lumps.

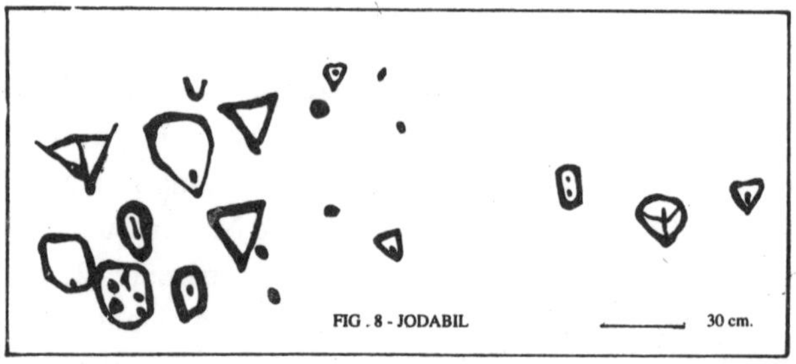

FIG. 8 - JODABIL

Imlimoda I

Situated right on the right bank of perennial Sapned nallah in Dhanubauns reserve forest in Lefripara Tahsil of Sundargarh district the massive rock shelter of Imlimoda I measures 17.55 m. in length, 8.45 m. in depth and 7.55m. in height. Besides the four grinding holes and a small occupational deposit, the rockshelter is featured by as many as 109 specimen of engravings,out of which 89 are identifiable female genital patterns executed poorly in shapes of ovals, apsidals and triagles with or without a central line and a shallow depression at the lower edge or

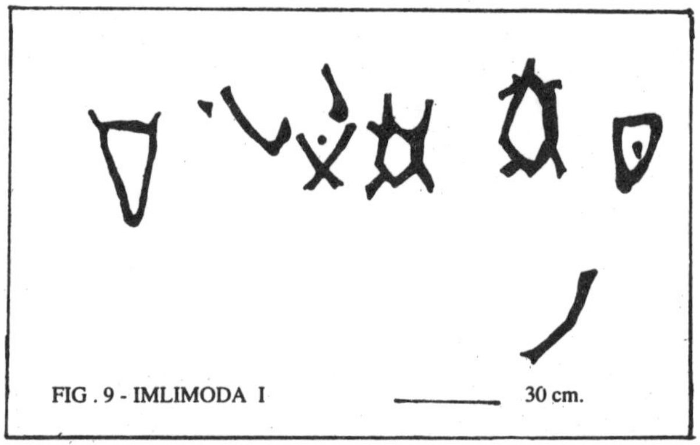

FIG. 9 - IMLIMODA I

at the centre (Fig.9). No other shape could be identified except a palm print. The size of the genital patterns vary from 40 cm. x 28 cm. to .07 x .05 cm with an average of 22 cm x 12 cm. in their length and breadth respectively.

Imlimoda II

Imlimoda II is situated on the right bank of the Kurkuti nallah, a tributary of Sapnei nallah in Dhanubauns reserve forest of Hemgir range in Sundargarh district. Oriented east-West and facing to the South the rock shelter measures 22m. in length, 6m in breadth and 9 m. in height. The shelter preserves 24 specimen of engravings. Except the lone specimen of an eroded and disfigured rhombic pattern, all the engraved forms are triangular female genitals with the usual traces of ochre in their grooves (Fig.10).

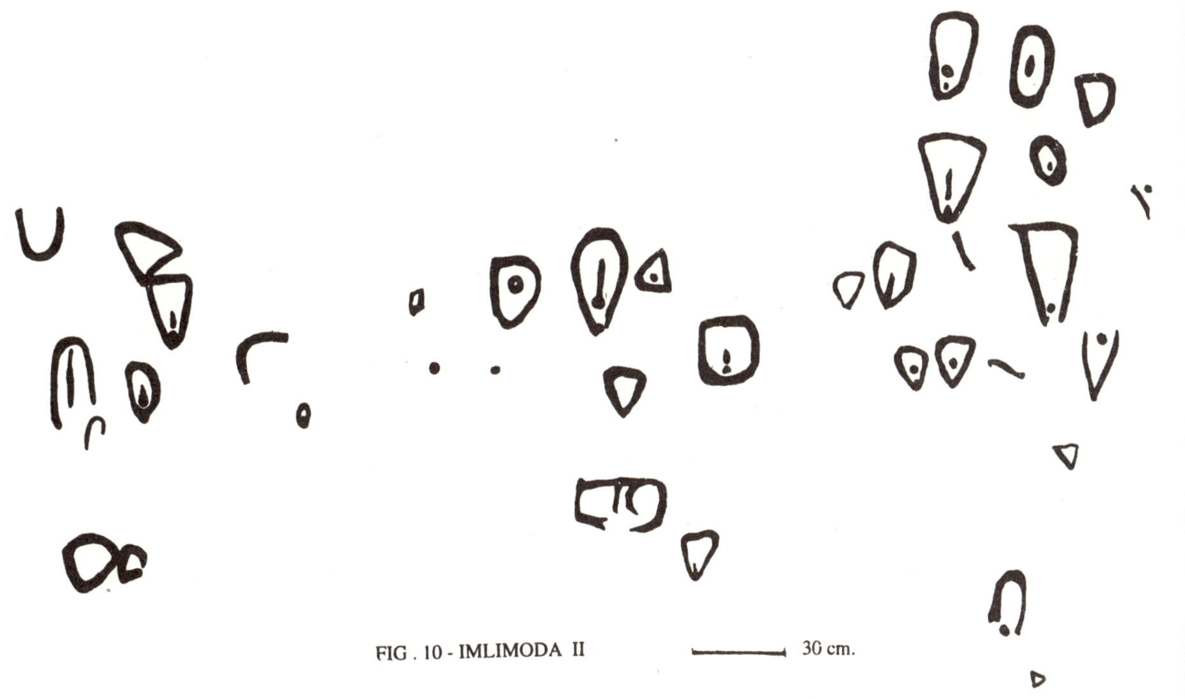

FIG. 10 - IMLIMODA II

In view of the above documentation the following discussions and observations are necessary for a better understanding of the rock engravings of Orissa;

(1) The engraved rock-shelters like the other painted rock-shelters do not follow any precise rule with regard to their position,orientation, size and concentration. In fact some of the bigger and better rock-shelters of this region do not show any trace of either painting or engraving. While some of them are easily approachable, others need stiff climbing risking even one's own life. Grinding holes and microliths of geometric and non-gemetric tools like blades,backed points, lunates, trapaezes, triangles, tned arrow heads, brins, fluted cores, flakes and chips are abundantly found in association with lumps of ground haematities from the occupational deposits and adjoining slopes of these rock shelters. Hand-made mat-impressed and engraved potteries have also been discovered along with-wheel made potteries from Lekhamoda VI. The other artefacts recovered from Lekhamoda VI are ringstones, hammer-stones, and celts suggesting an occupational deposit extending from the mesolithic period to the neolithic chalcolithic period.

(2) In the rock-art heritage of Orissa, engravings constitute a special feature along with the paintings, both being complimentary to each other, which is rarely found elsewhere in India.

(3) The treatment of the engraving is linear, boldly incised deep into the soft sandstone rock faces. The grooves of such engravings, measuring 20 mm x 10 mm (approx.) in width and depth, were mostly filled in with a paste of dark red ochre or were rubbed with moist haematite lumps, the most favoured colour of the Mesolithic paintings of Orissa.

(4) The engravings with their bewildering variety and pattern defy any chronological attribution due to the lack of any efinite evidence of superimpositions, stylistic differentiation and narrative pictorial depictions so common in Central Indian rock paintings. Though the forms and shapes have been executed with much care and precision, they are mostly abstract in their conceptions which might have had some kind of mystic and/or ritualstic significance as found in the wall paintings of the Saoras and engravings of the Juangs and Kondhs of Orissa.

(5) Anthropoforms are conspicuously absent in the rock engravings of Orissa. The geometric patterns like zig zag line, triangle, square, circle, grid of vertical and horizontal lines and spirals have been executed with so much of skill and precision that any geometrician would envy them which probably explains the transformation of some animal forms in geometric forms as found at Lekhamoda III.

(6) The popular motifs and patterns in these rock engravings are; female genitals, rhombic pattern, palm, foot, brackets and cobra hoodmarks with dots. Some of the intricate patterns like the rhombic ones have faint resemblance to the Central Indian paintings of the Mesolithic period. Orissan rock paintings are also pronounced with all such patterns and forms. The carving of a female genital from a serpentine form at Tongo is no less intriguing. What do they mean? Do they mean a Freudian interpretation of perversity? Do they have any association with fertility rites? Do they depict the primordial mother, the source of creation of all beings which recalls in one's mind the image of the large bellied and full bosom naked bas-relief of the Venus of Laussel or the Venus of Wilendorf. Symbols of fertility rituals always held a very important position in the religion of man.

(7) In this context in the absence of any satisfactory explanation as to what motivated the Pre-historic men for such graphic and abstract expression, an attempt at an Ethnographic interpretation may not stand irrational in view of the rich tradition of tribal art for which the state is so well known. The illiterate tribals like Saora, Kondh, Santal, Juang, Gond, etc. who constitute about one-third of the total population, living in the remote isolated hilly region of highland Orissa have a rich tradition of paintings and engravings executed in their pristine purity on their mud plastered house walls and other household objects and artefacts. V.Elwyn (1952:2) aptly remarked "the art forms and probably so also the process of production and even the underlaying ideas, have been inherited by the Saoras as the continuity of tradition". Ritual motifs in tribal art are more abstract in form and spiritual in meaning. To some tribals like Saoras, art is an essential requirement in their struggle for existence; to drive away diseases, calamities and evil spirits; to promote and preserve the fertility of the crops; to assist in easy child birth and for many such other purposes. they are worshipped as icons. While the tribals lie the Kondhs and Juangs practice wood carvings the Santhals and Saoras paint their houses in red and white and to a keen observer some motifs of rock art like spirals, honeycomb pattern, intricate designs, triangles, palm and foot prints are found in different degrees of execution in contemporary tribal art of Orissa. In the fitness of this an ethno-archaeological approach may be of help in solving some of the enigmas of rock engravings of Orissa.

REFERENCES

Behra P.K., 1992 "Pre-historic Rock Art pertaining to fertility cult and other subjects of Orissa, *Pragdhara,* No.2. 1991-92: 7-17.

Chakravarti, N.P. 1936. "The Vikramkhol Rock Inscription," *Annual Report of Archaeological Survey of India,* 1930-34. I: 229

Elwyn, V. 1951. *The Tribal Art of Middle India,* London: 2.

Fabri, C.L. 1936. "The Vikramkhol Rock Inscription."

Editorial remark, *Annual Report, Archaeological Survey of India,* 930-34, I : 230.

Gordon, D.H. 1960. *The Prehistoric Background of Indian Culture.* 2nd Edition, Bombay.

Indian Archaeology 1969-7-. A Review: 61.

Jayaswal, K.P. 1933, The Vikramkhol Inscription, Sambalpur District. *The Indian Antiquary,* Vol. 62;58-60.

Mathpal,Y. 1984. *Prehistoric Rock Paintings of Bhimbetka,* Abhinav Publications, Delhi.

Mohapatra, G.C. 1982. "Notes on the Vikramkhol and Ushakothi Rock - shelters in Orissa" *Man and Environment,* VI: 97-100.

Neumayer, E. 1992. "Rock Pictures in Orissa" *Puratattva* 22, 1991-92 : 13-2 Neumayer, E. 1993, *Lines on stone,* New Delhi.

Rajguru, S.N. 1950. *Journal of the Kalinga Historical Reseach Society* : 245.

Singh Deo, J.P. 1976." Prehistoric cave Painting of Jogimath Donger." *Orissa Historical Research Journal,* Vol. XXII, No. 2: 21-22)

Wakankar, V.S. and Brooks, R.R. 1976. *Stone Age Painting in India.* (D.B. Taraporevala sons and Co. Bombay) 96-98.

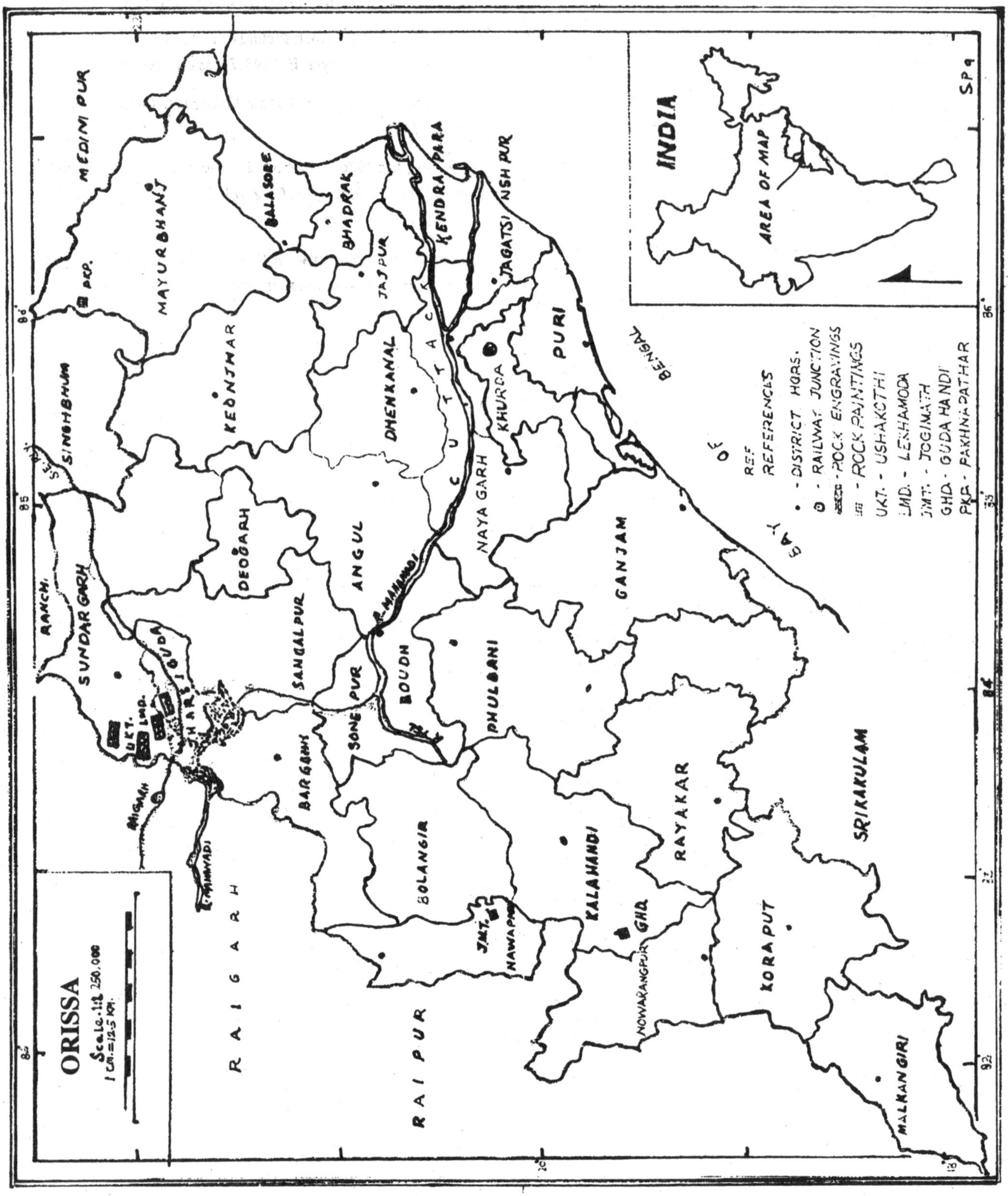
ORISSA
Scale 1:1,250,000
1 CM.=12.5 KM.
INDIA
AREA OF MAP
REFERENCES
• - DISTRICT HQRS.
⊙ - RAILWAY JUNCTION
ROCK ENGRAVINGS
ROCK PAINTINGS
UKT. - USHAKOTHI
LMD. - LEKHAMODA
JMT. - JOGIMATH
GHD. - GUDA HANDI
PKP. - PAKHNA PATHAR
BAY OF BENGAL
MAYURBHANJ
MEDINI PUR
SINGHBHUM
KEONJHAR
BALASORE
BHADRAK
JAJPUR
KENDRAPARA
JAGATSINGHPUR
CUTTACK
DHENKANAL
PURI
KHURDA
NAYA GARH
ANGUL
DEOGARH
SUNDAR GARH
RANCHI
JHARSUGUDA
SAMBALPUR
SONEPUR
BOUDH
PHULBANI
GANJAM
BARGARH
BOLANGIR
KALAHANDI
NAWAPARA
NOWARANGPUR
RAYAKAR
KORAPUT
MALKANGIRI
SRIKAKULAM
RAIPUR
RAIGARH
R. MAHANADI

Excavations at Sankisa 1995-96

B.R. Mani*

Sankisa, Lat. 27°20'N and Long. 79°20'E, is situated in Shamsabad tehsil of district Farrukhabad in Uttar Pradesh at a distance of about 320 kms. from Delhi and about 40 kms from the eponymous district headquarters. The nearest railway station is Pakhna and the police station is Merapur. The site is located near Kali Nadi, the river mentioned in Sanskrit literature as Ikshumati.

Sankisa has been unanimously identified with Sankasya, mentioned as the royal city and capital of Kusadhwaja, the brother of king Janaka in Valmiki's *Ramayana* and with Sankassa mentioned in Pali Buddhist texts. Chinese travellers Fa-hsien and Hsuan-Tsang visited the place and mentioned it as Song-Kia-She or Kia-pi-tha. According to them and the Buddhist tradition Buddha accompanied by Brahma and Indra descended at this site from the Trayastrimsa heaven by a ladder of gold or gem after preaching the *dhamma* to his mother Mayadevi. The place has been a centre of Buddhist pilgrimage. The Chinese travellers had seen the Asokan pillar, monastery, several stupas and *naga* tank in the city of Sankisa.

The mounds at Sankisa are scattered in almost a circular area within a periphery of about 5 kms. The present village of Sankisa is located on the high mound, measuring nearly 400m in east-west and 300m in north-south direction with a height of over 12 metres. Nearly 300 metres due south is another mound of solid brick work, supposed to be a stupa, topped by a late medieval temple of Bishari or Bisari Devi. An Asokan elephant capital is kept at the site under a shed towards northeast of the temple. The entire area within the earthen rampart is full of mounds of different sizes and heights. Outside the ramparts are also a few mounds. During the course of earlier explorations Painted Grey Ware, Northern Black Polished Ware and its associated red ware pottery and terracottas, coins, sculptures and other antiquities have been found from these mounds.

Although the site is known for more than 150 years, no scientific archaeological excavation was conducted there so far. Major General Sir Alexander Cunningham had discovered the site in 1842 and explored the ruins in 1862 at leisure. He has described the antiquarian remains noticed at the site, including the elephant capital, and on the basis of accounts of Chinese travellers he has also tried to identify the important places with the existing mounds. During 1876-78 Cunningham visited Sankisa three times and on the first occasion opened a few trenches in the hope of finding some portion of the shaft on which Asokan elephant capital might have stood. Due north of Bisharidevi temple he located brick walls and a square brick base which he thought was meant for the Asokan pillar but later on, during his excavations at the site in 1926, Hirananda Sastri laid bare the brick platform again and after re-examining it, he proposed that it was made of comparatively modern brick of late medieval origin and could not have supported the Asokan pillar. Both the archaeologists had collected a large number of antiquities from the site ranging from Mauryan period to the early medieval period. Earlier excavators had not paid any attention towards study of stratigraphy and cultural depos-

*Archaeological Survey of India, E.Br- II, New Delhi.

its at the site. Painted Grey Ware was reported from surface at Sankisa by B.B.Lal during his explorations in 1955-56. It was found in the earliest deposits during the present excavations.

In order to know the earliest antiquity and cultural sequence of the site and to get an idea of the archaeological potential of it archaeological excavations were taken up by the Excavation Branch II, Purana Qila, New Delhi of the Archaeological Survey of India from 1-5-1996 to 8-7-1996 for the first season under the direction of the author as Superintending Archaeologist assisted by K.K. Sharma, Vishnu Kant, L.S. Mamani, V.P. Verma, Vinod Kumar, Charan Singh and other members of the staff of the Excavation Branch II, New Delhi.

Before starting excavation work the entire site was surveyed thoroughly and it was noticed that the earliest ceramic remains are found only on the mound located towards south of the Bisharidevi temple. A new road is being constructed adjoining the archaeological area and for filling up the area for proposed road earth has been dug from the adjoining mound. A number of Painted Grey Ware sherds were collected from that site. It was, therefore, decided to lay out a few trenches at the spot. Trenches in forms of quadrants of 10 x 10 m square were laid and excavations were taken up in quadrants 3 and 4 of square A 1. Towards south of the mound on a separate smaller mound quadrant 3 of square E10 was also opened.

It was observed during excavations that in the area of A 1 the top three layers have a number of early and recent pits and as a result the material is very much mixed up. The habitational deposits of Sunga-Kushan periods at this spot have suffered much disturbance and early material, including sherds of Painted Grey Ware, Northern Black Polished Ware and black slipped ware have been found mixed up with the material of Sunga-Kushan period. Similarly, at E 10 the top two layers are formed in the shape of filling and levelling deposits.

At A 1 a mud floor having thickness of 8 cm with remains of circular post-holes were found in quadrant 4 which is sealed by layer 3 (Pl. I). The deposits below the level of the floor are quite reliable and two firm and thick layers of the deposits of Pained Grey Ware period were found in layers 5 and 6 with a thickness of about 1.25 to 1.50 m (Fig 1). It can be, therefore, presumed that the mud floor with post-holes may belong to the early NBP period. Total deposit in both the quadrants over the natural soil was found to be more than 2.5 m. In the quadrant 3 of E 10 the layers 3 and 4 have yielded material belonging to the Kushan period. The thickness of this deposit is about 40 cm. A 2.10 m long burnt brick wall having two extant courses of bricks was found which may belong to the Kushan period (Pl. II). The wall runs in east-west direction having a width of 0.75 m. It was found extending further towards both the sections. Maximum size of the bricks used in its construction is 44x27x6.5 cm. Layer 5 of this quadrant, which is 1 m. thick, has yielded material which can be dated to the first two centuries Before Christ. Layer 6 and 7 with a thickness of about 1.05 m. have yielded NBP with its associated red ware. Total deposit over the natural soil in this quadrant was about 4.0m.

The most important investigation in the first season's excavation work at the site was the confirmation of Painted Grey Ware period deposit which has yielded, besides usual shapes of PGW, black- and -red ware, black slipped ware and associaed red ware, important antiquities like terracotta bust of mother goddess, a similar terracotta female figurine(Pl. III), terracotta rattle with eight mini-balls, discs, *ghata* shaped bead, decorated and plain balls, gamesmen and other terracotta objects (Pl. IV), discs, bone points and bone arrow-heads, iron chisels and a stone bead which reflect the material culture of early iron age. Painted Grey Ware sherds have been found from top levels in square A 1 till the pick-axe touched natural soil. Its frequency was found more in layers 3, 3A and 4 in quadrant 3 and layer 3 in quadrant 4.

Surface finds from different areas of Sankisa and in particular from the village mound and area towards its north indicate that cultural deposits of other periods are surely to be encountered if further excavations are taken up in future. Cultural assemblage noticed at the present excavated site suggests deposits of following periods -

Period I- Painted Grey Ware period (*C.*9th century B.C. to *C.*6th century B.C.)

Period II-Northern Black Polished Ware period (*C.*6th

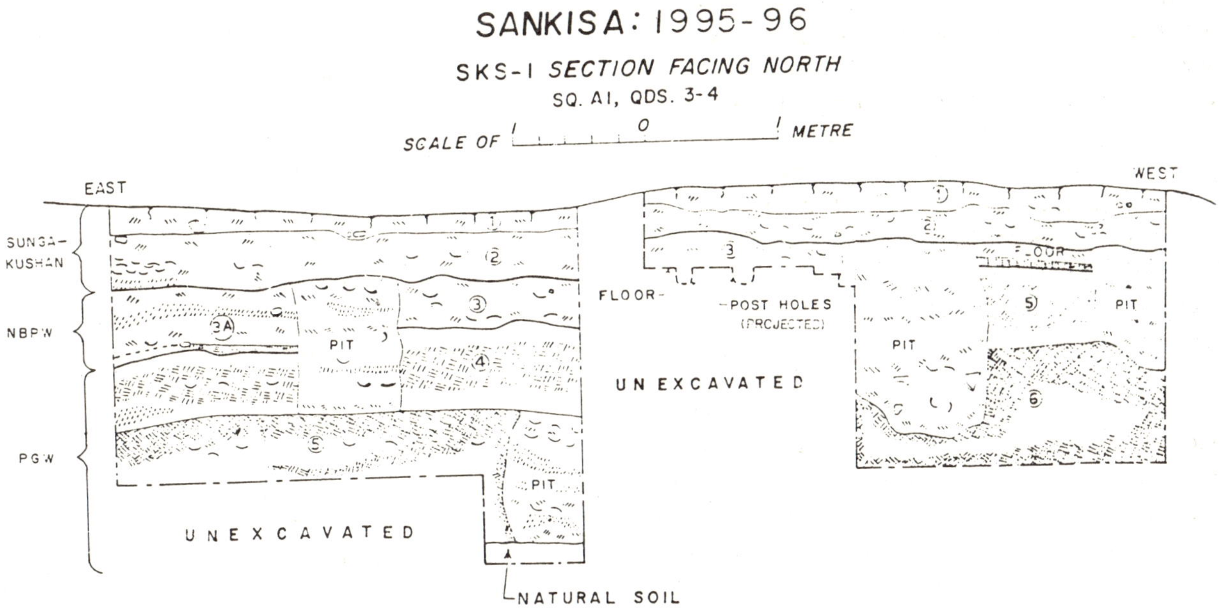

Fig. 1

century B.C. to *C.*3rd century B.C.)

Period III - Sunga period (*C.*2nd century B.C. to *C.* 1st century B.C.)

Period IV-Kushan period (*C.* 1st century A.D. to *C* .3rd century A.D.)

This classification is tentative and as per generally accepted divisions which can be confirmed later after further excavations, study of more antiquarian remains and scientific dating of the samples collected during excavations.

Layers 3 and 4 in quadrant 3 of square E 10 which represent the Kushan deposits have yielded tiles and a very few early shapes of sharp edged and incurved bowls in red ware besides a few black slipped ware sherds. The main ceramic industry was red ware, both plain and slipped. Handmade storage jars and wheel turned sherds comprising spout of sprinkler, lipped basin, medium size basins having nail headed variety also, bowls, including sharp edged bowls and thumb impressed incurved bowls with string-cut bases, small to medium size vases, spout, lamps and decorated pottery with incised multi-grooved designs and stamped decorations of *Srivatsa* and leaf design, have been found from layer 3. Shapes from layer 4 comprise thumb impressed incurved bowls, deep bowl with slightly out - turned rim, small to medium size vases, lids, handle, lipped basins, short neck vase with out-turned rim having multigrooved decoration on the exterior part of neck, medium size vase with applique shoulder design and handmade storage jars. Tiles have also been recovered.

Layer 5 of quadrant 3 of square E 10 which represents the Sunga period has also yielded red ware sherds which comprise base parts of bowls, spouted bowl with incised design, bowl with flat rim which might have also been used as cover or lid, miniature bowl with perforation at the side of the base part, small vases with short neck and out-turned rim, medium size vases with multigrooved design, vases of Ahichchhatra type X A, miniature pots, handle of jar, water vessels, carinated *handi,* knobbed lid, convex sided dish, medium size jar having flat top for provision of lid or cover, sprinkler, lids, deep bowl, bottle necked flask or water vessel, dish having externally flared rim, hand-made storage jar. hopscotches of grey ware and red ware and tiles have also been found.

Layer 6 and 7 of quadrant 3 of square E 10 represent the NBPW period. Layer 6 has yielded sherds of deep bowls and convex sided dishes in grey ware. Associated red ware shapes include base parts of bowls, deep bowl, funnel shaped lid, miniature pots, convex sided dishes, carinated *handi,* nail headed basin with soot marks on both the surfaces, channelled basin (dia. 36 cm.), plain basin, small to medium size vases, vase of Ahichchhatra type X A, small incurved bowl and handmade storage jars. A tile with hole was also found. Northern Black Polished Ware sherds were found from pit 1 sealed by layer 6 which comprise mostly dishes with black, golden and silver shades having medium to fine fabrick. A convex sided dish with golden shade has a diameter of 26 cm. Red ware sherds from the same pit comprise hand made plain and cord impressed storage jars with externally flared rim having husk impressions or storage jars with applique bands on the junction of rim and body, large bowl with incurved rim and tapering side (dia 36 cm.), convex sided dish, deep bowl, small to medium size vases including Ahichchhatra type 10 A, small incurved bowls, carinated *handi* and bottle necked vase. Deep bowl of black slipped ware and convex sided dish of grey ware were also found in the pit besides hopscotches. Layer 7 of quadrant 3 of E 10 has yielded convex sided dishes in grey ware and black slipped ware.

The associated red ware shapes include incurved bowls, string cut bases of bowls, deep bowls, convex sided dishes, basins, ledged and carinated *handis,* medium to large size vases, including Ahichchhatra type 5 A, miniature pot with soot mark, mat impressed and corded sherds of jars, one with applique band on shoulder, painted and incised decorations on sherds. Hopscotch was also found.

Layers 3, 3A, 4 and 5 of quadrant 3 of square A 1 and layers 3, 5and 6 of quadrant 4 of square A 1 have yielded a good number of Painted Grey Ware sherds besides its associated ceramics Fig. 2. Layers 5 and 6 of quadrant 4 of A1 are less disturbed and have provided definite evidence of habitational deposit of pre- NBPW period. A large unbaked storage jar has been noticed in the section facing west in this deposit which is sealed by layer 5. Layer 5 has yielded red ware of both handmade as well as wheel turned variety having coarse to fine fabric Fig. 3. The shapes are storage jars with applique band at shoulder, perforated footed bowl, fine convex sided dishes, incurved bowls, cord and mat impressed vases, medium size vases with externally thickened rim, lids with half folded rim, lids with flared rim, fine deep bowls, lipped bowl, miniature pot and carinated handi with externally thickened rim having mild depression on exterior. Clay lump with reed marks has also been found. The black slipped ware shapes include convex sided dish with mild depression on the exterior side of rim, deep bowls with concave profile, deep bowls with slightly out-turned rim, deep bowls with mild carination at the bottom and dish with slightly thicker section. The Painted Grey Ware shapes comprise convex sided bowls having vertical strokes with black paint in the inner and angular strokes on the exterior, convex sided bowls with black band on the rim, basal part of a bowl with red exterior and grey inner surface having circular bands in the middle and vertical strokes all around, a sherd having floral design made out of three hooks, dish with groups of vertical strokes on both the surfaces, bowl with black painted rim having vertical strokes below followed by loops further below, sherds with vertical and horizontal strokes in interior, one sherd with outer red surface and vertical strokes on both the surfaces and one thick sherd with black painting. Its associated grey ware shapes are convex sided dishes and bowls, one with slight depression on the exterior side of the rim. Some pieces have either interior or exterior red surface. The same layer has yielded a few sherds of fine variety of black and red ware of which one is a convex sided dish. A few sherds have outer black and inner red or grey surface. Some sherds of coarse variety of black and red ware have also been found.

Layer 6 of the quadrant 4 of A 1 has yielded the same material. Red ware comprise fine red ware dishes and bowls, handmade storage jars some of which have applique bands at shoulder, small to large size vases having prominent neck and some with externally splayed out rim, handmade vases with cord or mat impressed shoulders, channelled basins, perforated bowl, lid with folded rim, incurved bowls, convex sided dishes and miniature pots Fig. 4. Shapes of the Painted Grey Ware sherds are not very clear. Their paintings have vertical strokes, series of dots within two lines and floral pattern. Its associated grey ware have convex sided deep bowl and miniature pots. A few sherds have dark exterior and grey interior surface. Fine variety of black and red ware sherds comprising convex sided dishes and convex sided bowl with grooving on the exterior were also found. The black sliped ware include bowls with semicircular body, thick and thin convex sided dishes, some of which have mild depression on the exterior side of the rim, miniature bowl and bowls with concave profile have been found. A few sherds with powdery ochre surface were also found from the lowest levels in quadrant 3 of square A 1. Lowest level have yielded hopscotches made out of almost all the pottery types.

As many as of 343 antiquities were found during excavations besides a large number of antiquities collected from the surface during expolorations of different areas of the site. Among antiquities found from excavations terracotta discs form the largest group of 105. They depict different decorations. Antiquities in terracotta include 12 broken pieces, mostly from figurines, 9 human figurines(Pl.V), 13 animal figurines(Pl.IV), 16 toy cart wheels, 20 beads, 3 ear- studs, 15 bangle pieces, 23 sling balls, 6 gamesmen, 1 whistle, 1 pestle, and 1 rattle containing 8 mini-balls of clay. Among other antiquities mention may be made of 26 bone points, 40 bone arrow heads(Pl.VII), 7 copper pieces, including antimony rod, nail and a human figurine, 15 iron objects including nails, chisels and a piece of chain, 15 beads of semiprecious stones like agate, chalcedony, carnelian and quartz crystal, 1 glass bead, 3 ivory objects, including a pendant and a bead,3 stone weights, 2 rubbing stones, 2 bone objects, 1 stone architectural fragment, 1 microbead of paste and one square uninscribed copper cast coin.

Excavations at Sankisa are important in view of the fact that the great city site has never been earlier excavated with scientific methods and no proper record of the exposed structures and antiquities or stratigraphy is available besides the fact that its location in a zone where cultural trends from different areas might have influenced the inhabitants during protohistoric time also needs proper study which is possible only if different mounds of the site are excavated carefully in a wider perspective.

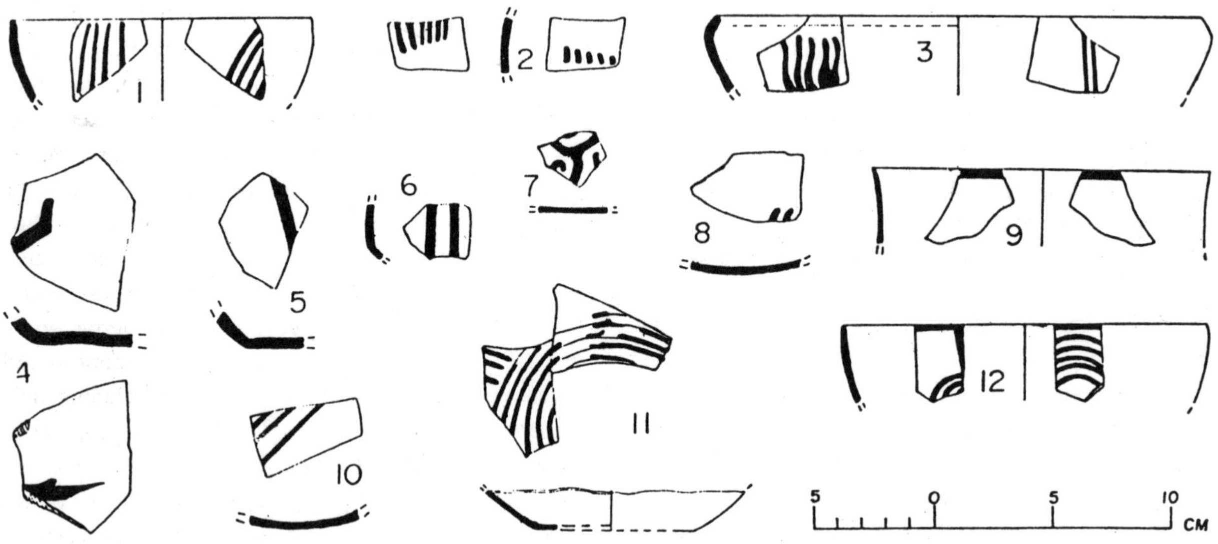

Fig. 2

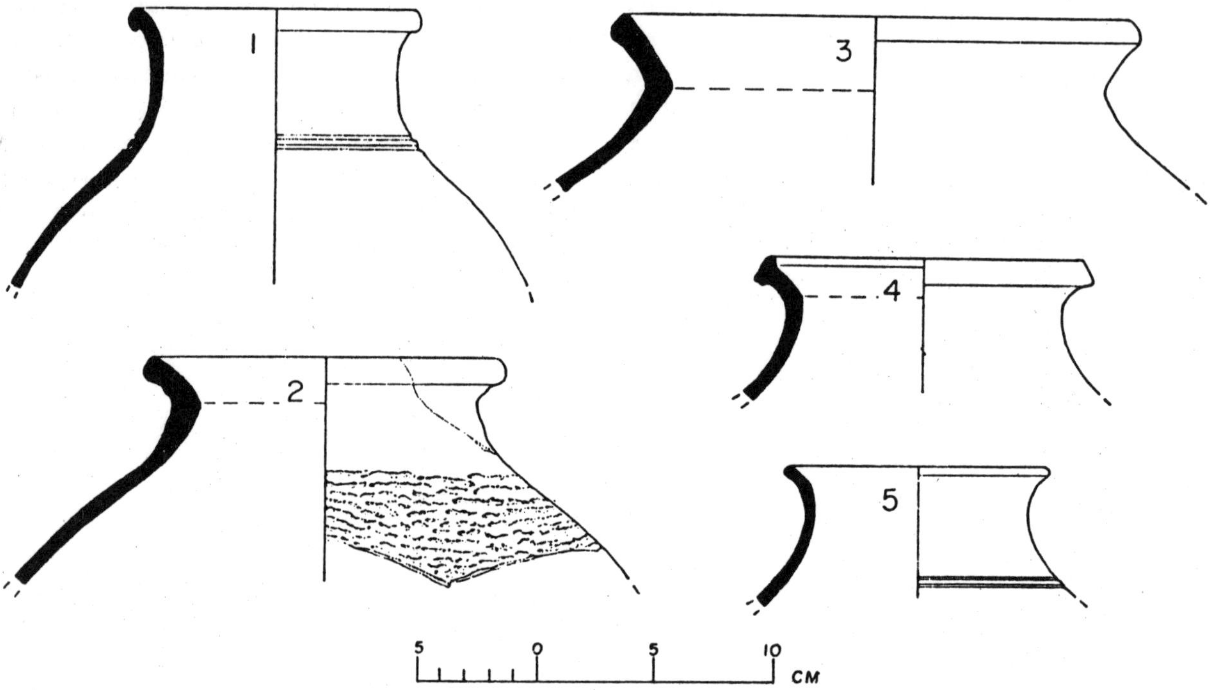

Fig. 3

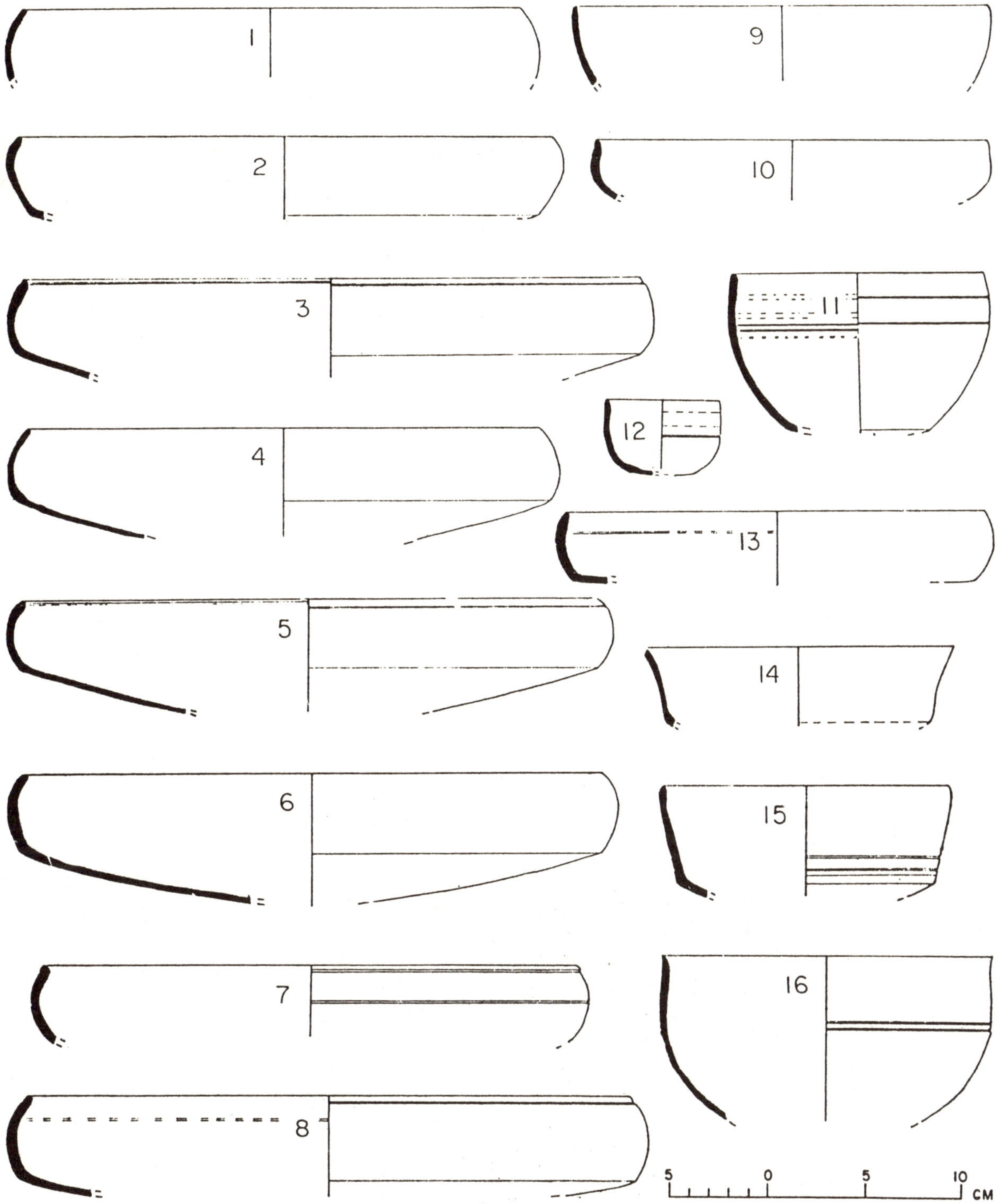

Fig. 4

Beyond Arikamedu : Macro Stratigraphy of the Iron Age-Early Historic Transition and Roman Contact in South India

SUNIL GUPTA*

The site of Arikamedu on the Coromandel coast of south India was excavated in 1945 by a team of the Archaeological Survey of India under the direction of Mortimer Wheeler. Arikamedu was excavated again in 1947 by the French archaeologist J.M. Casal. The Wheeler/Casal excavations were comprehensively reviewed by Vimala Begley in 1983. Begley also conducted excavations at Arikamedu in the early nineties with a joint Indian-American team. The full results of this excavation are yet to be published.

The Problem

Arikamedu has contributed to the archaeology of south India in three significant ways. Being the first excavated site in south India to yield material indicators of long distance Mediterranean trade, the Arikamedu stratigraphy has become the basic reference for studies of early Indo-Roman commerce in the region. Secondly, the ceramic sequence observed at Arikamedu (stratigraphic distribution of Rouletted Ware and Mediterranean ceramics especially) has been used to understand the profiles of other excavated sites in the region. Thirdly., the chronology imputed by Wheeler to the Arikamedu strata has been applied to date the sections of numerous sites subsequently excavated.

The emphasis upon the evidence from Arikamedu in studies of Indo-Roman trade and reconstruction of the Iron Age of south India has led, over the years, to "marginalisation" of evidence from other excavated sites in south India. Also, the "inadequacies" of the Arikamedu stratigraphy (such as surmising chronology from thickness of deposit by Wheeler) have been carried over into establishing space/time frameworks of some excavated south Indian sites and in discussions on Indo-Roman trade. This paper seeks to address these two issues central to Iron Age-Early Historic archaeology of south India. In this regard the attempt here is to delineate a "broader" stratigraphic and chronological framework in which to situate the evidence of Arikamedu. The macro-stratigraphic view would incorporate important cultural elements not emphasized in the Arikamedu stratigraphy. At the same time, in the process of generating the macro-stratigraphy, the paper will focus upon "contradictions" in the past applications of the Arikamedu evidence.

The Arikamedu stratigraphy as derived by Wheeler and Casal

The sequences recorded by Wheeler and Casal and subsequently consolidated by Begley are summarized below:-

Wheeler: Wheeler found a continuous single-culture occupation of the historical period at Arikamedu. In his diggings he discovered the occurrence of Mediterranean artefacts (amphorae) from the last but one layer. Excavations were undertaken at two areas of the site. These were classified by Wheeler as the Northern and the Southern

*Allahabad Museum, Allahabad

sectors. The basis for the subdivision of the Northern sector strata was Arretine ware that was found in the middle layers. Naming this the Arretine Phase, the deposits below and above were called the pre-Arretine and post-Arretine Phases. The Southern Sector was subdivided with structures as the basis. From bottom upwards these are: Pre-Structural Phase, Early Phase (3 sub-periods), Middle Phase (3 sub-periods) and the Late Phase. Chronologically, the Arretine Phase of the Northern Sector is in consonance with the "Pre-Structural" phase of the Southern Sector (Wheeler *et al* 1946:17-124,pp.50 for inter-sectoral consonance). Wheeler called the settlement an "Indo-Roman Trading Station" on the basis of his discovery of diverse Mediterranean artefacts (Arretine ware, Amphorae, Roman glass, Mediterranean lamps) in the context of a flourishing stone and glass beadmaking industry. Perhaps the most important interpretation of Wheeler related to the amphorae continuum he uncovered at Arikamedu. Wheeler (*et al* 1946:22) asserts that "the consolidation and development of Roman trade with the East was a product of the unification of the western world under Augustus (23 B.C.-A.D.14), and it is reasonable to suppose that previous trade with eastern India, if it existed at all, was of a spasmodic and indirect kind – *unlikely, for example, to have produced a continuous supply of amphorae at Arikamedu.*" (emphasis mine).

Casal: In contrast to Wheeler, Casal uncovered a multi-cultural sequence at Arikamedu. Digging at two areas of the site, Casal reported a Megalithic occupation in the lowermost levels indicated by the exclusive presence of the Black-and-Red Ware (hereafter BRW). This was followed by a transitional phase in which the Early Historic Rouleted Ware appeared while the BRW continued. The third period was termed "Roman". This period saw the appearance of Mediterranean artefacts in the form of amphorae and Arretine Ware (*Casal 1949*). Begley (1983:461-481), in a perceptive study of the Wheeler/Casal excavations, consolidated the evidence to present a revised stratigraphic sub-division of the Arikamedu profile (Fig.2).

BRW - RW - *Amphora/Arretine Sequence at* Arikamedu.

The Megalithic horizon at Arikamedu (Casal's Grp. II and Begley's Phase A), which precedes the Early Historic Phase at the site, is characterised by the occurrence of the BRW. The BRW is the diagnostic Early Iron Age pottery of southern India. It begins to occur at the point of Neolithic-Megalithic overlap at Payampalli (*IAR 1964-65*:22), Hallur (*1964-65*:31-32), Malaiyamputtu (*IAR 1970-71*:34-35) and Mallappadi (*IAR 1977-78*:50). In act it is neccesary to stress that the BRW is first and foremost associated with the beginning of the Iron Age in southern India and its association with the Megalithic culture is secondary to this reality (Ramachandran 1980: 43-76, 137; Begley 1983:464-467). Megalithism in south India, as a specific material culture complex, has been primarily identified with a funerary culture characterised by burials marked by stones (dolmens, cists, cairns etc.).

The transition from Iron Age/Megalithic Phase to the Early Historic in southern India is important. This transition marks the beginnings of the growth of towns, ports, industries and long-distance trade in the region. Southern India's commerce with the Mediterranean also needs to be situated in the context of the shift from Iron Age to Early Historic. A major issue with regard to the archaeology of Indo-Mediterranean trade in southern India has been to precise the point of Mediterranean contact, both stratigraphically and chronologically. At Arikamedu, Wheeler's excavation revealed occurrence of Mediterranean amphora (a primary indicator of contact) at all layers except the earliest (layer 15 of Tr. AKII). Wheeler (*et al* 1946:41) thought layer 15 of AKII to be part of the "old foreshore" (therefore a non-occupational deposit) and concluded that Mediterranean contact took place almost from the beginning of occupation at Arikamedu. However, as Casal's excavations later showed, there were rich occupational layers preceding the strata yielding Mediterranean amphora at Arikamedu (Casal 1949). Begley (1983:464-471) in her review of Wheeler's and Casal's excavation of Arikamedu, summarizes these antecedent layers as Phase A and Phase B. Phase A, corresponding to the "Megalithic" phase of Casal, has the Iron Age BRW as the principal ceramic industry. Phase B, corresponding to the "Intermediate" phase of Casal, reveals appearance of the Rouletted Ware in association with BRW. Amphorae begin to appear from Begley's Phase C onwards (Fig.2).

Macro-stratigraphy

The three-fold cultural sequence for Arikamedu, distinguished on the basis of appearance of diagnostic ceramics, is presented in Fig. 1 together with stratigraphic profiles of important Iron Age-Early Historic sites in southern India. The sites have been selected from all four southern states (Tamil Nadu, Karnataka, Andhra Pradesh, and Kerala) keeping in view the need for a regional distribution.

As Fig.1 shows, the transitions from Iron Age to Early Historic signified by ceramic indicators at Arikamedu are found to hold true over the south Indian landscape. The "broadened" picture of the three phases observed at Arikamedu adds a significant element to the basic pattern. Specifically, we notice that the ceramic which immediately post dates the BRW at many sites is the Russet Coated Painted Ware (hereafter RCPW; Sites no 4, 5, 6, 13, 15, 16, 17, 18, 20, 22, 24,26 in Fig.1). The RCPW, initially known as the Andhra Ware, was first recognised by Wheeler at Brahmagiri (Karnataka). He describes the pottery as "decorated with varieties of simple rectilinear or slightly curvilinear pattern in a paste of kaolin or lime under a wash of russet coated ochre...The two commonest types on which this characteristic decoration is found are dishes with an internally grooved rim and partially straight sided bowls..." (Wheeler 1947-48:236-237; Thapar 1957:72-73— redesignated Wheeler's Andhra Ware as Russet Coated Painted Ware).

At other sites (Nos.1,2,3,7,10,11,12,21 in Fig.1) the Rouletted Ware succeeds the BRW. Also, as Fig.1 shows, the RW is anterior to the RCPW at sites located near the coast in contrast to the anteriority of RCPW in sites located inland. In any case, the RCPW and RW, as new ceramics succeeding the BRW, manifest the transition from Iron Age to the more evolved Early Historic Phase in southern India. Significantly, Fig. 1 also reveals that Mediterranean artefacts and their imitations appear in the Early Historic horizon of southern India following the emergence of the RCPW and RW (Sites no 1,3,5, 7, 8, 10, 11, 13, 19, 21, 24, 25, 26). The appearance of Mediterranean artefacts and imitations, especially amphorae, indicate the point of Indo-Mediterranean long-distance contact. In the scheme presented in Fig. 1, the "Mediterranean-contact" sub-phase has been isolated from the RCPW/RW phase. The latter is situated under the nomenclature Early Historic 1 (E H 1) and the former under Early Historic 2 (EH2).

Now before we further discuss the stratigraphic profiles of sites listed in Fig.1 , it is necessary to clarify the chronological extent of Megalithic culture in southern India in the light of the three-phase scheme of material culture change presented in this study. The Megalithic culture, which we consider as part and not synonymous with the Iron Age , survived well into the early centuries A.D. in southern India (for recent dating of Megalithic in s.India see Rajan 1991:46-47). In this respect, the people believing in "lithic" burials were contemporaries at different points of time of the urbanising communities of the EH1 and EH2 periods.

The deposition of artefacts of Mediterranean origin or/and inspiration at a number of Megalithic burial sites in southern India is evidence of the survival of Megalithism at the time of Mediterranean contact (EH2 period). In the Coimbatore district of Tamil Nadu, a dolmen burial has yielded a denarius of Augustus Caesar (27 B.C.-14 A.D.; Ramachandran 1980:67-68). From a Megalithic grave at Savadipalayam silver punched mark-coins together with Roman coins have been recovered (Ramachandran 1980:75). A barrow (Megalithic) in the Nilgiris has yeilded a Roman gold coin issued at Constantinople in the 4 th C. A.D. (Ramachandran 1980:75). At Adichanallur, the important urn-burial site on the River Tampraparni, bronze mirrors and scent bottles of Hellenistic affiliation have been found and tentatively dated to 1st C..B.C.- 1st C. A.D. (Margabandhu 1973:21-22; 1996:233-243). At Navalai (Distt. Dharmapuri) a cairn-circle enclosing an urn burial and habitation mound has yeilded punch-marked coins and a (unspecified) Roman coin (Rajan 1991:51). At some places, the existence of Megalithic and Early Historic sites in close proximity and placed in same time-context, suggests interaction between two lifestyles. Begley (1983:464) has pointed to the possibility of interchange between Early Historic Arikamedu and the purely Megalithic settlement at Souttekeny lying only 20 km away. The Pandyan port of Korkai is only 15 km downstream on the Tamraparni from the Megalithic urn-fields at Adichanallur.

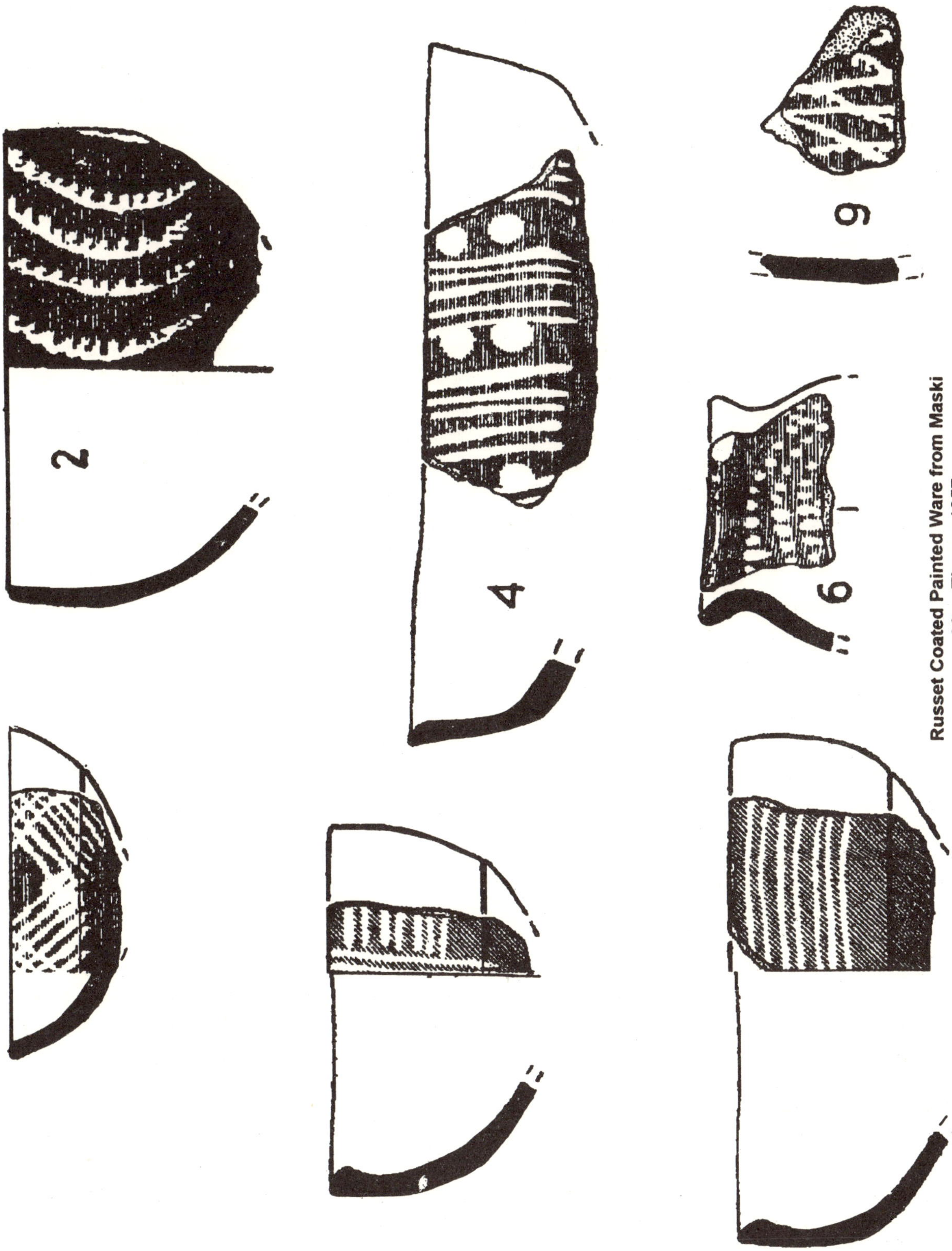

Russet Coated Painted Ware from Maski
After Thapar 1957

Figure. 7

In Fig.1 we have taken care to include sites revealing "Megalithic" strata only when the stratigraphy shows a Neolithic-Megalithic "overlap" or two-culture Megalithic-Early Historic strata. This criteria of selection excludes single-culture Megalithic sites which, in the absence of a cultural context (Neolithic underpinning or Early Historic succession), may have existed at any point in the three phases specified.

To recapitulate, with regard to the Iron Age-Early Historic change over there are two essential factors to be realised:

1. The stratigraphical shift from the Iron Age assemblage (BRW, Megaliths) to Early Historic phase was indicated, *inter alia,* by the appearance of the RCPW and RW. The impact of Mediterranean sea trade is descernible in the "intrusion" of Mediterranean artefacts (amphora, *terra sigillata,* Roman coins, glass, lamps, cameos,beads) subsequent to the appearance of the RCPW and RW.

2. The co-existence of Megalithic cultures survives into the 1st millennium A.D. with Early Historic complexes.The deposition of Mediterranean artefacts in the "late" Megalithic sites indicates involvement of the Megalithic communities in the international trade.

Iron Age - E.H. 1 Transition

Sites no. 2, 3, 4, 5, 7, 10, 11, 12, 15, 16, 17, 18, 19, 20, 21, 22, 23, 26. listed in Fig. 1 show Iron Age (Megalithic) levels succeeded by the Early Historic 1 Phase.

We shall attempt to demonstrate the viability of material indicators of Iron Age-Early Historic transition by analysing in detail the stratigraphic evidence from three widespread sites: Arikamedu, Chandravalli and Brahmagiri.

The sites of Brahmagiri and Chandravalli (no.4,5 in Fig.1) located in the heart of the southern Deccan, were excavated by Mortimer Wheeler and published in a single report (Wheeler 1947-48:180-308). It is at Brahmagiri and Chandravalli where Wheeler discovered the Russet Coated Painted Ware or the "Andhra Ware" as he called it. The experience of Arikamedu was fresh in his mind and as we have from the Brahmagiri/Chandravalli report, Wheeler was drawing from the ongoing excavation of Casal to understand the sections at Brahmagiri and Chandravalli (see extract below). That Wheeler had pegged the material cultural transition from Iron Age (Megalithic) to the Early Historic on diagnostic ceramics (including the RCPW) is clearly revealed by two critical observations of his on the Brahmagiri/Chandravalli stratigraphy:

"In 1947 J.M. Casal carried out further excavations at Arikamedu and at one point found pottery of the familiar 'megalithic' fabric in layers immediately overlying the natural soil. The maximum overall height of these 'megalithic' layers was 3 feet: the two lowest were free from admixture, but the two highest (1-$\frac{1}{2}$ feet) produced also typical 'Arikamedu' pottery, including Rouletted dishes. The overlap of these two cultures was clearly demonstrated and the equation between this evidence and that of Chandravalli and Brahmagiri is in this respect *absolute*" (Wheeler 1947-48: 273-274; underline mine).

Next we see Wheeler's use of the principle of ceramic seriation on the main section at Chandravalli:

"...the cutting of Ch.43 is consistent. The lowest stratum in this fairly extensive cutting contained only pottery of the 'megalithic' fabric, with neither coins nor painted sherds. Overlying this was a stratum again containing much 'megalithic' ware, but now in association with Andhra fabrics, including both the typically painted ware and fragments of 'beaked' dishes of the type to which rouletted decoration is sometimes applied. A little higher up, rouletted sherds were found immediately above the highest of the 'megalithic' sherds. The latter were completely absent from the remaining strata of the section" (Wheeler 1947-48: 271-273; section Ch.43 in Fig.3).

These two observations "dynamically" interlink the stratigraphies of Arikamedu and Chandravalli-Brahmagiri. Wheeler's observations constitute the first attempt to "broadbase" the ceramic indicators of Iron Age-Early Historic transition revealed at Arikamedu.

However, even though Wheeler highlighted a three-fold ceramic sequence at Chandravalli (BRW followed by BRW - RW - RCPW followed by absence of BRW) he did not *formally* divide his stratigraphy on the basis of the seriation principle. The scheme presented for Chandravalli was only a two-fold strata Pd.I (Megalithic) and Pd.II (Andhra). However, as is clear from the profile of the main section - Ch.43 - at Chandravalli, the intermediate phase is rather thick, occupying four complete layers (from top): layers 11, 12, 13 and 13N (Fig.3; approx. 6 feet of deposit according to scale of feet in Fig.3). These are the layers which display the BRW-RCPW ceramic association indicative of the EH1. period (see frequency Table in Wheeler 1947-48: 273). The earliest layer 13NE exclusively yields the BRW (Wheeler's observation above; Fig.3). The EH2 phase lies above layer 11 (discussed below).

Similarly, at Brahmagiri we find a substantial transitional phase between the Megalithic and Andhra (Early Historic) levels which Wheeler did not formally classify. We find no sub-phase between Pd.II (Megalithic) and Pd.III (Andhra) cultures in the report. The need for an overlap to be seperately defined becomes evident in the profile of the main section - Br.21 - of Brahmagiri (Fig. 4). Here we see the overlap or EH 1 phase represented by three complete layers (from top down): layers 4, 5, 6. (approx. one and half feet of deposit from scale of feet in Fig.4). The RCPW appears for the first time in layer 6 in which seven "yellow painted" sherds are counted. Significantly, the adjacent cuttings "equating with layers 5 and 6 of Br.21...produced 7 sherds of rouletted ware" (Wheeler 1947-48: 206). The consolidated evidence thus indicates the initial appearance of RCPW-RW after the BRW at Brahmagiri. The "pure" BRW phase at Brahmagiri section Br.21 is represented by layers 7 and 8. (Wheeler 1947-48:206).

The BRW-RCPW/RW shift, representing the Iron Age - Early Historic transition observed in the Arikamedu stratigraphy also finds expression at Chandravalli and Brahmagiri. In fact, in course of collecting data for this paper the author found that the ceramic indicators of cultural change delineated at Arikamedu/Chandravalli/ Brahmagiri had been "independently" observed by archaeologists in subsequent excavations. For instance, reporting trial digs around Cranganore (Kerala) the excavator comments: "... the discovery in Taluk Ponnani of the so-called Russet-coated Painted Ware, which overlaps with the Megalithic BRW in the early centuries of the Christian era is of great significance. The gap between the Megalithic and historical periods could thus be filled up to some extent" (IAR 1970-71:19). In similar vein the excavator of T.Kallupatti comments that the Megalithic site "continued to be occupied in the early historical period as attested to by presence of some copper coins and Russet-coated white painted ware" (IAR 1976-77: 46-47). Also in Veerapuram Pd.III we find a similar observation: "The layers belonging to this later phase of the Megalithic culture are overlapped by Early Historic culture in a few trenches. In this transitional phase antiquities belonging to Megalithic and Early Historic cultures were recorded. For the first time, the Russet Coated Ware and Rouletted Ware make their appearance..." (Kamalakar and Veerender 1991:4-5).

E H 1 - E H 2 Transition

Again, beginning our analysis with Arikamedu we quote Begley (1983: 471-472) who discusses the E H 1 - E H 2 transition in her revised stratigraphy of the site:

"Phase C, which corresponds to Wheeler's pre-Arretine ware layers in both Northern and Southern Sectors and to Casal's post 'overlap' layers in the Southern, is a period of rapid development and in many ways the most significant stage in the history of Arikamedu. For the first time amphorae and other items of undoubted Mediterranean origin are encountered."

The basis for demarcating Phase C is the appearance of amphorae and other artefacts of Mediterranean origin in the Early Historic horizon at Arikamedu. Begley also suggests a spurt in economic activity due to Mediterranean contact. In our scheme Phase C of Begley represents the beginning of the E H 2 phase which continues till Phase G.

At Chandravalli layers 10 to 2 in Section Ch.43 are reported by Wheeler as the Andhra Period layers. The occurrence of a denarius of Tiberius Caesar and the complete absence of 'Megalithic' pottery in these layers correlates with the Phase C to phase G stratigraphic assemblage at Arikamedu. The Roman coin at Chandravalli occurs in layer 5 of Ch.43. Since the basis of demarcating the EH2 phase are the earliest stratified Mediterranean/ imitation Mediterranean objects, it would therefore mean that E H 2 at Chandravalli comprises layers 5 through 1 of section Ch.43. However, there is an indication that the "Roman-contact" level may have been earlier. In his report Wheeler (1947-48:200) suggests that a coin of Augustus found at previous excavation at the site by the Mysore State archaeologists can be placed "at a low, but not lowest level of this (Andhra) culture" (bracket mine).

At the same time, there is evidence to push up the E H 1 phase at least to layer 9. Wheeler (1947-48:278) informs that the first occurrence of Rouletted Ware in Ch.43 is in layers 10 and 9.

Let us also take into account the stratigraphy of Chandravalli as revealed in the excavation by the ASI conducted in the seventies (reported in *IAR 1977-78:*27-29). Here also an Iron Age culture (Pd.II) is found to overlap with the succeeding Early Historic culture (Pd.III). In the main cutting (CDL-VI) the Iron Age is represented by layers (from bottom up):9, 8, 7, the overlap by layer 6 and post-overlap by layers 5 through 1.

The earliest deposit of Pd.II yielded the BRW in association with Black polished ware. The report emphasises that Pd.II "was found to overlap with the succeeding period." Pd.III deposits yielded the RCPW, Satavahana coins and "a jar comparable to amphora."

The section Ch.43 of Wheeler's excavation and section CDL-VI of the later ASI excavation at Chandravalli follow the same sequence as at Arikamedu: the Iron Age BRW followed by appearance of RCPW/RW followed by occurrence of Mediterranean artefacts.

At Brahmagiri, the 'post-overlap' layers are demarcated (from bottom up) 3a, 3, 2, 1. However these layers do not yield any evidence of Mediterranean contact.

Apart from Arikamedu and Chandravalli the following sites recorded in Fig. 1 show the EH1-EH2 transition: Alagankulam, Dharanikota, Dhulikatta, Kaveripattinam, Kanchipuram, Kodumanal, Peddabankur, Sengamedu, Uraiyur, Veerapuram. Additionally the sites of Karaikadu and Vasavasamudram show a single-culture stratigraphy yielding material evidence of long distance trade from the Mediterranean World.

Chronology of BRW-RCPW/RW-Amphora/ Arretine Shifts

In Fig.1 the three-phase sequence reflecting the shift from Iron Age to Early Historic in southern India is recorded with an attendant chronology wherever available (given under brackets). A review of the dates imputed to "common" phases of the various sites shows deep divergence. The disparate dating of common phases has been primarily the result of imputing time-frames to thickness of deposit. This estimation of chronology, first practiced by Wheeler at Arikamedu (Wheeler *et al* 1946:22-24), Brahmagiri and Chandravalli (Wheeler 1947-48:footnotes in 201), was later used prolifically by other archaeologists to fix the chronology of sites. Some of the sites dated recently on the basis of thickness of deposit are Sengamedu (Ramachandran 1980: 102-105) and Alagankulam (Nagaswamy 1991: 247-254).

The primary chronological indicators from excavations of Iron Age—Early Historic sites in southern India have been: (a) Mediterranean artefacts (primarily from Arikamedu): (b) Tamil-Brahmi and Prakrit inscriptions on pottery, (c) coinage of the Satavahanas and (d) carbon dates (till now used sparingly). The secondary indicators, loosely "datable", have been punch-marked coins, the Gangetic Northern Black Polished Ware sherds and the Red Polished Ware.

The need for a "standard" chronology for the Iron Age-Early Historic transitions in southern India cannot be ignored. In particular, the unearthing of more datable objects since Wheeler excavated Arikamedu and subsequent review of Wheeler's date for Mediterranean contact with Arikamedu / southern India generates the imperative for comprehensive re-assessment. Below, the primary chronological sources are discussed with the intention to provide clarity to the transitional periods, including the period of Mediterranean contact.

Mediterranean artefacts

The datable objects recovered from stratified contexts are Terra Sigillata, Amphorae, glassware, Roman coins, Mediterranean lamps, and Egyptian beads. All stratified Mediterranean objects from Arikamedu have been dated to the Augustan Period (27 B.C. +) and after except for a batch of amphorae from Arikamedu tentatively placed in the 2nd C.B.C. (Wheeler *et al* 1946: 17-124; Francis 1987; Begley and De Puma 1992; Comfort 1992:134-150; for amphora dates see Will 1992:151-156 and Slane 1992:204-215). At Alagankulam precise dates for the amphora are awaited. One of the Roman coins excavated at Alagankulam has been identified as that of Valentinian II (A.D. 375-392; Nagaswamy 1991:247-254). At Chandravalli the coins of Augustus (B.C.27- A.D. 14) and Tiberius (A.D. 14 - 37) mentioned by Wheeler as coming from the post-overlap layers of Ch.43 indicate a *terminus ante quem* at the B.C./A.D. changeover (Wheeler 1947-48:287). Similarly, the clay imitation of the coin of Tiberius (A.D. 14-37) from Pd.III B at Veerapuram can be placed not earlier than the 1st Century A.D. (Kamalakar and Veerender 1991:43). From the upper levels at Dhulikatta and Peddabankur was found one silver coin each of Augustus Caesar (B.C. 27- A.D. 14).

Inscribed Pottery

Ceramics in the Black-and-Red and Rouletted Ware fabrics inscribed with Tamil-Brahmi graffiti and occasionally in the north Indian Prakrit-Brahmi have been recovered from a number of excavations in southern India. From Quseir al-Qadim, the Roman port on the Egyptian Red Sea coast, a number of sherds containing Tamil-Brahmi inscriptions were excavated. A lone ostracon inscribed in Prakrit-Brahmi was also found at Quseir (Salomon 1991:731-736).

Arikamedu was the first site to yield the inscribed pottery. A batch of 18 sherds were recovered which were dated, on the basis of their paleography, to the 3rd-2nd Century B.C. According to Wheeler (et al 1946:109-110) the datation of these sherds was in "contradistinction" to the associated Mediterranean artefacts which were secured to the Augustan period and after (27 B.C.+). Mahadevan (1973:60-64), later reviewing the ostraca identified at least one of the 18 sherds (listed as Prakrit sherd no. 3, Fig.46 under inscribed pottery in Wheeler *et al* 1946:112) as carrying a 1st Century A.D. date. This single contradiction of the "consolidated" earlier chronology of the inscribed sherds makes the paleographical dating of the Arikamedu sherds from Wheeler's excavation ambivalent. In fact, N.P. Chakravarti, the epigraphist who reported the sherds in Wheeler's report discussed the possibility of a slow development of the Tamil-Brahmi which made it difficult to precise a paleographical chronology.

In another context, M.J. Filliozat (in Begley 1983:467) adopts a similar non-commital position with regard to dating an inscribed Tamil-Brahmi sherd from the Megalithic layers of Casal's excavation in remarking that "the characters resemble those of the 1st Century A.C. at Arikamedu, as well as those in use from the 3rd Century B.C." Begley (1983:467) surmises that this inscribed BRW sherd from Casal's excavation can be placed in the 2nd Century B.C. Her assertion is disputed by Nagaswamy (1991:251-252) who is of the view that the adoption of Brahmi to the Tamil language cannot be earlier than the 1st Ccentury B.C. Nagaswamy further suggests that the inscribed sherd from Casal's excavation should be dated to the 1st Century A.D.

There is thus a fair debate surrounding the inscribed Tamil-Brahmi and Prakrit-Brahmi sherds (of BRW and RW) recovered from the excavations of Wheeler and Casal at Arikamedu. The paleographic dates range from 3rd-2nd century B.C. to 1st-2nd century A.D. At other sites in Southern India the inscribed Tamil-Brahmi pottery occurs within the above date-range at Korkai (3rd Century. B.C.-2nd C.A.D.; Nagaswamy 1970:54), Alagankulam (1st Century. B.C. - early Centuries A.D.; Nagaswamy 1991:252-253), Alagarai (ascribed roughly to the 1st Century A.D., if not earlier *IAR 1963-64*:20-21), Uraiyur (1-2 Century A.D.; *IAR 1964-65*:25), Kodumanal (2nd C. B.C.; Rajan 1990:98) and Kanchipuram (2nd Century A.D.; *Ency.Ind.Arch.* Vol.II:200-201). The Tamil-Brahmi inscribed sherds from Quseir (Egypt) and the single Prakrit inscribed sherd from the same site have been dated to the 1st Century A.D. (Salomon 1991:731-736).

From the wide range of dating of inscribed sherds detailed above, we can say that the "palaeographic" chronology of inscribed pottery in south India ranges from 3rd Century B.C. to 1st-2nd Century A.D.

Satavahana/Associated Coins

Among the sites under review in this study, the coins of the Satavahanas are recorded in stratified contexts in the post-overlap layers of Ch.43 at Chandravalli, Pd.III B at Veerapuram, Pd. IIB at Dharanikota and upper levels of Pd. IA of the Kamakothi Math area of Kanchipuram. Satavahana coins have also come to light in Dhulikatta, Peddabankur and Kaveripattinam.

At Chandravalli two potin coins of Sri Yajna Satakarni were each found in layers 5 and 6 of Ch.43. Additionally, 15 inscribed coins of the Maharathis were found distributed across layers 7-10 of section Ch.43 (Wheeler 1947-48: 287-295).

At Veerapuram, two Satavahana coins, one with the legend *Satakarni* or *Pulumavi* and the other the coin of the Satavahana king *Pulumavi* was found in Pd. III B (Kamalakar and Veerender 1991: 11-12). A number of coins of the Maharathi dynasty also occur for the first time in this phase.

In Sub-period II B of Dharanikota late Satavahana coins were recovered (Ency.Ind.Arch. Vol.II:126).

Among copper coins of the Satavahanas recovered from upper levels of Pd. IA of the Kamakothi Math area at Kanchipuram (our phases EH1 and 2), the coin of Rudra Satakarni (dated 2nd Century A.D.) was identified.

All the coins at the above sites are of the Imperial Satavahanas. This study draws from the shorter chronology of the Satavahanas as recently constructed by Shastri (1987:89-92; Forthcoming). The shorter chronology puts the first Imperial Satavahana, Satakarni around 25 B.C. In this respect, the above kings which follow from Satakarni (at Veerapuram) can be placed in the bracket of last quarter of 1st Century B.C. to 3rd Century A.D.

Carbon Dates

From time to time carbon dates have been released by various Indian laboratories (TIFR, PRL, BSIP) after analysis of charcoal/wood samples from number of Iron Age and Early Historic sites in southern India. Though some of the carbon dates have been often quoted in research papers, there has been no attempt to draw a "structure" of ^{14}C dates for the Iron Age - Early Historic transition in southern India. A chronological "structure" is presented in Fig.5. A total of 21 ^{14}C dates are listed from 9 sites. The stratigraphic provenance of some of the carbon dates are clarified below.

Neolithic - Iron Age

It is noticed that the earliest dates available are for Neolithic-Megalithic overlap levels at Hallur (1105 and 955 B.C.). On the whole the 9 dates for the Iron Age range from 11th C. B.C. to 3rd Century B.C. (1105 - 260 B.C.).

There are two carbon dates from the "Early Period" at Dharanikota. The wood charcoal sample TF-246 (dated 475 B.C.) has been obtained from the layer 11 of cutting DKT-1 at a depth of 6.5 m below the surface (*IAR 1965-66*:86). The other wood sample of Early Period TF-247 (dated 390 B.C.) has been obtained from layer 8 of the cutting DKT-2 at a depth of 3.7 m below surface (*IAR 1965-66*:86). A third carbon date of 205 B.C. obtained from a wood charcoal sample TF-248 from layer 10 of the "fortification" profile of DTK-1 could not be related to any of the three phases due to absence of contextual data. The report of the excavator in the Encyclopaedia of Indian Archaeology informs that the lowest phase has been carbon dated to around 400 B.C. (Raghavachari 1989:126). The lowest levels at Dharanikota are associated with Iron Age Black-and-red Ware (*IAR 1962-63: 1-2; 1964-65*:2-3; Thapar 1957:19). Therefore the carbon dates deriving from samples TF-246 and TF-247 of 'Early Period' are placed in the Iron Age category in Fig.5.

E H 1 : The 6 dates for the E H 1 phase show a 4th-3rd /2nd Century B.C. range (380 B.C. to 200 B.C.). The 4 dates for Alagankulam have been derived from charcoal samples obtained from the digging AGM-2. The trench AGM-2 has a total deposit of 4.75 metres and is situated on the slope of the mound. (Nagaswamy 1991: 248). The concordance of layers between AGM-2 and the deeper trench AGM-1 (deposit of 6 m) has not been established by the excavator (Nagaswamy 1991:246-254). The earliest date of 380 B.C. has been obtained from a charcoal sample in AGM-2, layer 5 and at a depth of 2.80 m. The other 3 samples are posterior in layer and chronology to the lowest sample PRL-1299 (Fig.5). Layer 5, from which the earliest date has been obtained, has been designated "BRW and Rouletted Ware levels" (Agrawal, Kusumgar and Yadava 1991:329). The latter three samples, from layers 3 and 2, are designated as coming from BRW levels (Agrawal, Kusumgar and Yadava 1991:329). In all likelihood, the BRW in the layers 2 and 3 are of Early Historic affiliation as indicated by the typical E.H.1 BRW-RW association beginning in the lower layer 5. Keeping these considerations in view, we can place the four carbon dates derived from the BRW and Rouletted Ware levels in E H 1 phase.

The carbon date (320 B.C.) from sample BS-118 from Dhulikatta is derived from a wood charcoal obtained from a depth of 2.25 m. The other two carbon dates from this site have been obtained from depths of 15 cm (BS-119) and 55 cm (BS-117) (for dates see *IAR 78-79*:103). Dhullikata is essentially an Early Historic Buddhist stupa complex showing regular rebuilding activity. The excavator does not make clear the depth of his excavation in his report (*IAR 1977-76*:2; *1976-77*:4-5). The relative depths of the three samples suggest that sample BS-118 from 2.25 m comes from the early phase of the *stupa* at Dhulikatta. The earliest phase of the *stupa* is associated with Early Historic pottery in association with BRW. We therefore tentatively place the carbon-date from depth 2.25 m in the E H 1 phase.

Early Historic 2

All the 6 dates for E H 2 period lie in the 1st Century B.C. (70 - 10 B.C.).

The four dates from Peddabankur are generated from samples obtained from layer 2 of the site (*IAR 1972-73:63;* IAR 1978-79:103). Layer 2 constitutes the uppermost layer of the site if we do not take into account the "surface" layer 1. Layer 2 would thus fall in the uppermost Pd. IIB at Peddabankur. This period has yeilded a coin of Augustus Caesar as well as a terracotta figure modelled after a Roman (?) (*IAR 1967-68:*2; *1968-69:*2; *1970-71*:2; *1971-72:*2-3; *1972-73*:2; *1974-75*:5).

Similarly, the two carbon samples recovered from depths of 15 and 55 cm at Dhulikatta belong to the uppermost levels which have also yeilded Mediterranean artefacts (*ÍAR 1975-76*:2; *IAR 1976*-77:4-5).

The carbon dates are undoubtedly imprecise compared to other datable artefacts. However, in the consolidated state, the carbon dates are indicative of the chronological sequence that relates to the Iron Age-EH1-EH2 stratigraphic transitions. The carbon dates point to the 4th /3rd Century B.C. being the transition period from Iron Age to the Early Historic in southern India. Latest dates for Iron Age (315 and 260 B.C.) interface with earliest dates (380 and 360 B.C.) for E H 1. The transition from E H 1 to E H 2 is indicated by the 6 carbon dates from later levels at Dhullikata and Peddabankur (70 - 10 B.C.). The E H 1 - E H 2 shift can be placed in the end of 1st Century B.C. with the 70-10 B.C. range suggesting an emphasis towards the later part of the century. We know that E H 2 sub-phase has been demarcated on the basis of occurrence of Mediterranean artefacts. Both Dhullikata and Peddabankur yeild Roman coins (silver denari of Augustus Ceasar [27 Bel - 14 A.D.]) in the upper levels. The datation of beginning of 1st Century A.D. provided by Roman coins of Augustus and Tiberius at these two sites corroborates the B.C./A.D. changeover as the beginning of E H 2. indicated by ^{14}C dates.

Discussion

To recapitulate, the "standard" chronology for the three phases indicated by the carbon dates is 11 - 4th/3rd century B.C. for Iron Age, 4th/3rd - 1st Century B.C. for E H 1 phase and late 1st - 1st/2nd Century A.D. for the EH2 phase. Of course, the present projection is wholly preliminary and it will take more number of carbon dates in the future to bear out the chronology conceived here.

As for the inscribed sherds, none of them occur in the Iron Age levels. In the sites detailed in Fig.1 the Tamil or Prakrit inscribed sherds are to be found distributed in the E H 1 or E H 2 phase along a 3rd Century B.C. - 1st Century A.D. chronological continuum.

No imperial Satavahana coins are to be found in the Iron Age and E H 1 levels. At Chandravalli, Veerapuram and Dharanikota, where the stratigraphic sequences are clearly defined, the Satavahana coins occur in the E.H.2 levels in association with Mediterranean artefacts. We have dated the Imperial Satavahana coins according to the shorter chronology which commences from the last quarter of the 1st Century B.C. (Shastri 1987:89-92; Forthcoming).

Mediterranean artefacts form the basis of stratigraphic sub-division for the E H 2 phase. All stratified artefacts of Mediterranean origin are dated at the beginning of the Christian Era except for a batch of Koan amphora-handles from Arikamedu which has been tentaively placed in the late 2nd Century B.C. (by Will 1992:151-156). However, before we accept Will's 2nd Century B.C. chronology for the 'genuine' Koan handles (accounting for "little more than half of the double-handled fragments at Arikamedu" : Will 1992:151) the anteriority-posteriority of genuine Koan amphorae and the later pseudo-Koan/dressel 2-4 types in the Arikamedu stratigraphy needs to be clarified. At least we would expect the genuine Koan handles of 2nd Century B.C. vintage to occur below Wheeler's Arretine Phase where the *Terra sigillata* has been firmly dated from the last quarter of 1st Century B.C. onwards (Wheeler et al 1946:34-41; Comfort 1992:134-150). However, we find no amphora handles reported by Wheeler in the pre-Arretine Phase. Only 3 sherds are recorded from these early levels: 2 rim portions and 1 carinated shoulder fragment of amphora (Wheeler et al 1946:43). In this regard it may be noted that Wheeler (1946:42) illustrated in his report "all (amphora) sherds showing any part or shape of the vessel."

On the basis of the short review of the databale evidence conducted above a tentative chronology following the pattern of the carbon dates and supplemented by other chronological indicators for the three phases is suggested : 1000 - 300 B.C. (Iron Age); 300-50 B.C. (Early Historic 1); 50 B.C. - 250 A.D. (Early Historic 2).

Conclusion

The ceramic indicators representing the three-period cultural sequence at Arikamedu ('Megalithic' BRW/ BRW-RW/Amphora-Arretine ware) is reflected in the macro-stratigraphic classification of Iron Age/ Early Historic 1/ Early Historic 2.

The macro-stratigraphic profile of the Iron Age-Early Historic horizon in south India is presented here as a broader framework for understanding material culture transitions and precising the stratigraphy of long distance Mediterranean trade contact with the region. The macro-stratigraphy, while validating region wise the three-period cultural sequence derived at Arikamedu, concomitantly shifts the focus from single-site study to a more comprehensive analytical paradigm. The revised stratigraphic framework allows us to integrate elements not emphasised or not present in the Arikamedu profile. In this regard the Russet-coated Painted Ware (RCPW), which is absent at Arikamedu, appears in the macro-stratigraphy as a critical ceramic indicator of Iron Age-Early Historic shift at a number of excavated sites (especially at Chandravalli and Brahmagiri)

In terms of delineating chronology the macro-stratigraphy creates the scope to integrate a variety of chronological indicators (carbon dates, Satavahana coins, Mediterranean artefacts). The bracketing of a range of chronological 'markers' within relevant stratigraphic periods gives direction to evolving a 'standard' chronology for the three-period sequence.

The macro-stratigraphy reveals that Mediterranean artefacts consistently appear in the Early Historic horizon of south India subsequent to the first occurrence of the Iron Age ('Megalithic') BRW and RCPW/RW respectively. The posteriority of material indicators of Mediterranean contact in the macro-stratigraphic sequence serves to clarify the space/time context for Early Historic maritime commerce between south India and the Roman World.

REFERENCES

Agrawal, D.P., S. Kusumgar And M.G. Yadava. 1991. "Physical Research Laboratory Radiocarbon Date List Vi." *Radiocarbon.* Vol.33. No.3: 329-344.

Begley, V. 1983. "Arikamedu Reconsidered." *American Journal Of Archaeology.* 87 :461-482.

Begley, V. And Richard De Puma (eds.). 1992. *Rome And India - The Ancient Sea Trade.* Oxford University Press. Delhi.

Casal, J.M. 1949. *Fouilles De Virampatnam-Arikamedu.* C. Klincksieck. Paris.

Comfort, H. 1992. "Terra Sigillata At Arikamedu." in V. Begley And Richard De Puma (eds.) *Rome And India - The Ancient Sea Trade.* Oxford University Press. Delhi: 134-150.

Ency.Ind.Arch. Encyclopaedia Of Indian Archaeology, A.Ghosh (eds). Indian Council Of Historical Research. New Delhi.

Francis, P. 1987. *Bead Emporium.* Pondicherry Museum. Pondicherry.

Gupta, S. 1994. "The Dressel 2-4 Amphora In Ancient Indo-Mediterranean Sea Trade." Collection Of Papers Titled *Archaeology As Indicator Of Trade And Contact.* Academic Committe Of The 3rd World Archaeological Congress, 4-11 December 1994.

IAR = Indian Archaeology - A Review Kamalakar, G. And M. Veerender. 1991. Coins From Veerapuram

Excavations. Birla Archaeological And Cultural Research Institute. Hyderabad.

Mahadevan, I. 1973. "Arikamedu Graffiti: A Second Look." *Damilica.* Vol.II. Pt.III. 1973: 60-64.

Margabandhu, C. 1973. "A Note On Some Antiquities From Historic Sites Of Tamil Nadu And Their Cultural Significance." Damilica. Vol.II. Pt.III. 1973: 21-26.

Margabandhu, C. 1996. "Cosmetics In The Early Historic Period - A Study Of Cosmetic Holders." *Spectrum Of Indian Culture, Prof. S.B. Deo Felicitation Volume I. C.* Margabandhu and K.S. Ramachandran Edited. Agam Kala Prakashan. Delhi: 233-243.

Nagaswamy, R. 1970. "Vasavasamudram". *Damilica.* Vol.1. Dec.1970:48-49.

Nagaswamy, R. 1991. "Alagankulam: An Indo-Roman Trading Port." *Indian Archaeological Heritage (K.V. Soundarajan Festschrift).* Vol.II. C. Margabandhu, K.S. Ramachandran, A.P. Sagar And D.K. Sinha Edited. Agam Kala Prakashan. Delhi: 247-254.

Raghavachari, K. 1989. "Dharanikota." *Encyclopaedia Of Indian Archaeology.* A.Ghosh Edited. Vol.II. Indian Council of Historical Research. New Delhi: 126.

Rajan, K. 1990. "New Light On The Megalithic Culture Of The Kongu Region." *Man And Environment.* Vol. XV(I).1990 :93-102.

Rajan, K. 1991. "Archaeology Of Dharmapuri District. Tamil *Nadu.*" Man And Environment. Vol. XVI (1): 37-52.

Ramachandran, K.S. 1980. Archaeology Of South India - Tamil Nadu. Sundeep Prakashan. Delhi.

Salomon, R. 1991. "Epigraphic Remains Of Indian Traders In Egypt." *Journal Of The American Oriental Society.* Vol. III, No.4. Oct-Dec:731-736.

Shastri, A.M. 1987. "Dating Potential Of Early Satavahana Coins." *Numismatics And Archaeology.* Indian Institute Of Research In Numismatic Studies. Nasik: 89-92.

Shastri, A.M. Forthcoming. Monograph On Satavahanas Submitted For Publication In The Maharashtra State Gazetteer.

Slane, K.W. 1992. "Observations On Mediterranean Amphoras And Tablewares Found In India." *Rome And India - The Ancient Sea Trade.* V.Begley And Richard Daniel De Puma Edited. Oxford University Press. Delhi: 204-215.

Thapar, B.K. 1957. "Maski: A Chalcolithic Site Of The Southern Deccan." *Ancient India.* No.13: 4-142.

Wheeler, R.E.M., A. Ghosh And Krishna Deva. 1946. "Arikamedu: An Indo-Roman Trading Station OnThe East Coast Of India." *Ancient India* No.2:17-124.

Wheeler, R.E.M. 1947-48. "Brahmagiri And Chandravalli 1947: Megalithic And Other Cultures In Mysore State." *Ancient India.* No.4. Double Number. July '47 - Jan '48: 180-310.

Will, E.L. 1992. "The Mediterranean Shipping Amphoras From Arikamedu." *Rome And India - The Ancient Sea Trade.* V. Begley And Richard Daniel De Puma Edited. Oxford University Press. Delhi: 151-156.

Archaeological Remains of Sri Surya Pahar, Assam - A Brief Survey Report

SUKANYA SHARMA*

Sri Surya Pahar, 90°41' E Long. and 26°11' N Lat., is located 12 km east of Goalpara town, the main town area of Goalpara district, Assam.

The hills of Sri Surya Pahar are the northerly extension of the Shillong Plateau. The terrain is a mixture of hilly and plain lands on which can be seen a tropical deciduous forest dominated by Sal trees. A man-made water tank and a number of bubbling streams from the hills have enhanced the beauty of the place. Major rock type in the area is gneiss and the soil is red. But in the very low lying areas clay soil can be seen. The archaeological remains are scattered over an area of nearly 53 hectares.

Previous Study

Sri Surya Pahar was declared a protected site under the Archaeological Monuments Act, 1904, by the Archaeological Survey of India on 2-11-1925. Conservation work has been carried out from time to time and reports have also been published in the Archaeological Survey of India records. The Sri Surya Pahar ruins have been dated to 8th century A.D. Saraswati has expressed the view that the votive stupas are of 1st century B.C. or 1st century A.D. R.D. Choudhury has dated the Brahmanical sculptures to 11th- 12th century A.D. and has called them the product of the Pala-Sena School of Art (8th-12th century A.D.).

Nature of Remains

The archaeological remains at Sri Surya Pahar are of religious nature. Remains till now unearthed consist of rock-cut sculptures of both Hindu and Buddhist faiths; *stupas*, lingas with *yoni-pitha*, sandstone pillars, stone slabs and small square caverns were cut on artificially flattened rock faces.

Rock- cut sculptures

The sculptures are carved on gneiss rock. They are mainly bas-reliefs. On the basis of their size, the clusters have been titled in this paper as cluster I, II and III for the sake of convenience in describing them.

Cluster I

It is on the northwestern corner of the site and is referred to in the Survey-sheet as "Dasabhuja Devasthan" because of the presence of a deity which was originally thought to have had ten arms but actually has twelve arms. The image is approximately one metre high and is a male deity with a seven-hooded snake canopy over its head. It stands on a lotus. Due to heavy weathering of the gneissic rock the attributes of the deity are not clear. But on the basis of the lotus base and the seven hooded snake canopy the image can be identified as the image of Lord Vishnu.

*State Museum, Guwahati

Just below this image there is a panel facing east with eight sculptures, three on the right hand and five on the left. There was a central image on the panel which might have been of the presiding deity, but it has weathered beyond recognition. Siva and Vishnu have been depicted in the panel. Besides this, in this cluster there is a bas-relief of Lord Ganesh and another panel of four icons.

Cluster II

This cluster is located about half a km away to the south of Cluster I. At the slope of the hill there is a natural rock -shelter inside which there are three bas-relief sculptures carved on the interior face of the shelter. The sculpture in the middle is larger than the two on both sides. The middle image is standing on a *dharmachakra* and the image on the right seems to be standing on a four-legged animal which is sitting. It is either a bull or a deer which is hard to confirm as it is very indistinct. Some 75m above this rock-shelter there is a similar sculpture. These three sculptures have generated much controversy. They have been identified by some as those of Parshvanath, the first Tirthankar a of the Jain pantheon on the basis that the image is sky clad. But the image lacks the other criteria of a Tirthankara's image. The Tirthankaras generally have *srivatsa,* a triangular symbol on the chest, besides a triple umbrella above their heads and a symbol on the parasol. On the other hand the hanging ear-lobes of the sculptures suggest it to be a Buddha's image. Also, it can be said that this sculpture may have been carved nude under the influence of Tantric Buddhism.

Cluster III

A solitary sculpture of Lord Ganesh is present here besides a few lingas. This cluster is situated between Clusters I and II.

Stupas: Most of them are votive *stupas,* with size ranging from 30 cm to about 3 m in diameter. All of them have the *harmika* cut in stone. One large size *stupa* has a stepped square base which has floral patterns carved on it. A band has also been carved on the face of the *'anda'* or dome, all along its circumference. At most places these are seen occurring by the side of the *lingas.*

Lingas: There are *lingas* with *yoni-pithas* found all over the site.

Pillars: A bubbling stream has exposed on its bed and bank a few well-polished sandstone columns. Their diameter is approximately 30 cm. But as they are broken their heights could not be ascertained.

Slabs: The name Sri Surya Pahar has gained currency because of a square stone slab of about 80.5 cm in length. On one , having the figures of Adityas , two concentric circles, the outer circle of 60.5 cm in diameter and inner circle of about 30.4 cm in diameter, are carved. In the outer circle is carved a twelve petalled lotus, each petal having a figure of a seated Aditya. In the inner circle there is an image of Brahma. This slab is locally worshipped as Surya. Besides this,a few other stone slabs are seen in the bed of the stream where the columns can be seen. These are rectangular slabs which have sockets and also brackets cut into it. So, they are most probably part of a structure which was built for fixing these slabs.

Natural Niches: These are square niches of about 140 sq cm on the rock faces. Siva lingas are seen inside a few of them. They are believed to be places of meditation favoured by the mendicants

Discussion

The above analysis of the antiquities at Sri Surya Pahar makes it clear that these are the remains of a religious centre. But the type of religious practices in the centre is to be acertained. The material evidence point towards many directions.

(1) The name Sri Surya Pahar literally means "mountain of the sun". So, the mountain was either regarded as an abode of the sun or was dedicated to sun worship, which in Assam has great antiquity. The Grihya Sutras and the epics mention Pragjyotisha as a strong centre of the solar cult. The prevalence of the cult is also proved by a number of existing manuscripts of the period, like the one *Kamrpura Nibandhaniya Kandasadhya* of the 6th-7th century A.D. In the *Kalika Purana* it is precisely stated that the Sri Surya Mountain in Goalpara is the perpetual abode of the Sun. So,this place was already an established centre of the Solar cult when *Kalika Purana* was composed, before A.D. 1000. Thus the present name of the site and the literary

evidence indicate that it was a centre of Sun worship. But material evidence to support this view is only one, viz. the protected twelve Adityas carved in a circle and Brahma in the centre. This slab, worshipped locally as Surya, is the only evidence in favour of its being a centre of Sun worship.

(2) In Sri Surya Pahar, the lingas and also figures of Siva dominate the group of sculptures. There are also rock-cut images of Lord Ganesh and Lord Vishnu. These sculptures are belived to be of the Pala-Sena school of art which flourished in eastern India in the Medieval period. Their presence indicates the practice of Brahmanical cults, Saiva as well as Vaishnava. These cults flourished in Assam from about 4th-5th century A.D. and has continued till date. Huen Tsang, who was in Assam in the middle of the 7th century, mentions in his account that the predominant religion in Kamrupa included Brahmanical cults. The Pala-Sena School of Art flourished between 8th century to 12th century. So, the Surya Pahar temple-complex may have been built during this period.

In order to support a group of artists who could create such exquisite sculptures and bring up a whole temple-complex there must have been a strong royal power. The political history of Assam reveals the names of four dynasties which were ruling when *Kalika Purana* was composed before A.D.1000. Thus, rulers of Kamarupa from 7th century, to 12th century in respective order are the Varmans, the Solastambhas, the descendants of Bhagadatta, a mythical ruler of Asssam, and the Palas. All these were the followers of Hinduism. Except for King Bhaskarvarman of the Varman dynasty, who was much influenced by Buddhism and did help in legitimising this religion in Assam, they were all Hindus. All these four dynasties have left their marks in Assam through art and architecture. The sculptures, therefore, may have belonged to different rulers

(3) The next group of sculptures in Sri Surya Pahar are the Buddhist Stupas; Buddhism was practised in Assam only after 7th century in the form of Tantrik Buddhism of the Vajrayana cult. Before this period there are references to the presence of Buddhism but it is recorded that it was practised in secret by its adherents. The *stupas* in Sri Surya Pahar exist by the side of the *lingas* and other sculptures. Also, it was a known place of worship of the Solar cult. Thus, the prevalence of a secret cult in that place is not a very logical idea. Also the votive *stupas* are quite similar to the *stupas* of the rock-cut caves of western India. In fact one of the larger *stupas* has a band around the *'anda'* or dome and floral patterns in the base which are later additions in *stupa* architecture. So, Buddhism must have flourished in the place either in 7th century after Bhaskarvarman's acquaintance with Huen Tsang or between 11th-12th century when the Pala rulers or Kamarup a became the followers of Tantrik Buddhism.

The above are the three types of religious practices indicated by the material remains in Sri Surya Pahar. This situation of the co-existence of Brahmanic and Buddhist religious practices can be regarded as an expression of the popular Indonesian cult of 'Siva-Buddha' where Buddha is considered locally as the younger brother of Siva. Authorities have remarked on this aspect that this Tantrik cult must have emanated from India, perhaps from ancient Bengal. Major part of ancient Bengal was inside the kingdom of Kamarupa till about the middle of 12 century. In most parts of Southeast Asia the co-existence of Buddhist religious elements with Hindu elements is very common. Sri Surya Pahar, in the 'land of the rising sun', must have been a home of such a faith.

BIBLIOGRAPHY

Bapat, P.V.(Ed.). 1959. 2500 *Years of Buddhism,* Publications Division, Govt. of India., Delhi.

Borpujari, H.K., 1990. *The Comprehensive History of Assam,* Publication Board of Assam,Guwahati.

Chakraborty, J.and Battacharya, D.C.(Ed.) *Aspects of Indian Art and Culture,* S.K.Saraswati Commemoration Volume, Calcutta.

Choudhury, P.C., 1987. *The History of Civilization of the People of Assam upto the 12th cent. A.D.,* Spectrum Publication.

Gait, E.A., 1993. *A History of Assam,* Thacke Spink & Co., Calcutta.

Gupte, R.S., 1992. *Iconography of Hindus, Buddhists and Jains,* Taraporevala & Sons, Bombay.

Nath, Shyamasharan. 1991. *Sri Surya Pahar Bapujinagar, Goalpara.*

Sarma, Dimbeswar (ed.) 1981. *Kamarupsasnavali,* Publication Board of Assam, Guwahati.

Sarma, S.N., 1989. *A Socio-economic and Cultural History of Medieval Assam* (1200-1800 A.D.), Arunod Press, Guwahati.

Shastri, Biswarnarayan, 1993. *Kalika Purana,* (Trans) Nag Publishers, Delhi.

Siva And Sakti Worship In India

Urmila Agrawal*

The rising and setting of the Sun, shining of the Moon and blowing of the winds was as much a phenomenon of awe, wonder and devotion to the pure and simple mind of prehistoric Man as the natural urge in all living beings leading to creation and multiplication. Thus began the worship Siva and Sakti "in some prehistoric period when neolithic man looked upon the Linga (Phallus) and the Yoni (the female organ) in reverential amazement as representing the creating power"(Munshi, K.M.). The *Linga* and the *Yoni* represent the great generative principles of the universe-Purusha and Prakriti (Gopinath Rao). "The supreme god puts forth His active nature of *svaprakriti* and creates the *Jivas* (living beings), who work out their destinies along lines determined by their own nature." (Radha krishnan: 540)

Siva in his Pasupati form was the lord of the animals, the deity of "plenty and fecundity" (Munshi, K.M.). just as the Supreme Mother, Jagadamba was of "fertility and profundity"(Banerjea J.N:563). If Siva is the seed that grows, Sakti is the soil where alone the seed germinates; if one is desire, the other is its fulfilment; if one is penance, the other is its reward. They are one in eternal union; merely two aspects of the One supreme-indissoluble, undivided and never dividing. They are one in creation as well as in destruction. As destruction lies embedded in the cosmic dance of Siva, so also Sakti is destruction personified in her ferocity as Kali."Both are timeless Time, united and equal, both benevolent and terrific"(Munshi, K.M.).

The Harappan Pasupati gradually blended with the Vedic Rudra, the awesome god of Thunder "fierce and destructive like a terrible beast"(Munshi, K.M.). He is a "bull", "exalted", "the strong among the strong", rapid and swift", the "unaging Asura", "Lord Isana of the world"(Munshi, K.M.). Throughout the Vedic period Rudra is identified with Agni who has his abode in the sky as the Sun, in the atmosphere, as the lightning and on earth as fire; in other words "the sky",the atmosphere and the earth give birth to Agni in his triple aspect of the Sun, the lightning and the fire; hence he is called *Trayambaka* or three mothered"(Gopinath Rao)

He is also "wise", "beneficent", "auspicious Siva" (Munshi, K.M.). "the redeemer of mankind" (Bhandarkar, R.G:222-223). It is Siva who destroys the demons Tripura, Andahaka and Sarabha. It is He who unites with Uma to give birth to Skanda who would destroy Taraka, the demon and save the earth from his clutches. It is Siva again who swallows the poison (recovered from the churning of the ocean) when all other gods present looked askance as to who would die on the altar of self-sacrifice to save the world. Unhesitating and unflinching Siva drank the poison in one, and yet He lives on in His gulp glory redoubled, as Nilakantha- the blue throated (Munshi, K.M.). He opened "His matted locks to receive the mighty Ganga(Munshi, K.M.). — the mother of purity and plenty (Munshi, K.M.).

Siva, the insane lover, wanders all over the cremation

*E-7/ H 508, Area Colony, Bhopal

grounds, besmearing his body with ashes, carrying the lifeless body of his beloved wife Sati who had immolated herself in the sacrificial fire at the *yajna* performed by her father, Daksha, because her father had insulted her husband by not inviting him to the *yajna*. The ignorant father knew not that Siva was the Supreme Creator of the universe and Siva and Sakti were one in Eternal Love. Nay, the Two are not One in love alone. If Siva is a *tapasvi* (an ascetic), Parvati, as Uma becomes the tapasvini (a female ascetic), because marriage is a sublimated yearning and its only aim is not the fulfilment of desire or *kama*, creation and multiplication (Munshi, K.M.). Its ultimate aim is to lead the world on to a better and purer life, to subdue the carnal desires and attain love-sublime, the love which does not demand but bestows happiness. Such a love is based on complete understanding of one another, somuch so one feels what the other feels, one knows what the other wants and does what the other likes without feeling the stress of it. Attainment of this love turned Siva into Ardhanarisvara-half-man-half-woman. His right half was himself, but the left half became Uma and thus the two became one in reality. The real import of the Ardhanarisvara form of Siva is that "the male and the female principles are inseparable and are ever found together in cosmic evolution" (Munshi, K.M.). To this day Ardhanarisvara is the Hindu god of marriage and the attainment of this oneness through marriage is the ultimate aim of a Hindu couple.

"The great Asiatic mother goddess Ma and the father god Atthis, of prehistoric ages were associated one with lion, the other with bull, as were Sakti and Siva"(Munshi, K.M:42). As early as the Vedic times the "supreme goddess was associted with Rudra as his strength or Sakti and was most worshipful"(Munshi, K.M:42). — reference to which is clearly made in the *Devisukta* of the Rig veda.

Around Siva and Sakti religion philosophy evolved and literature and art soared high on the wings of imagination. Being so human in their appeal yet elevating in their sigificance, the divine couple never lost their importance in Hindu religion, and during the medieval period skilled sculptors set to translate the "sublime in stone"(Munshi, K.M:50). Worship of Siva prevails both in anthropomorphic and in aniconic forms.

Anthropomorfic Forms

In the numerous temples of the early medieval period that lie scattered all over the northern India, a large variety of Siva images have been found. The depictions of these images are not only based on the puranic stories, i.e., the stories given in the Puranas,but are also illustrative of the Vedic philosophy and the unflincing faith of the people. These images can be broadly categorised under two heads - the *Santa*, i.e., the calm, and the *Ugra*, i.e., ferocious,aspects. The *Santa* depiction conveys the benedictory aspect of Siva shown with his cosort or alone. Images of Siva with his consort are also named as Umasahita (with Uma) or Sukhasanamurtis.

The Sukhasana or Umasahita images show Siva's marriage with Parvati or they show the happy couple seated together in *alingana* (embracing) pose. Images showing the marriage are called Kalyanasundara Panigrahana images (which means holding the hands of the bride which is the important wedding-rite among the Hindu).

In these images Parvati is shown standing on the right of Siva. She is a graceful, slim and coy maiden holding a *darpana*(mirror) in her left hand and modestly covering part of her face with the mirror, but at the same time stealing a look at her lord. Her right hand is held in the right hand of Siva. This was a happy occasion and the gods and gandharvas (heavenly mucisians) are shown with musical instruments dancing and singing; and *Sivaganas* have garlands in their hands. To show that the images of the gods and *ganas* are subordinate to the divine couple they are made smaller and occupy the lesser place in the aureole of the main image. At times Surya - the Sun god, and Indra - the lord of heaven are shown witnessing the happy marriage. Brahma - the priest of the gods with his consort Savitri is shown performing the wedding and an attendant couple with *mangala kalasa* (auspicious water jar full of water) stands by as if to say - 'may the cup of happiness be full to the brim for you like the jars of water on our heads'.

Siva carries weapons like *chakra* (discus), *trisula* (trident), *gada* (mace), *parasu* (an axe), *damaru* (kettledrum) and *khadga* (sword), etc. Of all these weapons *trisula* is generally given in his hands. in some of the *Panigrahana* images Siva has four arms and in three of these, clockwise order (right upper, left upper and left lower) he has *kamal* (lotus flower), *trisula* with snake entwined over it and his fourth hand rests on his waist; or there are *trisula* and *khatvanga* (a weapon having a skull fixed on a staff) and the fourth hand is placed on Parvati's shoulder. In all these images his right lower hand is holding his consort's right hand.

To make the scene more realistic one image shows Brahma performing the marriage rites and giving offerings to Agni (Sacred fire) personified. Agni is shown lying down with his mouth open and flames of fire are rising from his mouth to devour the offerings.

In the other type of *Sukhasana* image which may better be called Umalinganamurtis (images) Siva is invariably shown embracing his consort Uma with his left lower hand. In these imges Parvati - now his wedded wife, sits on his left, keeping her right hand on the right shoulder of her lord. Both look fondly at each other or may be looking in front, but the unparallelled expression of heavenly bliss, contentment and supreme satisfaction is reflected on their faces. The half-closed eyes and smiling lips are the surest symbols of this. Their mounts the lion and the bull are shown couchant at their feet. Sometimes Siva fondly keeps his left lower hand on the left breast of his consort or is shown touching her chin. Parvati holds either a lotus or a mirror in her left hand. Siva holds a *kamala, a trisula,* or is shown in *abhaya* pose (pose for protection) with the *akshamala* (rosary). In some of the images Siva has four hands and the weapons in his hands vary according to the ideas or the impressions that the sculptor wants to convey.

To preserve his freedom of expression one sculptor shows Parvati seated on the right side of Siva - in stubborn defiance to the accepted rule that a wife's place is on the left and thus subordinate to that of her husband. This could also be interpreted as ignorance on the part of the sculptor. But it is difficult to believe that a person so well versed in his art and true to his representation could be ignorant of this fact. On the other hand it may be a genuine expression of the sculptor's devotion and greater faith in the Mother goddess. Another such example is the image in which Parvati also has four hands which represent greater power of the goddess.; once again the devotee voices his faith in the Sakti.

A beautiful image shows Siva playing on the *Vina.* This image remarkably gives an extremely human touch to the god by showing how he attempts to entertain his wife by the vibrating notes of sweet melody produced by the touch of his left fingers.

One panel depicts Siva and Parvati in *alingana* in the centre. On one side is a pose an emaciated follower of Siva; and on the other are Siva and Bhairava - the insane lover. Here it seems that the sculptor wanted to show the contrast by depicting lonely, grief-stricken Bhairava and Siva as a beggar with the begging bowl beside the happy couple in the centre.

The cosmic union becomes complete and the sacred couple have two sons Skanda and Ganesa. The slim maiden has now a round matronly figure and the family of four is shown together with Brahma and Vishnu (the two other gods of the Hindu trinity) on top.

The ingenuity of the sculptor is attested by the Ardhanarisvara images which combine both Siva and Sakti in one. As the name indicates these images are half-male and half-female, showing in one the *jata* (matted hair) of Siva with the chignon of Parvati; the *naga-kundala* (the serpent ear-ring of Siva) with the *karnaphula* (the flower tops of Parvati); the *bhujanga-hara* (the serpent necklace) with the *suvarna-hara* (Parvati's gold necklace); the *bhujanga-valaya* (serpent bracelet) with the *kangana* (gold bracelet) and bangles; and *kara* (gent's anklet) with the *payala* (lady's anklet) of Parvati. The right half with the jewellery of deadly serpents (whom Siva had no reason to fear having poison in his own body) is that of the god and the left half is the goddess with all the feminine fondness for gold jewellery. In the two hands these images have Siva's *trisula* and Uma's *darpana* and the prominent left breast specifies the female half of the god. To some these images have appeared grotesque and uncouth, but to the simple and pure minds aware of the mythology and deep significance their appeal lies in the unity of the two great forces of Nature. We cannot forget how extremely difficult it is to carve such an image.

The Ardhanarisvara images have four arms also and in the two right hands they carry the weapons carried by Siva while in the left ones they hold Parvati's mirror or the *dupatta* i.e. the thin flowing wrapper or stole.

A beautiful specimen depicts the god with his first hand placed on his bull-faced *yaksha* (his follower) and the fourth one is placed lovingly on the head of Skanda (their second son) who stands with his mount, the peacock.

From the detailed description of the images given above it would be evident how truly the sculptors were translating the religious beliefs and the mythological ideas of yore into stone.

Linga and Yoni worship

A thick veil of mist hangs over the worship of *Linga* and *Yoni* by the Hindus. Although the most popular form of Siva worship is in the form of *linga* and Parvati's in that of *yoni,* yet these are the most mis-understood principles by the world at large. Let us look into the meaning of the two.

In logic *"linga"* refers to the invariable sign which forms the basis of inference (Ranganathanda). *Lingasarira* means "subtle body" or the body which is the supprot of all i.e *Atma.*

Linga means the "creative aspect" of the mind which can be equated with the "creative organ" in the physical body. Thus *linga* worship stands for the worship of all creative urge in man.

Linga and *yoni* worship also typify the "generative-force or the creative energy."(Kanwar Lal:184)

Buddhist scriptures speak of the *"Vajra"* and *"Mani"* and the *"Linga"* and *"Yoni"* as symbols and signs of the same kind as algebraic signs and symbols in the study of mathematics and sciences. (Kanwar Lal:182)

Hindus have a class of "nature" symbols and the *linga* is one of them. These symbols are usually mathemtical in form. They not only represent a reality but are also the vehicles of the power within that reality. "The Lingam is an ellipsoid. It symbolises Siva-Sakti; that is the primary polarity principle of positive and negative forces. On this principle of opposites the universe is founded." (Howard Murphet:4:1)

Dr. Taimni (Dr. I.K. Taimni at the Theosophical Society's School of the Wisdom, at Adiyar, Madras) explains why an ellipsoid is used to symbolise the polarity principle, in the following way. "The ultimate reality, the Absolute or Brahman or God, or whatever we care to term it, has no polarity, no pairs of opposites; all principles are balanced and harmonised within it. Therefore, the ultimte reality is represented by the most perfect mathematical figure - the sphere."

If the centre of the sphere is cleavaged we would get the ellipsoid. Thus the figure of Linga gives a symbolic representation of the primary pair of opposites out of the original harmonious one. This first duality is the cause of all creation, all manifestation and all the multiplicity of things in the universe. Like *"aum"* the basic sound *"linga"* is the basic form of all creation.

Siva is not only one of the Trinity (i.e. Brahma, Vishnu and Mahesa or Siva) - 'the destruction-regeneration aspect, he is also the highest god' - the father of all gods, the cosmic logos.

Like all other gods of the Hindus, Siva has a consort Sakti or his female aspect. The male or positive aspect represents Conciousness and the female or the negative aspect is Power. Both are essential for creation or manifestaion of matter.

In Uttara-Gita, Lord Krishna says that *"lingam"* is from the word *"lina"* which means to be one with or to unite so that you lose consciousness of your own self. In this way the *lingam* makes possible the union of the lower self with the higher self and with God, i.e, the *atman* unites with *jivatma* and *parmatma.*

In the Jain text *"Ashtapahuda" linga* (Kunda Kundacharya) for Bhesha or any religious sect and Jina

Lingadhari (Kunda Kundacharya) means one who has faith in the Jina philosphy.

When understood in any of the above contexts *linga* and *yoni* stands for all that is the best and highest in Man. There is nothing lowly about it. But, sometimes, somehow and for certain unknown reasons obscenity was attached to linga and yoni.

According to Hindu Philosophy everything that is natural in man is divine. Nothing is obscene by itself. It is your feeling or pre-suppositions which make a thing good or bad, pure or impure, right or wrong. These are norms set up by man, but the impure becomes pure if you consider it so or if innocently done. Sex is divine, and Siva and Parvati form the ideal couple in anthropomorphic form. They unite in Ardhanarisvara and bless the newly weds. *Linga* and *yoni* are the aniconic representation of these two.

Aniconic forms or various depictions of Linga

1. The Jyotirlinga (i.e. Banner of light) is often represented like a small oil lamp or *deepa* lighted at the time of worship, stands symbolically for the streak of light or knowledge in the surrounding darkness or ignorance. This is the simplest representation of god. *Jyotih* the ensign, *ketu* or banner or *linga* of the unmanifested essence of the creator.

2. The *Sahasralinga* represents the all prevading power of Lord Siva by showing thousands of smaller *lingas* on the big main *linga*. There are Mukhalingas too having one, three, four or five faces respectively called Ekamukhi, Trimukha, Chaturmukhi and Panchamukha *lingas*.

3. The Ekamukia *linga* depicts only the face or the standing image of Siva on one side.

4. The Trimukhi *linga* combines in itself the faces of Parvati, Sadasiva (in the centre) and Chamunda. The big *Jatamukuta* unites and balances the three faces. The side faces in the dim light of the sanctum appear remote and unnatural in the presence of the glorious Sadasiva in the centre. In the centre is god the eternal, all knowing and unmoved witness of the play of sorrow and happiness in this world; the other two faces are always active creating (Parvati as Jagadamba) and destroying (as Chamunda). The two are the expressions of the same Sadasiva and emanate from Him alone.

5. The Chaturmukha Linga shows Brahma, Duttatreya, Vaikunthanatha and Harihara with their respective *ayudhas* (weapons) in their hands.

The Panchamukha *linga* represents the five aspects of Siva

The Isana on top; The Vamadeva with his compassionate young face on the north; Aghora Siva in fierce form on the south; Sadyojata or Siva as Supreme creator with calm benedictory face of Parvati on the west and Siva Tatpurusha invisible to the human eye facing east.

Even if *linga* and *yoni* stand for the procreative organs for men and women in their youth and prime when the blood is hot and heady, while desire is aflame and lust a living torrent, let there be free play of the passions, let the soul embrace the body and be mirrored in terms of sex. Yet these men and women should not forget that just as beyond dharma (*kartavya karya*-deeds to be done or the practice of social righteousness) and *Artha* (the pursuit of prosperity) is *kama* (the pursuit of pleasure), so beyond *kama* is *monksha* (the striving after liberation) man's supreme goal.(Kanwar Lal:176)

"There is nothing shameful in sexual life to a Hindu. It is a natural function. Even their gods are married. Thus sexualism has been transformed into divine by its assocation with religion. (Kanwar Lal:176) 'Man mated with woman to reproduce and in the same manner Nature performed this act of reproduction. So the generative organs were worshipped symbolically to mean the divine force of generation'. "The love of a woman or a stranger involves the surrender of all that the world values and is, therefore, inspired by a spirit of martyrdom such as should animate a religious devotee (Kanwar Lal:185). "Love consequently becomes a type of salvation". (Kanwar Lal:186).

"Love at its best extends far beyond the narrow confines of the reproductive act and as P.D. Ouspensky has pointed out, may provide for an ordinary man his nearest approach to a mystical experience."(Lawrence, D.H)

"The meaning and the purpose of the union between man and woman is to be found, not in the continuation of the species, or in its social import, but in personality, in its striving for the completeness and fullness of life and its longing for enternity."(Kenneth, Walker and Fletcher: 29-30)

That is why a Hindu worshipped the *linga* and *yoni,* as he worships to this day. The truth unravelled through *linga* and *yoni* leads him to salvation. Could there be an easier and purer expression of the soul uniting with God? Then why are the Hindus called the jungly phallus worshippers. the obscenity and purity have united in *linga* and *yoni* and the net result is salvation.

REFERENCES

Banerjea, J.N. *Development of Hindu Iconography* p. 563.

Bhandarkar, R.G. *Vaishnavism, Saivism and minor Religious Systems* , Chapter XVII, p.222-223.

Gopinath Rao, T.A. *Elements of Hindu Iconography* Vol.11,Part I, 58, 40-41, 59

Howard Murphet. *Sai Baba Man of Miracles* Chapter 4.

Kanwar Lal. *Immortal Khajuraho-Things Humanity Hides Away,* - pp.176-186.

Lawrence, D.H. From the essay "Love was once a little Boy."

Kenneth Walker and Peter Fletcher *Sex and Society* p. 29-30.

Munshi, K.M. *Saga of India Sculpture* :p. 41, 42, 43

Radhakrishnan, S. *Indian Philosophy*, p. 540

Ranganathananda Personal information

Sri Kunda Kundacharya. "Ashtapahuda" by Sri Kunda Kundacharya translated by Paras Das Jain Nyayatirtha in Hindi and Late Jagat Prasad into English, p.6 and p. 52.

Buddhist Monasteries in Mongolia

K.N. DIKSHIT*

Situated in Central Asia, the Mongolian Republic is a landlocked country bordering with Russia on the one hand and the People's Republic of China on the other. It is broadly divided into two geographical divisions: the Khangai zone in the northern part which has rich water resources and favourable weather conditon and the Gobi desert zone in the southern part with insufficient water. It is also known as 'Sunny country'.

India has played a distinctive role in shaping the cultural history of Central Asia which was the meeting place of various races, nations and religion. It is needless to say that Buddhism in Central Asia, which is highly composite in nature requires a detailed understanding of the development process of Buddhism in Tibet and other adjoining regions from where it travelled to China and other places. The original Indian art motifs and styles were modified enroute.

The earliest religion of the Mongols was shamanism but among the foreign religions Buddhism was most widely spread. The Mongols had contact with Buddhism much earlier than the establishment of Mongolian empire. During the reign of Ogodel Khan (1221-24) and Kublai Khan (1260-94) significant propagation of Buddhism in Mongolia took place when they introduced Saskya-pa branch of Tibetan Buddhism. The adoption of Lamaism by the Mongol ruling class also led to the establishment of Lamaist monasteries in China directly under the supervision of the Tibetan clergy.

Buddhism in Tibet is a form of Tantric Buddhism which was preached by the Indian saints and teachers like Padmasambhava, Atisa, Dipankara etc. This Buddhism is devoted to the worship of Tantric gods and goddesses like Tara, Dakini, Adi Buddha, Dhyani Buddha, Mahakala etc. Though Sakyamuni Buddha was not completely forgotten, it is the Boddhisatvas and Tantric gods and goddesses who were popular in Tibet. From Tibet, Buddhism spread to Turfan, Tung Huang, China and Mongolia. The third phase in the introduction of Buddhism began when Altan Khan invited the leader of Yellow sect of Tibetan Buddhism Gya-mtsho in 1576 which led to a mass conversion of Mongols to Buddhism. Influential nobles also adopted Lamaism simultaneously which contributed to the cessaion of feudal discord. A series of monastic rules were adopted and practice of shamanistic rituals was discontinued.

Architecture

The Buddhist monasteries in Mongolia evolved out of simple and basic roof forms widespread in Asia.(Fig.1). They were raised over the platforms of the hard rammed earth with timber columns and a frame of wood. It displayed the mixed styles of Tibetan and Chinese, but it is the Chinese superstructure which was used after certain modifications to suit the local climate. The special features were their planning and decorative principles. On the platform, the timber columns which were carved in different varieties were placed on stone bases to protect their base from dampness. The columns were then tied in both

* B- 322, Sarita Vihar, New Delhi, 110044

Evolution of Buddhist architecture

Fig. 1

directions by wooden beams. Sometimes more than one tier of beams of diminishing length was placed vertically over one another across the plan and separated by struts over which roof purlins were placed. The plan was extendable in all directions of the span by widening the bay and increasing the members of the beams. Above the beams and the brackets, the purlins commonly round in section carried rafters on which the boarding was fixed. An insulating layer of clay was also laid which was again interlocked with layers of segmented tiles. The flexibility of the frame-system with cantiliver arrangements provided different roof-forms,some with even eaves.

The walls of the building are raised over a low brick masonry mounted with a bamboo frame-work completed with beaten clay. The whole building was given a colour which served a kind of protection against decay and parasities.

The Mongols have given greater emphasis in the construction of their monasteries, for example the one at Erden Zuu on the left bank of Orhon river, specially on the curved roof lines, greater eaves overhang and brackets cluster. The interior is richly decorated with the exquisite colour schemes.

In later monasteries for example at Ulan Bator the roof was treated in a new way by which it appeared rather to float above the structure. The part of the roof which admitted decoration is the central ridge and the projecting eaves at the sides which in course of time became more or less purely decorative forms. The buildings were found set in courtyards but not specially designed and treated for this purpose.

Art

The art of Mongolia having its genesis in the Stone Age travelled through the Bronze and Iron age has its firm roots in the so called 'deer stones' of Turkic and Mongol tribes. The carvings executed over them are of highly stylized manner. In one of the deer stones, a hairless human figurine with prominent cheek bones and hooked nose having round ear-rings and neck ornaments is carved. Other images were those of Moon and the Sun. During 6th-8th centuries A.D. "stone men" were portayed as warriors and the same were executed on a higher level of artistic mastery.

With the introduction of Buddhism in 16th century A.D. Tibetan influence was exerted on the development of indigenous art. A few Tibetan images served as models for the early productions. In China also an independent stylistic evolution of Lamaist art was noticed in the 16th century. The Chinese craftsmen decorated lotus pedestals with two draped stoles.

Zanabazar (1635-1723) from the family of Chingiz Khan's lineage put Mongolian sculptural art on a different footing and his creations confirm his knowledge of cannonical proportions and adherence to the 10-palm *Dasatala* proposition of Indian art. The Buddhist metal statues were hollow cast. The figures are graceful and well proportioned and as a rule Buddha, Avalokitesvara, Amitayus, Manjusri, Siyama-Tara, Sita-Tara, etc. were seated on round lotus-shaped pedestals. The tradition of these statues continued vigorously in later centuries and even in other idioms such as coral, wood and clay mixed with paper (*papier mache*) also contributed to the development of sculptural art. The preparation of masks of gods and beasts in different sizes was another tradition started in the 19th century. Wood was generally used for making folk-sculptures.

Paintings

Prehistoric man left traces of paintings on rock suface and painted the figurines in red pigments. During the Bronze Age and Hun period distinctive colour designs developed. The fragments of wall murals of Uighur and Kidan periods were found in excavations. The portraits of the Yuan rulers are the continuation of Kidan portrait. With the coming of Buddhism in Mongolia, the tradition of painting reached the level which was started by Zanabazar. The paintings are, however, not exclusively based upon the philosophical teachings depicted in texts. The visuals are often based upon the dreams of the saints. In order to understand the pictorial representations including iconography the actual practices of Buddhist monks living in the Mongolian monasteries have to be observed. In the 19th century alone 140 life size paintings of Ugra school were produced. In the 20th century with the begining of national movement, the artists commenced painting on social themes.

Harhorum

Located at a distance of about 360 km from Ulan Bator, the first Buddhist Monastery of Erden-Zuu was built in 1586 by Abatai Khan in the ancient city of Karakorum after his long pilgrimage to Tibet (Fig.2). Since then Lamaist Buddhism began to spread into other parts of Mongolia. Some scholars feel that 'Lamaism and its monastic system brought into Mongol nomadic life, a series of changes and strengthening of cultural value, social mobility, economic diversification and establishment of political linkages.' The translation of Tibetan Buddhist literature into Mongolian language was also started. In Mongolia more than 700 monasteries existed before the formation of Peoples Republic of Mongolia. The architecture of this monastery which combined Mongolian, Tibetan and Chinese styles was of high skill and produced a characteristic trait developed by Mongolian architects. In 17th - 18th centuries, it was known as Buddhist Mecca and is a treasure-house of Buddhist religio-conographic material of Zanabazar School and of later times. Located in an area of 18 hectares it was girdled by a fortification wall having 108 exquisite *suburgans* (votive *stupas*) built into the wall. These votive *stupas* are dome-shaped memorial structures similiar to Indian shrines; each of them is devoted to some enlightened person or god of the Buddhist pantheon. Inside the structure is an icon depicting a heavenly being.

On display inside this monastery are icons; the important amongst them are the gilded statue of Maidar, the god of the future, a silver icon depicting Buddha and the Bodhisattvas, a gold statuettee of Bendze-Dharampala and gilded bronze statue of Padmasambhava. Other objects include *tankas,* paintings and ritual objects. In 1941 the State took over the monastery and 14 years later a Museum of Culture and Religion was opened. It houses materials of historical and cultural value, bronze statues and deities, ritual masks and objects and beautifully decorated mural paintings and samples of ceilings and articles made by craftsmen. The monastery was repaired in 1961.

The monastery contains a temple called the 'Eye of Divine Purity' and the "temple of three gods". The "temple of three gods" is a good piece of wooden architecture. The principal gods of this temple are made of mixed technique of early 20th century. They are sitting over Lamaist altar with numerous cast images on the sides. The roof purlins and curved roofs including wooden beam of the temple roof which cannot be seen from the ground have been intricately carved and beautifully decorated. It is approached from an entrance gate which leads to another main gate opening in a courtyard. The "temple of gods" is in one alignment and this complex represents the model for all those later construction in Mongolia.

The Tibetan temple is a latest addition. The main *'suburgan'* - the 'Eye of Divine Purity', has nine minor *'suburgans'* and base of the main one has painted panels.

Bagdo Khan's Palace, Temples and Museums

Situated on the southern edge of Ulan Bator, this

ERDEN ZUU

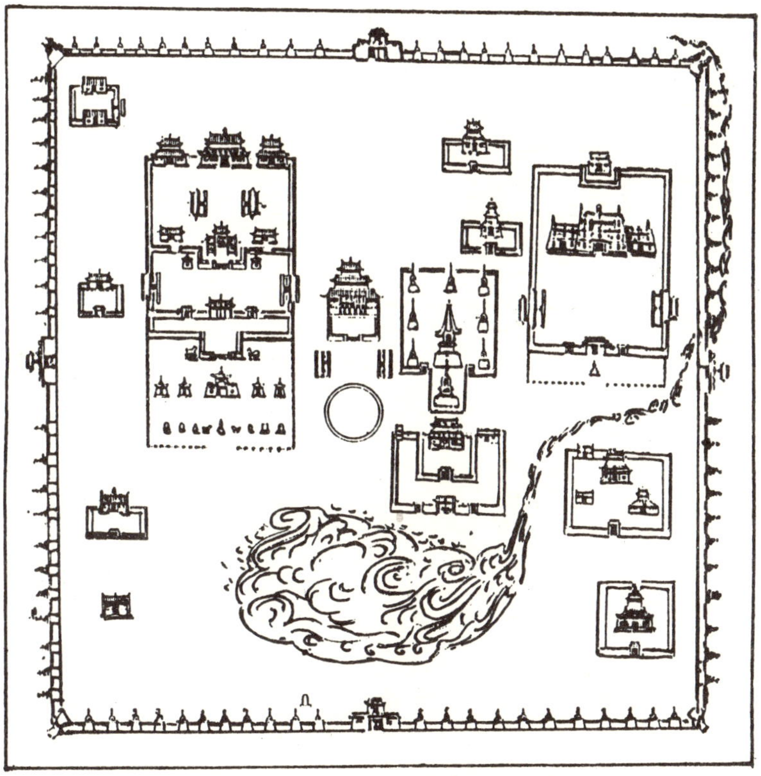

Erden Zuu - the first monastery in Mongolia

Fig. 2

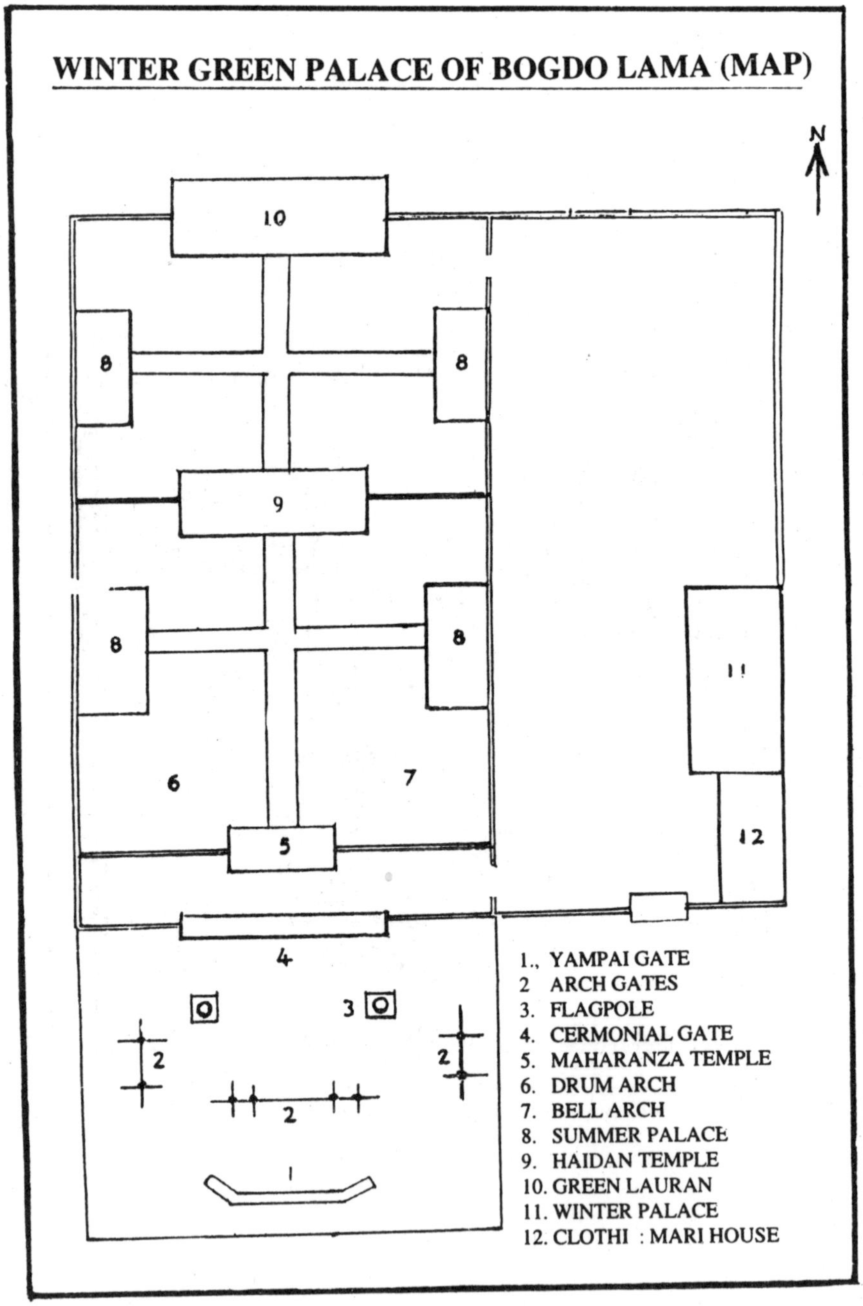
WINTER GREEN PALACE OF BOGDO LAMA (MAP)
N
10
8
8
9
8
8
11
6
7
5
12
4
3
2
2
2
1
1., YAMPAI GATE
2 ARCH GATES
3. FLAGPOLE
4. CERMONIAL GATE
5. MAHARANZA TEMPLE
6. DRUM ARCH
7. BELL ARCH
8. SUMMER PALACE
9. HAIDAN TEMPLE
10. GREEN LAURAN
11. WINTER PALACE
12. CLOTHI : MARI HOUSE

Fig. 3

Summer Palace was constructed in 1893 for the eighth Bogdo Khan who was brought from Tibet as the 8th re-incarnate of Zhavzandamba and installed as the head of the Yellow sect of Buddhism in Mongolia. It was taken over by the Government in 1924 on the death of Bogdo Khan. The Palace was renovated in 1960-61 and in 1982 (Fig.3).

The two storeyed modern building housing the present museum was the winter dwelling of Bogdo Khan located adjacent to the Summer Palace and temples outside the walled enclosure but again within the complex. Inside the enclosure starting from the direction of main entrance in a south-north axial line through a painted gate building, rectangular on plan, and a series of courtyards with temples of single storey on either side, and towards its end is a double storeyed structure surmounted by an ornamental roof known as Summer Palace. The area of this palace enclosure and temples, which are predominantly painted in green colour prepared out of mineral ores with adhesives or without, may be roughly around 5 acres (exact measurments were not available). The whole palace is painted but is damaged at a few places due to flaking but gilding work is in a better state of preservation. Paintings occur on walls and ceilings of various rooms, verandahs and enclosures of the temples and palaces.

The main roof of the structure is designed and framed first and then put over the wooden columns resting on the stone bases. Subsequently the roof of the corridor is framed and then raised on the smaller columns which constitute its enclosure. In order to provide light inside the intervals between the columns rising above the corridor roof are generally filled with screen work constituting a clerestory.

The outer surfaces of the temples standing just opposite to other, have a series of panels depicting narrative paintings having lightly coloured figurines. Inside these temples are kept bronze statues and *tankas* along with other objects of rituals.

The triumphal wooden gate of the palace built in 1912 and restored in 1989 has two side gates with wooden balconies over them and surmounted by four diminishing tiers of curved roofs. The main gate and side gates have paintings of over expressive of life sized deified human beings derived from Central and Eastern Tibetan Tantric mythology. Above these gates are small painted panels and on the main gate are five panels. The curved roofs which are painted in green colour have terracotta figurines on the corner and in the centre along with the State emblem in the middle. As the country is known as Sunny country, the colours which are receiving direct Sun rays have faded. From the wooden columns of these gates some paint were taken out as sample which revealed on examination in laboratory traces of cement.

The paintings which are of green, blue and red colours, are required to be repainted by using mineral based pigments. In some cases the purlins of roof also need to be repainted.

As most of these temples in the Summer Palace and in the museum have Buddhist *tankas* and *gilded* and ungilded bronzes of Tantric gods and goddesses genetically related with the Tibetan Buddhism, the preservation of these items is also of utmost importance.

The Tankas

The *tankas* depicting Samvara, Kalachakra, Mahakala, Yamantaka, Tsamba, Mandala Yamantaka, Mandala Ushnishasita, a hundred Buddhas, Amitayus, Yama, Vajradhara, Buddha, Mangla, Ushnishavijaya, Vajravarahi, Hayagriva, Zanabazar, seventh and eighth reincarnation of Jebzundamba, are important Buddhist iconographic representations influenced by Tibet and other Himalayan countries belonging to Bogdo Khan museum. A majority of them belong to the latter half of the 19th century.

Thee *tankas* and paintings are brittle due to surface accretions and soot. Their surface has a series of micro-cracks due to the natural shrinkage of medium on ageing.

The Bronzes

In the latter half of the 16th century when the Yellow sect of Lamaism established itself in Mongolia, Tibetan language became a means of communication. This gave rise to artistic conceptions and iconography based on

Tibetan tradition. In the time of Zanabazar a large number of Buddhist statues gilded and non-gilded bronzes were cast in one piece. They were physically well proportioned with defined muscles, straight shoulders and rounded waists. As rightly pointed out beautiful are the faces of the gods in deep meditation with high-bridged nose, slightly parted lips, half-closed lotus leaf-shaped eyes and the eyebrows radiating the harmony of youth. Most of them are seated on lotus-shaped pedestals. These bronzes are in monasteries, museums and private collections. In Bogdo Khan Palace Museum, gilded and non-gilded bronzes ranging in date from 17th - 19th centuries such as Syam - Tara, Buddha, Amitayus, Mahakala, Vajrapani and Yamantaka are beautiful representations of Buddhist pantheon. The objects made of clay mixed with paper, of wood and bone also made appearance at about this time. The *papier mache* painted in different colours or glided are continung even today.

Some scientists drew attention to a hitherto unnoticed form of basic copper chloride and basic copper corbonate formation on bronze items which are kept in museums.

Choijin Lama Monastery

This monastery which is located in the town was built in 1904 - 1908 by Choijin Lama brother of Bogdo Khan. It was in use as a residence till 1938 but from 1942 it was turned into a museum. Repairs to this monastery took place in 1960-61.(Fig.4)

Located within an enclosure, it is approached from south-north axis through an entrance gate opening into an open courtyard leading to Maharanza temple. From here one has to go to the main temple of Tsogchin Dugan. By the side of this, are located the temples of Zuu and Undur Gegan. The external paint of the temples have faded at a few places and requires repainting by using mineral based pigments.

The Tankas and Bronzes

The temples have a good collection of *tankas* and gilded bronzes. The paintings of Shangad/heaven, and Buddha are important pieces whereas gilded bronzes of Maitreya, Sitasamvara, Vajrasattva, Amitayus, Mintugwa, Mangla belong to Zanabazar school of 17th century. There are also gilded bronzes, masks and *papier mache* of 19th century in the collection.

As in other monasteries, the timber columns are placed on stone bases to protect them from capillary action (Fig.5). As at this place the water table is too high, a water disposal system has to be evolved to lower down the water table. Being an alluvial plain land and concentration of living apartments nearby, the rain water having no regular outlet stagnate in the region and creates the situation of dampness. In the month of July, it was observed that the stone bases were quite wet in the temples.

WOODEN PILLAR ON STONE BASE

Fig 5.

In Mongolia, wall *tankas* are available in plenty sometime they are painted with mineral colours or made out of applique design. It is observed that they are in need of chemical conservation and to rectify this situation a programme for its scientific study and chemical preserva-

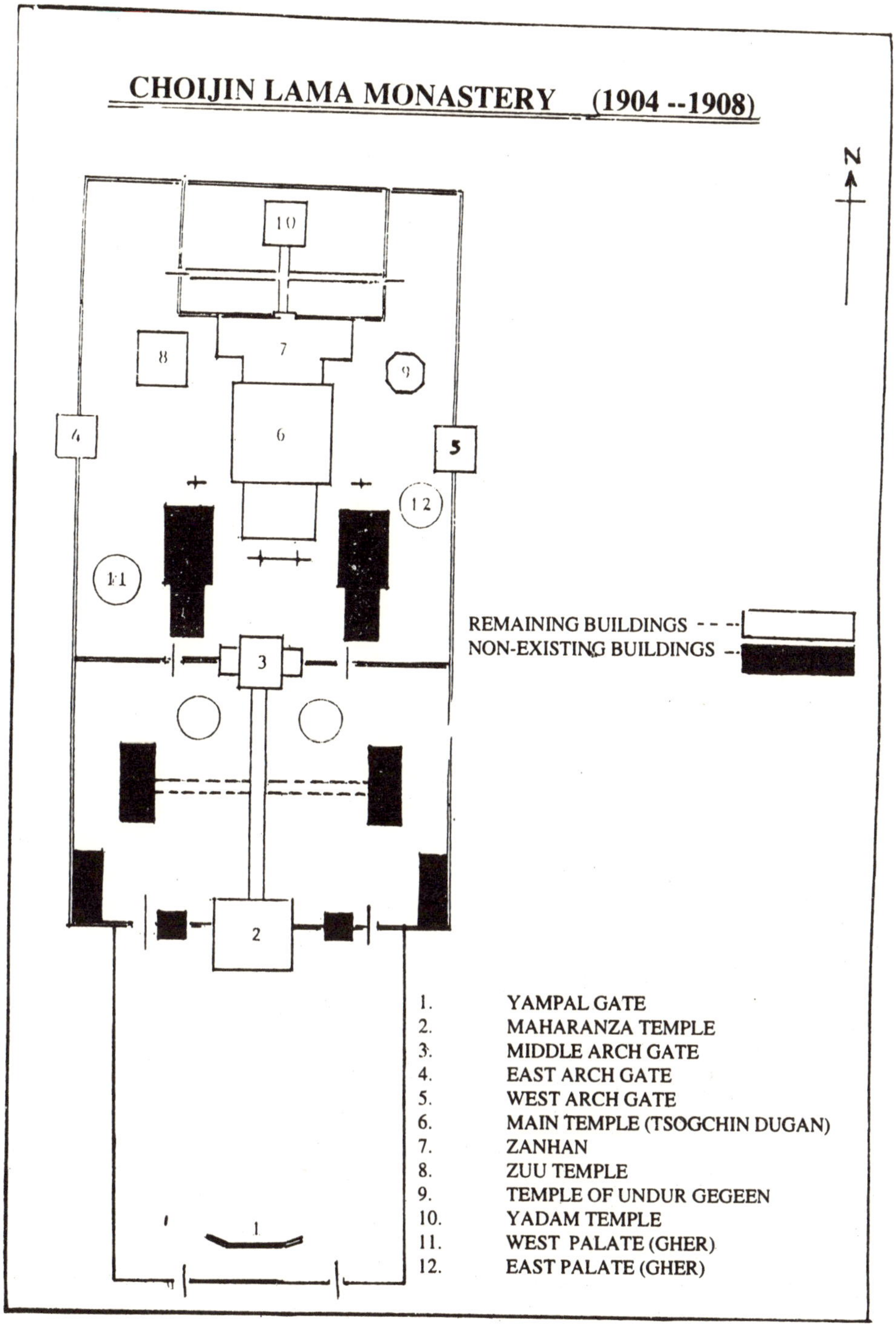
CHOIJIN LAMA MONASTERY (1904 --1908)
N
REMAINING BUILDINGS
NON-EXISTING BUILDINGS
1. YAMPAL GATE
2. MAHARANZA TEMPLE
3. MIDDLE ARCH GATE
4. EAST ARCH GATE
5. WEST ARCH GATE
6. MAIN TEMPLE (TSOGCHIN DUGAN)
7. ZANHAN
8. ZUU TEMPLE
9. TEMPLE OF UNDUR GEGEEN
10. YADAM TEMPLE
11. WEST PALATE (GHER)
12. EAST PALATE (GHER)

Fig. 4

tion may be taken up. However, the condition of the objects should be documented before conservation.

Gandan Living Monastery

This monastery which is a living one is located in the heart of the town. There is a sign on the gate engraved in three languages : Sanskrit, Tibetan and ancient Mongolian: "Storehouse of Wisdom of the Great Chariot Holy Shrine". One of the temples of this monastery is housing a library which is having an extensive stock of publications on Tantrism as well as on meditation, tantric rights and sermons.

Conclusion

The survey of the Mongolian monastries clearly proves beyond doubt that Buddhism in Mongolia is different from the Tibetan Buddhism not so much in spirit as in content. There are of course major similarities in terms of Buddhist life, scenes, the root of which goes back to Indian Buddhism, but the stories were not only elaborated, multiplied but also adopted to the liking of the local monks who were determined to have their own kind of Buddhism, a process which is found not only in Mongolia but also in Russia for example in Buriyat Republic where also there is a big and powerful monastic establishment. However, there is difficulty in tracing the connection between one School of art and another except that all of them are the extension of Central Asian Buddhist thought.

BIBLIOGRAPHY

Boy, Andrew, 1962, *Chinese Architecture*, London, pp.163.

Dani, A.K. and V.M. Masson (Ed.), 1992 *The History of Civilization of Central Asia*, Vol.1, *The Dawn of Civilization : Earliest Times to 700 B.C.* UNESCO, France, 535.

Information Mongolia, 1990, Academy of Science MPR, Pergamon Press, pp.505.

Lattimore, Owen, 1962, *Nomands and Commissars*, New York, pp.238.

Sandagdorzh, D(Ed.) 1986 *Development of the Mongolian National Style Painting*, '*Mongōl Zurog*' in Brief, State Publishing House,Ulan Bator 1989, *Mongolian Sculpture*, Ulanbator - Mongolian Architecture, Ulanbator.

Sharma, R.C. and Bira, S. 1991 *India and Mongolia*, New Delhi, pp.290.

Zeng, Dan, 1987, *A Survey of Tibet*, Tibet People's Publishing House, Hongkong.

Conservation of The Taj Mahal

P.B.S. SENGAR*

Introduction

The Taj Mahal, aptly described as dream in white marble, is a masterpiece of Indo-Islamic architecture. It represents the remarkable engineering skill and perfection of constructional devices as well as aesthetic ideals of the period. The monument was built by the Mughal emperor Shahjahan (reigned 1628-58) on the right bank of the river Yamuna as a garden-tomb for his most favourite queen Mumtaz Mahal following her death in 1631. The work of construction of this great monument started from the very foundation in the fifth regnal year i.e. January 1632 under the superintendence of Makram Khan and Mir Abdul-Karim. The inscriptions on the exterior of the western grilled door, southern arch of the centotaph chamber and northern arch of the main gate bear the dates of A.H 1046 (A.D.1636-37), 1048 (1638 - 39) and 1057 (A.D 1647- 48) respectively, denoting presumably the year of completion of various parts on which the inscriptions occur. Information revealed first that foundations were laid by excavating down to the sub-soil water level, second, that masonry below the ground is of stone-in-lime and third, that platform above the ground is of brick-in-mortar (Begley and Desai, 1989, pp. 65-86). Owing to the proximity of river, the whole fabric together with the four corner minars were made to rest on a firm bed of masonry, which seems to have been supported on piers sunk at close intervals in accordance with the usual Mughal practice. It has been later on confirmed through excavations carried out by the Archaeological Survey of India that the terrace on the river front has been raised on well foundations with filling of rubble masonry in between.

The principal material used in the core of the tomb proper, its minarets and other accessory buildings is essentially brick (*Lakhauri*) and lime mortar. The external surface of the tomb-building including its dome, drum, minarats, and interior of cenotaph chamber are lined with white marble veneering, whereas all the other interior surfaces are in lime plaster. Similarly both exteriors and interiors of all the other accessory buildings such as mosque, guest house, gates, etc. had been veneered with red sand stone except the exterior surfaces of domes which are veneered with white marble. Besides, in the accessory buildings a coat of red ochre was applied over a thin layer of special lime plaster invariably provided on red sandstone surfaces basically for the purpose of proper protection of the stones as well as for the decorations. Further, all the important external and internal surfaces of the monument were embellished with rich variety of highly artistic and delicate inlaid or *pietra dura* ornamentations. The chracteristic materials used in the inlay work include black marble, yellow marble, varieties of agate and jasper, coral, carnelian, turquoise, jade, crystal, lapis-lazuli, garnet, onyx, chalcedony, amethyst, diamond,etc. These precious and semi-precious stones were imported from different parts of the world, whereas white marble and red sandstone came from the quarries of Makrana, in District Nagaur of Rajasthan and Fatehpur Sikri in District Agra of Uttar Pradesh, respectively.

* Suptd. Archaeologist. Archaeological Survey of India, Agra

The main tomb–building measuring 57.30 m in width as well as height above the plinth level and identical in elevation on all four sides is located on a square platform of size 95.65 m. The plinth itself rises about 6 m above the ground level. The predominant feature of the structure is its 23 m high dome, from the springing to the base of 9.8 m high gilded finial or pinnacle,resting on a cylindrical drum of 18.4 m in internal diameter and rising 12 m above the terrace roof. The drum is supported by eight octagonally arranged piers interconnected with arches. The octagonal main hall or cenotaph chamber thus created below the double dome measures 17.74 x 17.74 m in plan. This central hall is surrounded by four octagonal corner chambers measuring 8 x 8 m and four square chamber of size 4.8 m. These surrounding chambers also exist on the floor above and are interconnected by vaults at both the levels. In addition, four minarats measuring about 5.8 m in diameter at the base and 41 m in height are located at the four corners of the plinth platform.

With the varied nature of component materials and extremely complex architectural scheme of the Taj Mahal, the problem of proper maintenace, upkeep and conservation is simply of very high magnitude. Due to its age, effects of environmental and geotechnical changes, besides its own massive weight over the years some specific visible signs are noticed which need due attention. These include leakage of water inside, cracks in the veneer stones,out of plumb minarates,loss of inlay pieces, and loss of cohesion in the mortar. Since so many different types of factors are involved, it would be prudent to make a full geotechnical and other relevant studies before undertaking any major conservation project. Otherwise, the conclusions drawn may be totally faulty. The Archaeological Survey of India, which is responsible for the repairs, conservation and maintenance of the Taj Mahal has taken adequate measurs to protect and preserve the monument without, of course, disturbing the originality of the monument. The basic principle of archaeological conservation is to retain the ancient character of the monument at all cost.

History of Conservation Measures

The earliest record of deterioration of the Taj Mahal is given by prince Aurangzeb to his father Emperor Shahjahan in December, 1652. Specifically the letter menttions that during the preceding rainy season, extensive leakage had occured in various parts of the tomb and adjacent mosque and assembly hall. To resolve the general leakage, a new layer of mortar over the flat roof of the dome was proposed.

In 1810, Captain Joseph Taylor under the guidance of Col. Hyde, replaced the missing slabs on the outer surface of Taj and renewed the damaged mosaic work. But Captain Taylor's use of coloured *chunam* in place of the inlaid stones proved a failure as ornamental work done by him was bady damaged during rains. In 1874, cracks were once again noticed. The principal items of his work carried out were the removal of the broken marble, the substitution of new pieces in the vaulted opening, the restoration of some of inlaid work, the regilding of finial surmounting the main dome, rendering of main dome with Portland cement and the resetting of the pinnacles of the gateway which had fallen down. The conservation work was mainly confined to the main building of the Taj complex.

In December, 1903, Lord Curzon of Keddlestone, then Viceroy of India, visited the Taj Mahal and since then, it received constant care and attention. During this period, the work of conservation of subsidiary buildings of the Taj Mahal was energetically pushed orward. Proper efforts were made for the first time to analyse the conservation problems of these buildings and accordingly one by one buildings were taken on hand for their systematic conservation. The Fatehpuri Masjid on the right and the Saheli Burj corresponding to it on the left of approach road, were rescued from a state of sad neglect. The colonnades flanking the approach were opened out and repaired and the untidy quadrangle which preceds the main entrance,was converted into well grassed and presentable court. Within the precincts of the tomb itself the gardens, with their water course, fountains and flower beds were laid out more strictly in accordance with their ancient designs and considerable improvements were made in water supply while the mosque and its *Jawab* (*Mehmankhana*) were structurally repaired and beautified by the renovation of their incrusted ornaments and sculptured panels.

In 1936, on account of the leakage of main dome, continuous cracks in the vaulting of all the chambers and passages of second floor, vertical cracks in marble facing and splitting and bulging of marble slabs, vegetal growth, deplorable condition of corner *chhatris*,etc. an the necessity of closer attention was felt towards the comprehensive investigations of various factors affecting the stability of structure. But before implementing any extensive scheme for the conservation of the Taj Mahal, an Advisory Committee of five experts was appointed by the Govt. of India in 1941 to investigate into the causes of deterioration and to suggest adequate measure of repairs. A number of studies on scientific lines were conducted and several accurate drawings including plans and cross sections, both central and diagonal, stress diagram for calculating the intensity of presure at various points of the structures were prepared. The Survey of India was assigned to record the levels on each floor of the building. Their observations indicated that there is no settlement in the foundation. However, the four minarats at the corner were found out of plumb. The formation of cracks was attributed to rusting of iron dowels, combined tension and decay of masonry core, squeezing of mortar in the joint, expansion through variation of temperature, inherent defects in particular piece of marble, excessive stresses coming on masonry of dome and drum, etc.

This Committee was expanded in 1943 and five more members were included to review the recommendations submitted by it in 1942 with a view to report whether the measures suggested therein constituted a suitable cause for action in the light of defects found in the structures of Taj Mahal and whether any modification or additional measures were necessary. In general, the expanded Committee agreed with the observation of the Advisory Committee in regard to visible defects and damage but they were of the opinion that the cracks appearing in the marble facing are not due to any excessive stresses on account of loading of the structure namely its dead weight and wind pressure.

Extensive repairs already started in 1941 and some of the items of repairs of emergent nature were completed in 1944. The recommendations of the Committee relating to marble facing of drum, dome and inlay work thereon were attended, leaving the rest of the recommendations to be taken up later.

During 1947-49 one of the recommenations of replacement of relating to work of special repairs of the split pillars, broken chhajja stones, lintels, etc. to four *chhattries* round the main dome was implemented. The repairs and replacement of *chhajjas* of four *chhattries* were also completed without dismantling them. The decayed plaster upto a height of 19 m from the interior of the drum was removed and entire surface re-plastered with weak mixture of cement mortar (1 cement : 10 sand). The intention of applying weak mortar was to draw out the salts. This process of eliminating salts will have to be repeated after èvery 2nd or 3rd year till the wall is completely free from salt. The modern accretions from the berm round the main dome and the corner *chhatries* as well as the parapet all round the terrace were removed and made water tight. On examination the berm, it was found that to an approximate depth of 40 to 45 cm and the upper cell 22 -25 cm in depth was loose than the stuff below it. Having removed all this above here and there, it was filled with 30 cm grouting and concreting.

From 1949 - 55 loose inlay parts and pieces were refixed and water tightening of monument was carried out. The Geodetic Branch of Survey of India which had laid out 104 points on the whole monuments checked the levels,

In 1956-57 some ill–founded Press Reports were published regarding deterioraion of monuments and a body of the engineers and conservators was constituted to examine the monument and review the implementation of the recommendations of the expanded Committee of 1943. They were satisfied about the stability of the monument and also conservation measures taken. They advised fixing of tell-tales all along the cracks in the underground vaults on the river front and some repairs to dislodged south-west pilaster of main mausoleum, such as removal of flat strips of stone fixed on either side of plaster and re-setting of the dislodged veneer stones in position by clamps and dowels after thorough grouting of voids behind them. The tell-tales were immediately fixed and the said repairs to pilaster were taken up and completed in 1957-58. Instead of iron clamps, copper ones were used for re-setting the dislodged veneer stones. The appearance of cracks and presence of water in the underground vaults on the river side led to opening of the drain running at the base of the wall among the river front. The percolation of water was due to longitudinal cracks; some of them were 72 m long thoroughly grouted with hydraulic lime and cement mixture.

On the recommendation of the Expanded Committee the foundation strata was exposed by laying out trial pits measuring 15 x 5 m along the outer wall on the river side. The trial digging exposed a series of wells rubble stone masonary used as foundation. One of the series of such wells was found supporting the weight of the Mausoleum which was on the foundation wall, whereas the other series which was provided as a precautionary measure was to check any erosion of bank which might take place in future. On examination it was noticed that in the last 350 years except the deposition of flood no other material was found. The depth of these wells could not be assertained as the water has hampered further digging after four feet.

The Geodetic Branch of Survey of India checked the levels of Taj Mahal and verticality of minars once again. To minimise errors a permanent bench mark was constructed in the garden.

From 1962 to 1983 various conservation works were undertaken to keep the Taj Mahal in presentable position. The predominant works were, changing of veneering stones, replacement of inlay pieces on the main mausoleum and other subsidiary buildings including the main gate. The foundation of the north-east *dalan* was strengthened as a portion of which had settled. The north-west corner *burjee* and northern wall were threatened by the scouring action of the river and in order to prevent any damage two spurs were constructed to deflect the river-flow.

In order to consolidate and strengthen and to prevent further deterioration between 1984-94 repairs to south west minarat were carried out. In October, 1985 water leakage was observed from the north-east side of the inner dome. On the close inspection, it was observed that the octagonal berm round the base of the drum of the outer dome had been provided with lime concrete, which had been fully pulverised and decayed at places and could not prevent rain water entering inside the structure. In order to stop absorption of rain water inside structure, the decayed and worn out lime concrete of the berm around the drum and corner *chhattries* was carefully removed and fresh lime concrete was laid after grouting the open joints and gaps in the masonny with liquid cement and giving water proofing treatment to the whole surface. The entire surface of the roof terrace was rendered water tight by pointing of expansion joints.

In order to prevent moisture entering inside the veneering stones and causing rusting to the iron dowels, the open joints of entire exterior surface of Taj were pointed with special lime mortar consisting of marble lime, marble dust, *rumi mastagi, batasa*, gum and *belgiri* water mixed with a small quantity of epoxy.

In the year 1984, the Government of India constituted a committee of eminent experts at the initiative of Archaeological survey of India with an object to examine the various aspects relating to structural, scientific, aesthetics and tourism,and to suggest appropriate measures for better preservation and conservation of the monument. The Committee after due deliberations expressed its satisfaction on the condition of the monument and its maintenance and conservation measures. However, it was felt necessary at the same time to get the scientific studies conducted with an aim, at first, to identify the causes of deterioration and then to prepare action plan to minimise the loss. Accordingly, the assistance of many scientific institutions is being taken for detailed investigations on the materials used in the construction, foundation, geotechnical survey, seismic activities, etc. Some of the institutions have already submitted their premilinary reports on the following aspects.

The chemical cleaning of Taj Mahal is being carried out by the Archaeological Survey of India periodically by using physical absorption technique with the help of activated clay pack method. The result of this technique seems quite satisfactory as original colour and luster of marble is restored.

The environmental factors affecting the Taj Mahal has not been considered in this paper as many detailed reports are already available on this degradational aspect. All of them have recommended development of Green Belt around Taj Mahal.

NOTES AND NEWS

Early Stone Age in Tansa Valley

Tansa river, in Thane district of Maharashtra, a tributary of the Vaitarn, rising near Kharda in Shahpur taluk cuts across the dark-coloured volcanic lava flows and laterites. After having a westerly flow by the north front of the great hill of Mahuli, passing through the holy places of Akloli, Ganeshpuri and Vajreshwari, it joins Vaitarn at Chimana about 12 km from the Arabian sea. The predominantly basaltic composition of the lava is usually dark grey to grey and bluish grey in colour and is hard, compact and tough and fine to medium grained in texture. It has a tendency to form flat topped plateau. There are numerous dykes that criss-cross the area.

In the bed and on the banks of the river Tansa, a large number of hot springs, mostly found on the fringes of dykes, are located, mainly near the villages Akloli, Ganeshpuri, Nimbavli and Vajreshwari. The temperature of the water ranges between 42°C and 55° C. These waters having therapeutic value, spring areas have been converted into religious spots with temples coming up from ancient times. The valley extends between 18°42' and 20°20' North latitude and 72°45' and 73°45' East longitude.

The 30-60 km wide coastal strip of Maharastra known as Konkan, well forested due to plenty of monsoon rain and fertile soil obtained from the weathering of horizontal sheets of lava, has revealed the existence of Early Stone Age man as well as Late Stone Age man in the area. During Terminal Pleistocene, palaeolithic cultures adopted to laterite plateaus and deep entrenched valleys flourished in the foothills near the sea, for instance, near Bombay in Tansa Valley. During the course of our investigations we were able to locate Early Stone Age sites at Parol, from the bed of a stream that runs down the eastern side of Tungae Hill and from the bed of Shantanu river, a tributary of Tansa, near village Akloli. In these streams atleast two cycles of deposition and erosion could be noticed. The deposit contains rubble gravel with occasional large boulders or pebbles of basalt, laid in a matrix of sandy clay over the basal rock. From bottom upwards there is rock, clay rubble gravel with sandy partings at places and at the top few cms. of dark clay generally formed due to deposition of decaying vegetal remains.

As the area had no dearth of perennial supply of fresh water-food, both in the form of animals and vegetation, in the thickly wooded forests and abundance of easily available raw material in the form of basaltic rock, olivine dolerite and fine grained variety of trap, which occur as dykes in the Deccan trap formations, for making tools, early man considered the area ideal for occupation. It is likely that the hot springs in the bed of Tansa and around, which are now being regularly frequented by modern man, might have also been frequented by his ancestors Early Stone Age men. Though from Kandivli, near Bombay, Todd (Todd 1939) reported rostrocarinates, choppers , etc. Malik, Sankalia and others did not find handaxes, cleavers and other tools of truly Abbevillio-Acheulian facies. Sankalia (1966 and 1974) declared that 'Early, Palaeolethic industry is absent at Kandivli. But the tools recovered by the author from Tansa Valley are in true Acheulian (few early Acheulian) characters. The tools recovered from the beds of the streams are in generally rolled condition and made on fine grained basalt. They comprise hand-axes, cleavers, choppers, discoids, flakes and cores. They are generally dark grey and olive green in colour. Middle Stone Age tools were also recovered from Parol and Tungareshwar.

A. Shantanu: Plate I

1. Scrapers-*cum*-point on a thick triangular flake which is Levallois like. The upper surface has three flake-scars with a prominent mid-rib running upto pointed end. The underside having a bulb has also been trimmed so as to give a point and a scrapping edge. From the section of the river. Size: 17.1x12.6x3.7 cm.

2. Cleaver on a flake with a thick untrimmed butt. The junction of two sloping surfaces forming the cleaving edge while only one side having chipped sharp edge. Butt end flat, working edge convex, section triangular. Size 13.9x15.5x3.8 cm.

3. Hand-axe like tool with cortexed butt on dorsal side and oblique edge. Heavily rolled from the river bed. Size 15.6x10.00x6.7 cm.

4. Scraper on a roundish Levallois like flake. On one side some context is present. Surface bears marks of trimming to obtain sharper edge almost in the two third of the margin. From the bed of the river. Size 13.5x12.8x5.0 cm.

B. Parol-Plate II

1. Hand-axe, pear-shaped or ovate, rolled, shaped out of fine grained greenish dolerite, high protuberance near the butt on the upper side, section roughly biconvex, beautifully flaked by stone hammer and soft-hammer techniques resulting in almost a symmetrical form. From the bed of nala. Size 15.4x11.0x5.3 cm.

2. Hand-axe, heavily rolled, ovate with pointed end, flaked along the margin on the upper side retaining context on entire dorsal side. Section plano-convex. Raw material greenish fine-grained dolerite. From the bed of nala. Size 14.5x9.5x4.8 cm .

3. Hand-axe, rostrocarinate form, slightly rolled, thick butt with steep rising body having an uneven median ridge, deep scars due to bold flaking on one side while the other is almost flat. Section plano-convex. Shaped out of greenish fine grained basaltic rock. From the bed of nala. Size 17.7x10.1x7.2 cm.

4. Hand-axe, heart shaped, made on a large flake, section roughly plano-convex. Could have been used as a cleaver also. Raw material fine graind variety of trap. From the bed of nala. Size 15.1x12.6x4.2 cm.

Plate III

1. Cleaver, shaped out of basaltic rock. Of large size but only lower half present, with straight edge. The two longitudinal sides as well as the working edge have been retouched. Portion of under side flaked and is almost flatt. Section plano-convex. Slightly rolled, from the bred of Nala. Size 10.8x 17.4x5.6 cm .

2. Cleaver shaped out of basaltic rock, heavy duty tool, straight butted but 'U' shaped working edge. One side is well trimmed by cylinder-hammer technique whereas the other side is flat, unworked. Plano-convex in section. From the section of nala, Size14.2x15.2x4.1 cm.

3. Side scraper with 'U' shaped thick butt, elongated-oval in plan having roughly convex working edge. Underside is flat being the primary flaked surface Raw material basaltic rock. From the bed of nala. Size 18.4x11.5x 6.6 cm.

4. Cleaver similar to No.1, but of smaller size. From the bed of Nala, slightly rolled; raw material basaltic rock, greenish black in colour. Straight butt, 'U' shaped working edge, median ridge prominent, oblique sides, edge trimmed by cylinder-hammer technique; butt end retaining cortex on flat, straight top. Section plano-convex. Size 11.1x13.43.8 cm.

Acknowledgement

I am grateful to Shri M.N.Deshpande for providing me the opportunity to study the area and also for his scholarly guidance.

BIBLIOGRAPHY

Joshi, R.V., 1991. "Prehistoric Archaeology of Coastal India," in *Archaeological Heritage*, Vol.I (eds.) C. Margabandhu, et al.

Joshi, R.V., and Bopardikar, B.P., 1972. "Stone Age Culture of Konkan," Archaeological Congress.

Sankalia, H.D., 1966. Prehistoric Man and Primitives in South Gujarat and Konkan," *J.A.S*, Bombay .Vol. XII.

______, 1974. *Prehistory and Protohistory of India and Pakistan*, Poona.

Todd, K.R.U., 1939, " Palaeolithic Industries of Bombay", *J.R.A.I*, LXIX.

Todd, K.R.U., 1950,The Microlithic Industries of Bombay, *Ancient India* No.6

A.K. SHARMA

F-8/5,Sector III
CBD, New Bombay-400614

Prehistoric Rock– Paintings In Bihar

One of the most remarkable archaeological discoveries made in the state of Bihar is that of the pre-historic rock-paintings and rock– shelters at ISCO, Thathangi, in the district of Hazaribagh; Ranigadar, Naadiha, Fioluhar (Kauwakola), Sarkanda (Kakolata Fall area) in the district of Nawada; Baltharva, Sankarpur in the district of Gaya and at Mukwa, Pateshar, Jhapla Hathidah in the district of Kaimpur by the author and his team.

Geographically there is a vast plateau south of the Ganga viz. Chhotanagpur. It comprises the Kaimur plateau in the north-west, and the Rajmahal plateau in the north-east. The plateau consists of a large number of hills and valleys in the south. Chhotanagpur is composed mainly of Archaen granite and gneiss rocks with patches of Dharwar series. The plateau also forms the catchment basin of several streams. Chhotanagpur is a land with hoary antiquity and glorious past.

Appearance of rock-paintings at several caves in the district of Hazaribagh, an area of *Vratya* tradition, are indicating the essential element of artistic expression. The available evidence suggests a widespread uniform development. The highest achievements were reached in the limited area of ISCO(Hazaribagh). The people who painted on cave walls may also have painted on skins - as many people had no caves available. This art vanished abruptly at the end of Pleistocene period with no reawakening of aesthetic skill untill many thousands of years later. It is true that the finest development had no visible effect on the future and mere a dead end just as the highly specialised *Vratya* tradition was itself a dead end in terms of the subsequent evaluation of Bharatiya culture. More the way it presents an interesting problem in culture process. An engraved lady figure in ISCO cave speaks of Paleolithic man's skill for engraving and carving. Flint burins of various types and sizes were employed. For painting the pigments used were red with hematite or other oxides of iron and lime. Most of these compounds were usually available in the nearby area. The painting was done with the fingers, and perhaps with a spatula, a crude brush such as the frayed end of a twig or a pad of fur. The powdered pigments must have been made into paint by the addition of a liquid binder, whose identity has not been established. The paintings involve a major intellectual break through, the epock-making discovery of how to represent in two dimensions what is perceived in three.

With the development of pastoral economy deities are predominantly male. With this concept of socio-economic and spiritual development of human heritage the ISCO rock-paintings are being observed. They reflect the organized akheta (catching of Animal). We see men in row trying to catch animals for domestication in broad day light. In the row a man is shown carrying a baby animal over his shoulder. A tall superman with prominent phallus is shown standing as a leader divinity and observing the *akheta* (the catching of animal). The trioanthropomorphs are gracefully introduced. There are some complicated linear compositions and elaborate polychromic diagrams are illustrated, perhaps representig magical ethics and practices.

Other prominently illustrated figures are tree, bird, lotus, sun in the natural background, jumping deer, ring of circles, hill and the most important and surprising representation is dinosaur-like animal. A dancing female figure has been engraved marvellously adopting the method of petroglyphs with the help of sharp stones. The figure looks very charming and has supported the method of petroglyphs adopted by the Stone Age people.

In the Kaimur district of Bihar rock-paintings have been found in five rock-shelters namely two at Pateshwar and one each at Mokwa, Jhapia hill and Dugha in a recent exploration carried out in the Kaimur range covering the Kaimur hills and the Kaimur plateau. In these rock-shelters the paintings are mostly ochre coloured and besides human figures, both male and female, in different actions, animal figures such as deer, lion, antelope, dog, elephant, bison, etc., as well as decorative and geometrical designs have been also depicted in these paintings either singularly or even in groups. The rock-paintings in Dugha are especially remarkable as they depict community dancing as is even now prevalent among the aboriginal tribes of this area.

The Kaimur hills and the plateau which extends along the southern boundary of the Kaimur district forms the eastern limit of the Vindhyan range. The rock-shelters which have rock-painings in them prove to be very promising from the archaeological point of view as they provide sufficient evidence of the rock-art and other human activities in and around the area right from the mesolithic period and even thereafter, although their exact date can be determined only after further extensive investigation and scientific analysis.

Despite the considerable artistic expression, there is a definite homogeneity in subject matter, composition and the realism with which this is portrayed. This is essentially religious and animal art. It is nearly always inspired by the animal world. Portrayals of human figures are also dominent. There are also a good number of signs and geometrical figures (may be magical or Tantric) whose significance is unknown. Bu it is the animals that are the obvious concern of the prehistoric *Vratya* artists, and not all the animals with which they must have been familiar, but precisely those that were hunted and around which their lives revolved. Wild cattle, bison, deer, boar, rhinoceros, bear, bird, reptiles and dinosaur-like animal are represented. Animals are shown in their customary attitudes. Poses are often rigid and execution is sometimes clumsy, but the subjects are depicted running, leaping and grazing. the aim was to represent the animal as they really looked. Cave-art is associated with living sites dating middle Paleolithic. It throws light over the middle Paleolithic cultural habitats. Certainly the preoccupation of cave-art with animals suggests a connection with hunting, and the location and nature of the sanctuaries suggests magic or religious motivation.

Unfortunately, a systematic and detailed study of the prehistoric culture in Bihar has not been made as yet. More attention has been paid to the historic culture whereas the scientific study of prehistoric culture has remained neglected.

Z/11, Ashiana Nagar, Patna, 800025

Prakash Charan Prasad

Iron-Ore Element In The Microlithic Industry Of Kirandul, Madhya Pradesh

Microlithic industries of Mesolithic tradition are reported from varied eco-zones across the country. The onset of Holocene not only marked a favourable atmosphere for the rapid growth and spread of mesolithic cultural phase but also encouraged and later, forced the culture to venture into new and difficult accessible environments such as the sand dune of the Thar desert (Misra 1995), the high altitude of Eastern Ghats (Issac 1960 : Murthy 1966: Srinivasa Murthy 1986), the hilly terrains of the Central India (Wakankar 1975; Joshi 1978) and the north eastern states (Sharma 1978; Ramesh 1989) which were hitherto presumed to be bereft of any prehistoric evidence, supposedly because of heavy rainfall (Misra 1985: 114). Kirandul in the Bastar district of Madhya Pradesh is one such environment zone which the Mesolithic man has occupied and exploited iron ore, besides quartz and chert, for tool-making. The present paper discusses the significance of the use of iron-ore as raw material in Indian Mesolithic.

The Kirandul Environ

Kirandul (19° 9' N - 81° 40' E) is a small industrial township in the Bailadila iron ore hill range in the Bastar district of Madhya Pradesh (Fig.1). To its east (about 100 km) is the border of Orissa and to its south (about 100 km) and South-west (50 km) is the border of Andhra Pradesh. The prehistoric site is located at the foothills of one of the hills in the Bailadila hill range which has several iron ore deposits. Large number of microliths are found scattered over an area of about 10 sq.m, quite adjacent to the mouth of cave near iron ore deposit no. 4 of NDMC.

Bailadila, which is one of the largest iron-ore reserves in the country (about 10%), is locally known by the Muriya tribals as Bail ka Dilla meaning 'a hump of an ox'. It is remote, inaccessible and replete with wild life, roaming the dense forests and guarding the secret treasures of the earth. This verdant territory, rising to a height of 1,260 m above MSL is about 32 km in length and 4 km in width. Copious rainfall, averaging 350 cm a year, keeps the region green and refreshing, and the temperature pleasant, throughout the year. The region which is part of

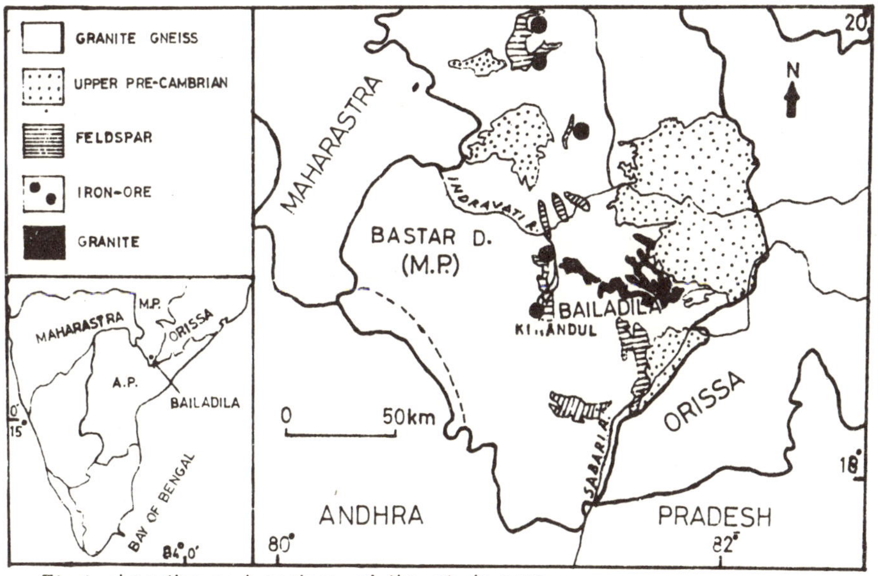

Fig.1 Location and geology of the study area.

the Bastar plateau, is formed of highly folded Dharwar metamorphosed sedimentary rocks.

The region has a well connected seasonal drainage system with two hill streams namely, Sankani and Dankani, flowing across the Kirandul region, starting from Nandiraj peak (935 m) of the Bailadila hill range. The hill streams fall into the Danteswara channel (near Danteswara township to the north) which is a tributary of Indravati river, flowing about 30 km north of Kirandul. In fact, Sankani is the stream, flowing very close to the prehistoric sites.

The Microlithic Industry

The microlithis are scattered over 10 sq.m area in front of the cave mouth near deposit no. 4. A total number of 143 artifacts, including 57 finished forms, were collected from the area (Table 1). Raw material wise the industry is dominated by quartz (77.6%) followed by iron ore (16.1%) and chert (6.3%). Interestingly, however, iron ore forms a sizeable portion of raw material types. Similarly, quartz (44) numerically dominates over iron-ore (10) and chert (3), in the finished forms category. Quartz and iron ore (which is of haematitic nature) are locally available in bulk, while chert occurs scantily.

Although there is typological similarity among most of the tools in quartz, iron ore and chert, the size of tools and technique of manufacture vary according to the rock type used. The tools made on iron ore are fairly large (4 cm - 6 cm) in comparison to the tools made on chert and quartz (below 4 cm). Secondary retouch is intensive in some of the quartz specimens, whereas the iron ore tools show only simple flaking and occasional retouching. Technological simplicity is manifested in flaking out iron ore tools, the quartz and chert tools show the use of baking and blunting technique for some specimens. Typological diversity is marked in the case of quartz tools obviously because of frequent and extensive use of the raw material in tool-making.

Most of the microliths on quartz are made from micro blades by steeply blunting one or more of their margins by removing minute flakes through pressure flaking. The micro blades are produced *en masse* by the removal of thin, almost parallel sided, flakes from the cylindrical cores which are prepared or dressed before detachment. Pointed and other simple forms of cores are also used for the removal of flakes for tool-making. Tools on chert are fashioned out similarly but the size of the blade varies only marginally. The iron ore tools are made on larger flakes although a small proportion of blade is also used. In fact, occurrence of an almost cylindrical core with fluted marks suggests the use of stone technology on iron ore.

In the context, therefore, iron ore tools may be considered as heavy duty tools in the industry. The way they have been manufactured (without in its metal form) indicates a poor knowledge of iron.

Discussion

Iron tool-bearing microlithic industries have been reported only from the central-western India; that is from sites such as Bhimbetka, Langhnaj, Bagor and Lekhahia, etc. (Sankalia 1965; Malik 1966; Misra 1973, Jacobson 1970; Wakankar 1975; Luckacs et al. 1983). But nowhere iron ore has been reported to have been employed for tool-making. The occurrence of iron ore element in the Kirandul microlithic industry, therefore, is the first instance in the prehistoric era when the Indian Mesolithic stone industry were guided more or less by the law of local availability of raw material for tool-making Whatever is the rock and how ever much it may be inferior or superior, if it is even little convenient for tool-making, prehistoric man exploited it. It is more so during the Mesolithic; so is the case at Kirandul. Both quartz and iron ore are locally available. However, use of iron ore, instead of only quartz and chert, for tool-making, may have something to do with the Mesolithic people opting for more durable tools, even if it might have been difficult and laborious to produce tools in iron ore.

Very little evidence of the prehistoric cultural phases has been reported from Bastar, so far. Barring Cooper's study (Cooper 1983) the district has hardly unveiled any significant prehistoric record. Interestingly, only Mesolithic evidence has been recovered from the district (Krishnaswami 1953; Jha 1968, 1969; Cooper 1983). and in all these studies the element of iron/iron ore does not form a part of raw material exploitation suggesting that the iron ore element is very much confined to the Kirandul Mesolithic.

Kirandul being an isolated instance in the region, the use of iron ore in tool-making during Mesolithic becomes interesting. The predominance of quartz and the typologies thereof are in concurrence with a common regional microlithic characteristic and the association of similar artifacts (as on quartz; see Table 1) on iron ore, albeit in larger forms, suggests that the iron ore artifacts are a part and parcel of the same industry. Probably the durability of the tools made out of iron ore encouraged the microlith users to make tools on iron-ore. Production of arrow heads exclusively on iron ore is a good example which corroborates this observation.

Occurrence of the iron element in Mesolithic industries is not new to India, as has already been discussed. In fact, in many central Indian microlithic industries iron forms a part of advanced or final phase of Mesolithic or microlithic industries surviving into the Iron Age (Misra 1989:26). Iron arrow-heads are found to have been associated with the topmost levels of the microlithic deposits at Bhimbetka, Langhnaj and Lekhahia sites (Misra 1985: 121). However, in these instances iron is found in its metal form and the tools are suspected to be in contact with the local, contemporary iron-using cultures (Misra 1985: 120). While this may be true, could the same be applied to Kirandul microlithic industry? It is, probaly, the first of its kind in India where haematitic iron ore has been found to have been used for producing tools during Mesolithic. The evidence has, therefore, added to our present knowledge regarding the Mesolithic phase in India. However, more intensive and extensive studies, especially trenching, need to be carried out in order to comprehensively understand the place of iron ore element during Mesolithic India.

REFERENCES

Cooper, Z. 1983. CRT-19: A Mesolithic site in Bastar district (M.P.), *Man & Environment,* 3:1-30

Issacc, N. 1966. *The Stone Age Culture of Kurnool,* Ph. D. Thesis. Pune: Deccan College.

Jacobson, J. 1970, Microlithic Contexts in the Vindhyan Hills of Central India, Ph.D. Thesis, New York: Columbia University.

Jha, V.D. 1968, Prehistoric Archaeology of Bastar, *Bulletin of Ancient Indian History & Archaeology,* University of Saugar, 2:63-65.

Jha, V.D. 1969, New Light on prehistory of Bastar, *Journal of the Madhya Pradesh Itihas Parishad,* 7:23-26

Joshi, R.V. 1978. *Stone Age Cultures of Central India,* Report on the Excavations of Rock-shelters at Adamgarh, Madhya Pradesh, Deccan College, Poona.

Krishnaswami, V.D. 1953. Prehistoric Bastar , *Proceedings of Indian Science Congress,* 40: 5-41

Luckacs, J.R, V.N. Misra and K.A.R. Kennedy 1983. *Bagor and Tilwara; Late Mesolithic Cutures of North-west India,* Vol.I, The Human Skeletal Remains, Pune: Deccan College.

Malik, S.C. 1966. The Late Stone Age Industries from excavated sites in Gujarat, India, *Artibus Asiae,* 28:167-174.

Misra, V.N. 1973. Bagor : A late Mesolithic Settlement in Northwest India, *World Archaeology* 5 (1): 9-110.

Misra, V.N. 1985 Microlithic Industries in India, in V.N.Misra and P. Balwood (eds.) *Recent Advances in Indo-Pacific Prehistory:* New Delhi: Oxford and IBH, 111-122.

Misra V.N. 1989. Stone Age India: An Ecological Perspective, *Man & Environment* 14,1 : 17-64.

Misra, V.N. 1995. Geoarchaeology of the Thar desert, Nothwest India, in S.Wadia, R.Korisettar and V.S.Kale (eds.) *Quaternary Environments and Geoarchaeology of India,* 210-230. Bangalore: Geological Society of India.

Murty, M.L.K. 1966. *Stone Age Culture of Chittoor Dist. A.P.* Ph.D. Thesis, Deccan College, Pune.

Ramesh, N.R. 1989. *A Study of Geomorphology, Quaternary Geology and Associated Cultural Remains of East Tripura, Dist. Tripura,* Ph.D. Guawhati: Guawhati University.

Sankalia, H.D. 1965. *Excavations at Langhnaj: 1944-63* Part-I Archaeology, Deccan College, Pune.

Sharma,T.C.1978.A note on the Microlithic Iindustries of the Garo Hills in Pramolilekha and V.L. De Leewz (eds) *Seharat Paranavitana Comm.* Vol.: Leiden: E.J. Brill, 215-217.

Srinivasa Murty, K. 1986, *Stone Age Archaeolgy of Araku Valley, Visakhapatnam, Dist. Andhra Pradesh,* Ph.D. thesis. Visakhapatnam: Andhra University.

Wakankar, V.S. 195. Bhimbetka - the Prehistoric Paradise, *Prachya Pratibha,*3(2):7-29

Table 1. Raw Material Frequency of Microliths from Kiraṇdul

Artifact type 1	Frequency 2	Frequency 3	Frequency 4	Total 5	% 6
Core	08	02	01	11	7.7
Flake	22	04	03	29	20.2
Chip	20	05	02	27	18.9
Nodule	06	-	-	06	4.2
Unfinished tool	04	02	-	06	4.2
Broken tool	07	-	-	07	4.9
Backed blade	06	-	-	06	4.2
Simple blade	17	03	-	20	14.0
Triangle	01	-	-	01	0.7
Side scraper	03	02	02	07	4.9
Concex-Concave scraper	-	01	-	01	0.7
Concave scraper	-	-	01	01	0.7
Bi-convesx scrapher	01	-	-	01	0.7
Plano-convex scraper	01	-	-	01	0.7
Thumb-nail scraper	01	-	-	01	0.7
End Scrapr	01	02	-	03	2.1
Arrow head	-	02	-	02	1.4
Point	05	-	-	05	3.5
Borer	04	-	-	04	2.8
Burin	04	-	-	04	2.8
Total	111 (77.6%)	23 (16.1%)	09(6.3%)	143	100.00

Dept. of Anthropology, Utkal University, Buhubaneswar — ALOK RATH
Dept. of Anhropology, Andhra University, Waltair — P. VIJAY PRAKASH

Mesolithic Rock-Shelter and Megalithic Rock-cut Caves in Kerala

Mesolithic Rock-shelter at Maruthuwamalai

Kerala has only a few Stone Age sites. An important discovery made recently was the discovery of a Mesolithic rock-shelter at Maruthwamalai near Agastheeswaram (8°4'N and 77°36'E) 52 km away from Thiruvananthapuram. The south-western part of the Western Ghats extends from 8° 30' N to 12° 30' N latitude and 75°15' N to 77°45' E longitude. The southernmost reaches of the Western Ghats, known as the Agastyamalai Range, extends from Mahendragiri near Kanyakumari to Ariyankavu pass in Kollam District. The Idamala pass lies across the group of hills which form a ridge, about 3 km to the north-east of Maruthwamalai. Further, this region has proximity to the township of Thirunelveli through the Anchugramam and Punnakulam passes. Physiographically, situated on the undulating midlands near the coastal tract, the Maruthuwamalai forms one of the most important isolated hills in south Kerala. The region comprises pre Cambrian khondalite group of rocks. The rich tropical moist forests in the Western Ghats are in this stretch. Hence the hill has abundant vegetal resources and is regarded as a garden of economically and medicinally useful plants.

The rock-shelter situated on the top of the hill did not yield any cultural deposit due to frequent human intervention. But as in the case of majority of Mesolithic sites the rock-shelter has been preserved in a better condition since significant changes are not obvious in the land-form of this region except for cultivation carried out in villages surrounding the hill. The rock-shelter has a sterile layer of earth which thins down as it goes into the interior, where the cave roof slopes down to the floor. Inside, on the left, there is a rectangulr opening on which the cave roof partly rests.

The discovery of this rock-shelter is important in different ways This is the second rock-shelter in south Kerela after the one explored at Thenmalai in Kollam District and has an important place in the prehistoric map of Kerala. Secondly, human burials mark their presence in archaeological record in mesolithic cultures. Thirdly, it is interesting in this context that the Idamala, Anchugramam and Punnakulam passes near Maruthwamalai give access to Thirunelveli, especially to the Teri sites, resulting in a conglomeration of Mesolithic sites in the region. Further it should be noted that unlike Tirunelveli, which forms one of the driest regions in peninsular India, the environment of the Western Ghats in south Kerala has provided the settlement base to varied number of ethnic groups, whose very survival was entirely dependent on its diverse ecosystems: This is especialy so since the Mesolithic communities liked a greater variety of habitats than their predecessors.

Megalithic Rock-cut Caves at Vazhamuttam, Thiruvananthapuram

The term "Chambered megalithic tombs" is used to denote various types and sub-types of megalithic chamber– tombs. Among them the burial caves were confined entirely to north Kerala. However, the discovery of megalithic burial caves at Vazhamuttam, near Vizhinjam, (latitude 8° 05' N and longitude 77° 15' E) 12 km away from Thiruvananthapuram is significant for two reasons. Megalithic burial caves have been explored for the first time in south Kerala. Secondly, they are not sporadically distributed in north Kerala but has proved their presence throughout the coastal tracts of Kerala. These burial caves at Vazhamuttam are located above the sea level and encircled by a sacred grove, thin growth of vegetation due to the rocky nature of the area. The caves have cut marks on the entrance as well as inside the chambers which shows that it underwent masonary work.

The excavation of these caves was dug a pit into the rock by scooping out the solid laterite. But the vertical opening carved out at the entrance is not too narrow like the burial caves at Chovvannur, Kandanisseri, Kakkad, Porkalam, Eyyal and Kattakampal in Kochi in north Kerala. The interior portion become comparatively narrow in the caves at Vazhamuttam. They have neither top openings nor benches, nor steps.

The cave on the right side has a height of 1.9 m and a width of 0.50 m. The internal chamber becomes narrow as we proceed inside and is 5.4 m long from the entrance. At the basement of the internal chamber there is a dividing wall, linear and slanting having a length of 0.93m.

The cave on the left side goes down vertically inside. The length between the entrance and internal chamber is 3.5 m. The entrance has a height of 1.2 m and a width of 39 cm along with a narrow disfigured ventilation on the dividing wall. The caves have been left unfinished as is obvious from the deep scars on the surface of the entrance. At present these caves are used for snake worship.

These two sites are closely interrelated, since the Iron Age burial caves are located 50 km away from the Mesolithic sites where human burials marks their presence in archaeological context. Proper excavation can unearth the material remains in these sites.

Deccan College, Pune

B.S. Hari Shankar

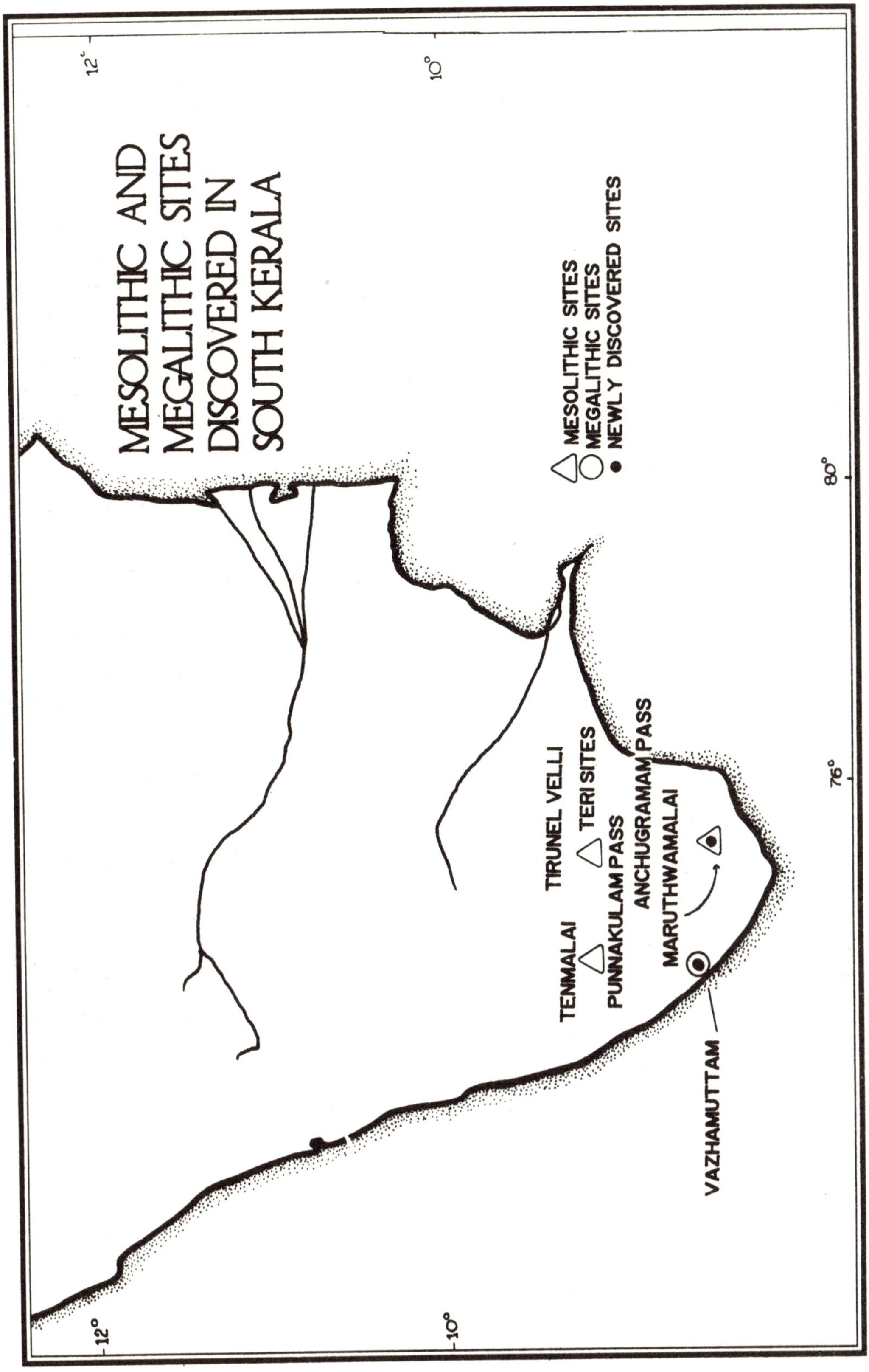
MESOLITHIC AND
MEGALITHIC SITES
DISCOVERED IN
SOUTH KERALA
MESOLITHIC SITES
MEGALITHIC SITES
NEWLY DISCOVERED SITES
TIRUNEL VELLI
TERI SITES
ANCHUGRAMAM PASS
TENMALAI
PUNNAKULAM PASS
MARUTHWAMALAI
VAZHAMUTTAM
12°
10°
80°
76°

Animal Skeletal Remains from Mirzapur, Kurukshetra

Mirzapur (Lat. 29°58' N ; Lon.g76° 49'S), District Kurukshetra, having a low mound, small in size, about 200m to the east of Raja Karna Ka Qila,was excavated by the Department of Ancient Indian History, Culture and Archaeology, Kurukshetra University, Kurukshetra, Haryana, on a small scale from 1972 to 1976. Topographical features indicate that during the earliest period of habitation in the mound, river Saraswati which now flows nearly four km. away from the site, passed adjacent to Mirzapur.

Excavations have revealed that the earliest habitation, (1800 to 1500 B.C.) having a deposit of 1 to 1.5 m in thickness belonged to the Late Harappan phase of the Harappan Civilization. This period is characterized by mud brick structures of three phases. Evidence of a fireplace, a refuse pit, an oven and a corn bin have been found inside a room. The other finds of the period include: a large number and variety of beads of semiprecious stones, such as agate, crystal, jasper and carnelian and a few steatite disc beads; terracotta bangles,beads, discs, marbles, toy-cart frames, toy-cart wheels, terracotta cakes, both circular and triangular, plain as well as painted bull figurines and a painted curved figure, probably of a snake; faience bangles, balls with incised decoration, a beautiful figure of a stag in faience with a horizontal hole, probably used as an amulet; and copper objects, including a complete spear-head without mid-rib. The pottery is represented by a sturdy red ware, painted in light black colour with geometric and linear designs of plant, fish and bird motifs. The painted designs and shapes are very similar to those from sites like Bara, Sanghol, Chandigarh, Mitathal IIB, Daulatpur and Bhagwanpura.

After the Late Harappan occupation the mound remained uninhabited for a long time, probably due to the shifting of the river, apparently as a result of tectonic movements in the area; and was re-occupied during the early historical period datable to the early centuries of the Christian era. Remains of the late medieval period, in *Lakhauri bricks* and brickbats were encountered just at the top. During this period this site was used as a graveyard which greatly disturbed the entire remains.

During the excavation,several animal skeletal remains were collected from all three periods, but it appears that the emphasis was given more to those from the earliest period. Nature and amount of collection under present study also indicates that primary sorting was done at the site before removal to the headquarters for storage and study. The bones which were found in association with other remains of human habitation, have a lot of tales to tell; about the animals to which they belonged, ecological and climatic conditions of the time, domestication of the selected species useful for man, food habits of the people, their use, and use of their skeletal remains for various purposes such as tool-making, etc.

Collection, Packing and Labeling

Animal skeletal remains recovered from different layers of different periods, have been packed separately, after initial cleaning. Each bone has been marked, generally giving locus, layer from which it was recovered and the depth at which it was found. Bones belonging to smallest animals have been packed in paper packets in order to avoid further damage. In case of large animals, it appears that, generally, only the extremities of bones, and sturdly ones were retained and shaft portion along with other splinters and fragments were discarded at the site itself. Out of the collection, 155 pieces of bones have been selected for study and report. Out of these 84 belong to the

Late Harappan Period, 60 to early historical period and eleven to the late medieval period.

State of Preservation

Most of the bones, in full or in pieces, recovered from the excavation are in considerably good state of preservation. Almost all of them have gained weight and some from the lower layers have got encrusted due to high percentage of salt in the soil. The presence of encrustations have sealed the pores of the haversine canals thus preventing entry of organisms and developing matter. The bones from the lower levels, particularly from the Late Harappan levels, are dark brown in colour, whereas those from the upper levels are muddy brown with a yellowish or whitish tinge. Some of the specimen display greenish brown colour mainly due to the ashy deposit from where they were recovered. Some have developed surface gloss. While the collection from the lower levels are heavier and comparattively intact, those from the upper levels are mostly fragmentary and have developed numerous cracks, probably due to the arid atmosphere and other disturbances.

Nature of the collection

In all, 155 pieces of bones were subjected to examination for this report. The animals are represented by complete or partial lower or upper jaws, lower and upper teeth, astrgali, calcanea, vertebrae, rib fragments, metatarsals and metacarpals, ephiphyses and shafts of long bones, phalanges and horns. The collection includes a good number of charred bones, the intensity of charring varying from light to very heavy. It appears, many of them got charred in the process of roasting, obviously for meals. This is further supported by the presence of cut marks particularly on cattle and deer bones. Amongst the charred specimens deer bones predominate. There is an evidence of religious offering, from the early historical levels. Canine of Equus was recovered in heavily charred condition, which was later on further used most probably for medicinal purposes, as it was rubbed a number of times to obtain paste for cure for some specific ailment.

Some of the parts, particularly shafts of cattle and deer, and ends of long bones and ribs were used as tools, generally after subjecting them to some degree of charring, either the entire piece or only the end. so that the contained fat oozed out making the piece stronger and smooth. The collection could be broadly classified into the following categories:

1. Those animals which were either domesticated or were in the process of domestication.

2. Those animals that lived in the houses or in the vicinity of habitation.

3. Wild animals included those that were hunted for food.

Species identified

From the collection twelve species of animals could be identified. In all the periods cattle bones out number all other species followed by sheep,goat and deer.

A. The Late Harappan levels have yielded skeletal remains of the following species:

1. *Bos indicus* Linn - the domestic cattle.
2. *Bubalus bubalis* Linn - the Indian buffalo.
3. *Capra hircus aegagrus* - the goat .
4. *Ovis vignei Blyth,* race domesticus - the sheep.
5. *Equus caballus* Linn - the horse.
6. *Axis axis* (Erxleben) - the chital or spotted deer.
7. *Canis familiaris* Linn - the dog.
8. *Sub scrofa cristatus* Wagnes-The Indian domestic pig.
9. *Lepus nigricollis ruficandatus* F. - the rabbit .
10. *Carps* - fish.
11. *Rattus rattus* Linn - The common India rat.
12. *Unionid* - Fresh water muscl.

B. Early Historical levels have yielded the skeletal remains of the following species:-

1. *Bos indicus* Linn - the domestic cattle.

2. *Bubalus bubalis* Linn - the Indian buffalo.

3. *Capra hircus aegagrus* - the goat.

4. *Ovis vignei, Blyth* - race domestic - the sheep.

5. *Axis axis* (Erx)- The spotted deer.

6. *Canis familiaris* Linn - the dog.

7. *Equus cabalus* Linn - the horse.

8. *Carps* - fish.

Percentage of animals periodwise

Species	L.H.P.	E.H.P	L.M.P
Cattle	58%	46.6%	66%
Sheep and goat	8.2%	20%	-
Horse	3.5%	1.8%	-
Spotted deer	18.3%	16.6%	9%
Dog	3.4%	8%	16%
Pig	1.2%	-	-
Rodents	1.2%	-	-
Fresh water muscl	1.2%	-	9%
Fish	5%	7%	-
	100%	100%	100%

C. Late medieval period

From the number of bones representing this period, in this collection, two things are quite obvious- a) a very limited area of this period was exposed, and b) most of the bones, being from the top and disturbed areas, being extremely fragile were probably discarded at the site itself. Among the excavators, the general tendency found is to discard the bones from upper levels, not giving them due importance. The bones representing this period belonged predominantly to cattle, dog and fresh water muscla were also present.

Cattle (Pl-I-III)

In the collection from Mirzapur bones of cattle out number others. The domestic species are distinguished by two skeletal characters. These are the broad, flat, cleft *spina dorsalis* of the thoracic vertebrae and the flattening of the median condyle of the trachlea of the humerus. Evolutionary changes are also noted in the horn-cores which point side-wards in the wild prototypes and not upwards as in the modern Indian cattle.

Both *Bos indicus* Linn (the Indian humped cattle) and *Bubalus bubalis* Linn (the Indian buffalo) are represented at Mirzapur in all the three periods. There were distinctly two varieties of cattle, one of the massive size and the other comparatively of dwarf size and lighter built. Generally bones of cattle from Late Harappan period, , belonged to massive size. The cattle population outnumbering the population of other species represented in the site indicates that animal husbandary was one of the major source of economy along with agriculture. Statistics worked out indicate decrease in population of cattle in Period II i.e. Early Historical period, coupled with increase in the percentage of sheep and goat. This increase is more than double, i.e, from 8.2% in Late Harappan period to 20% in Early Historical period. This is probably indicative of the economic pattern of the two societies which was more dependent on animal husbandry. The population of cattle increased steeply during late medieval times showing that the people started giving more attention to agriculture, milk and milk products as not much pasture was left due to heavy deforestation, for sheep and goat, whereas the cattle could be fed on agricultural fodder. The sharp decline in the number of deer bones also indicates heavy deforestation. Large number of bones of cattle, particularly ribs and long bones from Late Harappan period bear cut-marks (butchering, skinning, dismembering, etc.) and only one or two pieces display these marks from those belonging to Early Historical period. This is a clear indication that during Late Harappan period people used more meat of cattle in their food whereas during Early Historical period, it appears from the available evidences, that cattle meat was not popular.

A close of examination of third phalange of cattle shows the increase of pedosis and exostosis pointing to the increasing dependence of men on cattle, in Period I and II, for draught purposes. The presence of marked anchylosis also indicates that the people in both the periods were practising a lot of agriculture that required extensive use of cattle both for ploughing and drawing of vehicles.

Cattle belonging to massive variety was more in percentage during Late Harappan times. Such type has also been identified from other Harappan sites like Kalibangan, Lothal, Surkotada, Malvan and Bhagwanpura. Total absence of rarefication of bones shows that during this period there was plenty of green fodder available in the area. Rarefication is caused due to deficiency of calcium content in fodder which mostly affects either milch cattle or cattle grazing on pastures with low vitamin content.

None of the bones belonging to buffalo show any cutmarks. Their percentage shows steady increasing trend from Period I to III. It is evident that this animal was not reared for food but for procuring milk. The earliest domesticated buffalo remains come from Adamgarh in India (*c.* 5500 B.C.). It is generally believed that the Indian buffalo was domesticated within the subcontinent and is a direct descendant of *Bubalus palaeindicus* found in the Siwaliks. The domestic buffalo, osteologically, has changed so litte that it is regarded as only semi-domesticated and continues to inter-breed with wild species. The domestic buffalo was introduced from India into Iraq and into the Jordon valley in 725. A.D.

Sheep and Goat: (Pl. V-2, Pl. VI - 2,9,11)

All the bones of sheep and goat recovered from the collection belong to domesticated variety. These animals are represented in the collection mostly by limb bones, ribs, vertebrae and a horn core. Short and straight nature of the horn shows that the animal belonged to the domesticated variety. There was more than double fold increase in the population of sheep and goat in the site from Late Harappan times to Early Historical times. Unfused epiphyses of long bones indicate that these animals were slaughtered when young. The large number of charred bones, particularly radius, ribs and vertebrae indicate that at times the animals were roasted for food. In view of the cold climate of the area, sheep was generally reared to obtain wool for warm clothing.

The five species of the wild goat occurring in the subcontinent area: *capra falconei* and *capra ibex*, both found in the region between Afghanistan, Kashmir, Punjab and Kumaun: *Hemitragus jemlabicus,* Himalayan Tahr; and *Hemitragus hylochius,* Nilgiri Tahr, are reported respectively from the Himalayan and sub-Himalayan belt and the Nilgiris.

Of the four wild species of sheep existing today, *Ovis orientalis,* the Asiatic urial, *Ovis amonion* algali are found in India. The Indian domestic sheep, as also these of Tibet and South-East Asia, are essentially derived from the urial stock.

The most notable skeletal changes that have occurred with domestication are a convexity of the nasals, shortening of the facial bones and decrease in the size of the animal but increase in the degree of wrinkling of the horns.

Horse: (Pl. V 5-8)

Bones of horse (*Equus caballus* Linn) have been recovered from Period I and II. The parts recovered are metatarsals and canine, which are very distinctive bones. The evidence clearly shows that during Late Harappan period horse was very much known in the area, and was reared for transportation. The heavily charred canine recovered from this period, which has on one side heavy rubbing marks, indicates that the animal was also used for medical and religious purposes. Probably the paste obtained from the charred canine, as it has been used many times, seemed to have been used as a cure for specific ailments.

The bones recovered belong to medium sized variety. In India the earliest evidence for the domesticated horse occures in *c* 4500 B.C. at Bagor. Subsequently, the true horse is also reported from the Neolithic levels at Kodekal and Hallur.. At Surkotada, a Harappan site in Kutch, bones of *Equus caballus* Linn occur from Period IA to IC (2500 - 1700 B.C.) along with those of *Equus asinus and Equus hemionus* (Sharma, 1974). In this site also some of the horse bones were found to be charred; possibly the older animals were killed and sacrificed for religious purposes. Horse bones have also been reported from the late Harappan levels at Mohenjodaro (Sewell, 1931. Ropar, Harappa, Lothal and Bhagwanpura and proto-Harappan site of Malvan in Gujarat have also yielded bones of domesticated horse from mid to late levels of the Harappan deposits. (Alur and Sharma, 1995) Cut-marks on the bones of horse from Hastinapur (Period II) also suggest the slaughter of the animal. Now, with the evidence of cut marks and charring coming from many sites, doubts should not remain that horse was also used as a sacrificial animal and probably for food, at least on rare occassions religious or non-religious.

Deer: (Pl V-1,3, Pl VI 1-6)

Next to the cattle the largest percentage of bones were that of spotted deer in all the three periods represented at the site. From Period I, which had 18.5 %, there was slight decline in Period II (16.6%), whereas in Period III it formed 9% of the total bones. The presence of large number of bones of deer clearly indicates that the environmental conditions in the area was very favourable for the animal to exist. There was plenty of grass land, swamps and greenery around. Deers freely move in the area rightupto the late medieval times. As per records, plenty of them inhabited the area even upto the first half of the 20th century. Steady decline and then its almost disappearance in recent times is the natural corollary of urbanization, coupled with deforestation and increase in hunting activity both for flesh and pleasure.

Majority of the deer bones including the antlers, are in heavily charred condition and many of them bear cut-marks. Shafts of long bones have also been used for toolmaking also. The roasting of the animal after the hunt appears to be a common practice in the site. Roasted flesh, being more tasty, was preferred. The light burning, and in many cases approaching the stage of charring, shows that roasting was done under field condition, using mostly dry grass leaves and small branches of trees. A fine specimen of stag with antler, shaped out of faience, standing graciously and looking alarmed, was recovered from the Late Harappan levels.

Dog: (Pl, V-9, VI-12)

There is steady increase in the percentage of bones of dog in the collection from 3.4% in Period I to 8% in Period II and 16% in Period III. As in the case of other small animals, the bones of dog are fragile and disintegrate faster. The specimens obtained indicate that they belong to *canis familiaris* Linn and their size was not more than the present day medium sized dog. Zeuner (1963) holds the view that the Indian wolf is the probable ancestor of the domesticted dog because of the close morphological similarity, notably the dentition and complete interfertility between these species. Jackals also inter- breed and have affinities with dogs. The earliest evidence of domestication has come from the mesolithic levels of Adamgarh in

M.P. (5500 B.C.),followed by evidences from the neolithic sites of Burzahom and Gufkral(Sharma, 1968), in Jammu and Kashmir. The type recovered from the late Harappan period of Mirzapur, resembles the pariah. Remains of this variety have also been reported from Ropar, Lothal, Kalibangan, Surkotada, Rangpur, Bhagwanpura and Mathura.

Pig: (Pl. V- 13)

Bones of this animal were recovered from the levels of Late Harappan period only. Two feral races of the pig are found in the main land today; *Sus salvanicus,* in the foot hills region of the Himalayas; and *Sus scrofa cristalus,* common throughout peniusulr India. *Sus cristatus,* is regarded as the ancestor of the Asian domesticated pig. The earliest evidence for the domestic pig is associated with the begining of agriculture and domestication of the cattle, at the Neolithic sites like Burzahom and Gufkral (3000 B.C.) though bones of domestic pig have also been reported from the mesolithic levels at Adamgarh and Bagor. In the Harappan context, bones of this animal have been reported from Harappa, Mohenjodaro, Ropar, Lothal, Rangpur, Surkotada, Bhagwanpura and several other sites. The pig, it appears, was bred for meat and fat, and rarely used as a sacrificial animal. It appears that during Early Historical Period and Late Medieval times pig was not liked by the people in the area or at least they were not allowed to roam freely in the main habitation area on hygenic grounds.

Fish: (Pl. IV -II)

Only the vertebrae of carp (medium sized fish) were recovered from Period I and II. Fish bones being very fragile, are hardly supposed to survive. The presence of a few vertebrae shows that fish formed part of the diet of at least a section of Mirzapurians during the Late Harappan and Early Historical times. At Mirzapur, Late Harappan pottery was profusely decorated with fish (carp and dog fish) apart from other birds and animals.

Fresh water muscla: (Pl. V- 10)

Specimen recovered from Period I and III belong to class Gastropoda. Family- *unionidae,* species, *Lamellidens* marginalis. They are found in sandy bottoms in clean running water of rivers, pools and tanks.

Cut -marks and bone tools: (Pl IV,Pl.V-3, Pl.VI-6,10)

In the collection of animal bones from Mirzapur a large number of specimens revealed hunting, slaughtering and consumption marks. They also carry the marks of scavenging animals like dogs and at time wolves. Fragments of bones recovered from the garbage of the settlement mostly contain the modfication brought about by human and non-human agencies. In the case of scavenging animals teeth leave marks on the bones. At Mirzapur animal bones were also shaped into tools for various purposes. Most common tools recovered are points, scrapers, piercer-*cum*-scraper, diggers and polishers. Generally the shaft of long bones of cattle and deer and other convenient parts have been used. Mostly in order to give strength to the tools, bones were charred when green. Due to charring they not only gained in strength but also acquired smooth surface due to oozing out of contained fat. Such specimens with smooth surface were easy to use as polishers for pottery.

Cut-marks may occur during butchering, skinning, dismembering and filleting. During butchering a hunted or captive animal such marks are produced as a result of cutting and chopping. Nature of these marks depend on the nature of tools used. Cut-marks made as a result of use of metal tools are very thin, almost hair line in size, and are generally long and obliqely placed, leaving an overlapping small 'shelf ' of bone. Marks from stone tools are generally short and occur in groups of parallel marks and have rugged appearance and do not appear through the contours of the bone as the pressure with which stone tools are used is not great.

Cut-marks resulting due to skinning process gnerally encircle a bone at a particular point. Such marks are generally noticed on the shafts of lone bones, on the skull, particularly around the base of the antler, horns and around the mandibles.

Since dismembering of parts involves disarticulation, cut-marks are generally found near points of articulation such as removal of the head from the neck and mandible from the skull. Other parts that possess dismembering marks are vertebrae, ribs, sternum, pelvis, sacrum, femur, tibia, tassals, metatarsals, scapula, humerus, radio-ulna, carpals, metacarpals and phalanges.

Filleting in the process associated with dismembering when the dismembered parts are further segmented for storage and/or for finally preparing the kill for consumption. In the process the appendages are removed from the long bones, etc., so that it becomes easier to remove meat from the parts. Filleting marks are mostly longitudionally oriented on the bones on which they are caused so that the bone could be easily pulled free from the meat and could be severed from muscle attachments. Filleting process produces only superficial scratch marks unlike deep cut marks produced during butchering or skinning. They are generally in clusters in irregularly shaped bones like radio-cubitus, lateral side of tibial crest, etc.

Gnawing and Breaking for Marrow

During consumption, like animals, man is also required to gnaw and break the bones in order to obtain marrow. In the case of man it is always the green bones that are subjected to this process, whereas in case of animals while feasting on the thrown parts, scavenging animals like dogs and wolves leave marks on the scavenged material. Teeth produce punctures, pits, scars and furrows. The bones cracked by man do not show crenulated edges as in the case of animal cracked bones.

Plate IV

1. Rib fragment of cattle from pit 1 sealed by layer 4. The fragment which is 10.5 cm long and 4.2 cm broad, on the dorsal side bears two horizontal deep cut-marks, 1.2 cm and 1.3 cm long. They seem to have been caused in the process of skinning.

2. Shaft of cattle from pit 1 sealed by layer 4. It is 8.4 cm long and 3.0 cm boad. It contains on the dorsal side at least eight horizontal cut-marks probably caused by very sharp instrument for removal of flesh.

3. Shaft of long bone of deer, 5.2 cm long and 2.1 cm broad. It bears several cut-marks and is heavily charred.

4. Heavily charred shaft of long bone bearing slicing marks. One end being pointed, appears to have been used as a digging tool; 6.4 cm long and 3.2 cm. broad.

5. Proximate end of tibia of *capra* from layer 6, it is 4.9 cm. long and 2.6 cm. broad. On its dorsal side it has three shallow skinning and dismembering marks.

6. Rib fragment of cattle from pit 1 sealed by layer 4. On its one edge it contains deep vertical cut- marks.

7. Metatarsal fragment of cattle, 9.7x 3.1 cm, lower dorsal end used as a polisher. The area used is 2.7 x 2.6 cm. From trench D.1, layer 5.

8. Heavily charred shaft fragment, 2.7 x 1.3 cm, dorsal, convex side used as polisher. Due to constant use surface has become very smooth and has developed shine like N.B.P. ware. from pit 1 sealed by layer 4.

9. Heavily charred rib of cattle, 6.5 x 2.70 cm, used as polisher particularly the dorsal side taking,advantage of the convex shape. From pit 1 sealed by layer 4.

10. Shaft fragment of cattle of massive size, from pit 1 sealed by layer 4, 10.6 cm long and 4.4 cm wide, splintered to give one side very sharp end and edges. Used as piercer and side scraper.

11. Shaft fragment, from trench D.1, layer 5, used as piercer on the sharper, pointed side. It is 8.0 cm long and 2.4 cm broad.

Pl V- 3

Heavily charred shaft of long bone of deer from trench B-3, layer-5, 9.4 cm long and 2.0 cm broad, used as a tool with a 0.25 cm. wide socket at the narrower end.

Pl. VI

6. Femur of deer from layer 6, the surface is pitted displaying teeth marks.

12. Heavily charred shaft of long bone, 8.1 x 2.8 cm, having teeth marks of the scavenging animal, on the dorsal

side at the broader end of the shaft from layer 7.

13. Femur fragment of *capra*, 6.3 x 3.5 cm, having at least three deep 'U' shaped teeth-marks, near the proximal end. These marks are caused during the attempt made for extraction of bone marrow.From layer 6.

Environmental conditions

The study of the animal bones from Mirzapur indicates that the site was having a well forested, grassy area nearby where wild animals like deer moved freely, and in plenty. The conditions of the bones, particularly from the Late Harappan levels, show that in the area plenty of green fodder was available to supply the grazing animals with enough of calcium carbonate for the healthy development of the bony tissues. Occurrence of fish bones, plenty of fish designs on pottery from Late Harappan levels and depiction of stork, a fishing bird and occurrence of fresh water musclas, indicate the presence of a running water stream or pond in the vicinity. There seems to be drastic reduction in forested area during the Early Historical period and later on.

Food habits

Durng Late Harappan period Mirzapurians substituted their meal of the grains and cereals, with the roasted meat of deer, fish and occasionally with cattle meat as the cut marks on the bones of these animals indicate. Sheep and goat meat was also consumed. Apart from these in all the three periods under study, people were mostly dependent on agricultural products for their food. They reared large number of cattle, including buffaloes, for milk. Presence of very limited number of bones of pig shows that the people did not relish pork. It appears, due to drastic reduction of forested area, as the reduction in the number of bones of deer indicate, during Early historical times and Late medieval period, there was less hunting. People became more dependent on agricultural products and milk food. During all the periods people reared good number of sheep and goat, both for meat and wool. Presence of cut-marks on bones and their charred condition, necessarily does not indicate that the entire population in the habitation was non-vegetarian.

Discussion

Study of animal skeletal remains from excavations at Mirzapur have revealed the following facts regarding environmental conditions, agricultural activities, economic role of animals in the site and food habits of the people during different periods of occupation.

1. Amongst the domesticated varieties cattle population outnumbered all other species. During all the periods, animal husbandry was widely practised. Apart from obtaining meat from them, they also seem to have been used for draft purposes. During the Late Harappan period massive size of cattle breed was available.

2. Sheep and goat were reared both for meat and wool, which was a necessity due to severe cold conditions.

3. Amongst the wild animals spotted deer was widely hunted for meat. Bones were also used for making tools. With the decrease in the population from Period I to III, hunting activities also became less frequent and people started paying more attention to animal husbandry and agricultural activities.

4. Condition of the bones, their study, nature and total absence of raefication due to lack of calcium carbonate in the fodder, indicate that the area had sufficient fodder for the healthy growth of the animals. Presence of good number of deers also shows that the area around Mirzapur was well forested. Slow decline in the wild animals from Period I to III shows that as the human population increased, in order to get more food, jungles were cleared to convert the land into agricultural fields. Though there was plenty of forest around, absence of bones of carnivores in the collection indicates that such animals, probably were rare due to vigorous hunting activity by the people.

5. Presence of bones of buffaloes,fish and fresh water muscla indicates that in the near vicinity, there was plenty of fresh water. Topographic study also shows that the river Saraswati was earlier flowing adjacent to the mound of Mirzapur.

6. During Late Harappan period, people ate plenty

of roasted meat of deer, meat of capra, fish and occasionally cattle meat along with the agricultural products. Consumption of roasted meat of deer continued during Early Historical period but it sharply declined during the late mediaevel period due to scarcity of the animal.

7. Presence of only few bones of pig in the collection shows that pig population was not much in the area. Probably people did not like the animal to roam about in their habitation and also did not relish pork. This fact was observed, at Bhagwanpura also, which falls in the same belt.

8. Horse was very much known to the people right from the Late Harappan times. The animal though only few in number was of dwarfish variety. It might have been used for transportation by the well-to-do people. Strangely enough, evidences indicate that the animal was also sacrificed for religious purposes and its teeth was used for magico-medicinal purposes.

9. Absence of fresh water muscla in Periods II and III, probably indicates that source of running water shifted from the area. Stork, a fish catching bird, particularly in the streams, finds good depiction in Late Harappan pottery along with fish designs but suddenly it disappears from the pottery of Early Historical period and Late mediaeval period. Probably it was after the Late Harappan period that the river shifted away from the site due to heavy silting and tectonic movements.

10. Due to fertile nature of soil, which got renewed every year as a result of silt brought by river and air borne soil,people practised plenty of agriculture making them economically sound. This resulted in spare time for them for indulgence in other creative activities. Creation of a beautiful piece of deer on faience, artistic paintings depicting fish, stork, etc. on pottery and clay toys speak of their artistic taste and creative instinct.

Acknowledgements

I am extremely grateful to Prof. U.V. Singh for inviting me to Kurukshetra University to study the animal skeletal remains from Mirzapur which was excavated by his team from 1972 to 1976.

I am grateful to Prof. S.P. Shukla and B.K. Kathial with whom I had very fruitful discussions that helped me in the preparation of thispaper. I am also thankful to S/Shri Surinder Vashisth and Sukhdeo Saini, both Research Assistants, for arranging the material, cleaning it and packing it. My thanks are also due to the photographer S.P.Bali for good photographs, and to Shri Ishwar Chand for typing the manuscript.

F-8/5, Sector III
CBD, New Bombay-400615

A.K. Sharma

Further Exploration at Gopalpur, Orissa

The site was discovered in December 1991 by a team from the P.G. Department of Anthropology, Utkal University (Tripathy and Kar, 1993). Subsequently in January 1996, the author explored this site. His findings are given below.

Gopalpur, lat. 20° 01' 52" N and long. 85° 21' 19" E is situated in Nayagarh District of Orissa. The nearest railway station is Kaluparaghat about 16 km from Gopalpur. The nearest bus stop is Chandpur on NH 5, about 12 km from Gopalpur.

At present evidence of Chalcolithic culture in Orissa has been found at three sites, i.e. Sankerjang in Angul District (Dash 1986; Yule et al 1990), Kuanr in Keonjhar District (Ray 1993) and Golbai Sasan in Khurda District (Sinha 1993). The aim of the author was to find a few more sites. Gopalpur was the fruit of his efforts.

The Site

Towards the north of the village Gopalpur there is a mound known as Jagati. It is oriented north-south and is cut by a small stream along the north-south axis. The dimensions of the mound are 140 m x 115 m x 9m representing length, breadth and height respectively.

The stream has exposed a section of the mound. This is seen from the eastern side. The section contained many varieties of neolithic celts, potsherds, burnt clay fragments of rubbing stones and bones.

Tools

The neolithic celts are fashioned from chlorite and basalt. Their sizes vary; one is larger and the other smaller. The larger one is triangular on plan and flat; the smaller one resembles a trapezium. 11.5 x 6.5 x 1.5 cm and 6.5 x 4.5 x 1 cm; the dimensions representing length, breadth and thickness.

Pottery

Red, red slipped, grey, black and dull red wares have been found. The shapes noticed consist of vase, handi, dish, shallow dish, bowl, ring-based bowl and lids. Some miniature pots were also observed.

Stone objects

Fragments of rubbing stones, pestle and querns and ring-stones were seen lying scattered.

Bones

Charred bone fragments and antlers have been noticed.

Iron smelting process

Iron slags and fragments of terracotta pipes found here point to smelting of iron.

Sculptures

Close to the mound is a pond locally known as Godipohari pond. An image of Mahishamardini in Khondolite is seen lying on the field bordering the pond.

A figure of headless Dhyani Buddha is being used as washing stone by the villagers. The image is lying at the water's edge of another pond known as Banushabhandi pond.

Conclusion

The finds mentioned above indicate that Gopalpur has a long history extending from the present to the far off neolithic — chalcolithic period.

REFERENCES

Dash, R.N. 1986 Sankerjang- a chalcolithic site in Orissa, *Orissa Historical Research Journal* 32.

Ray, Ranjana. 1993 Discovery of a chalcolithic site near the source of River Baitarni, Orissa. *Journal of the Indian Anthropo logical Society*, 28, pp. 97-101.

Sinha, B.K. 1993 Excavation at Golbai Sasan, Dist. Puri, Orissa. *Puratattva*, 23, pp 48-50

Tripathy, K.C. and S.K.Kar 1993 Microlithic Industry of Tangi,Orissa, *Manava, The Journal of Anthropological Society of Orissa,* Vol.4, pp. 151-155.

Yule, P., B.K.Rath and K.Hojgaard 1990 Sankerjang- A Metal Period Burial site in the Dhenkanal uplands of Orissa in M.Taddei (Ed.) *South Asian Archaeology 1987*, pp. 581-584.

Behind Ranger's Training College
Angul. Orissa - 759122

SUSHANTA KUMAR KAR

Recent Exploration In Saraswati - Ghagghar Basin

Haryana with Saraswati as its major river was well known even in ancient times because of its rich flora and fauna. The new State of Haryana by its very name, based on '*harita*' or green, signified a land abounding in greenery and vegetation. This has been referred to in ancient text as *bahudhanyaka*, in the *Mahabharata.* The important archaeological finds of proto–historic sites here are Banawali, Rakhigarhi, Mitathal, Siswal, Daulatpur, Bhagwanpura, Balu and Kunal The excavation at Bhgwanpura (Haryana) has brought to light for the first time juxtaposition of the Late Harappan and the Painted Grey Ware cultures.

The ancient Saraswati originated, according to local tradition, from the Shivalik hills near Adibadri (Ambala District, Jagadhari Tehsil) though presently it is hardly larger than a nullah. Though anciently, we are told, it ended up in the Western ocean, presently it joins the Somb Nadi and, following an easterly course, it discharges it waters into the Yamuna Khadar region, near Dadupur, in Haryana. But at one time it ran parallel to the Ghagghar through the present Rangoi bed until it met the latter near Satrana in District Patiala, Punjab, having passed through the present townships of Thanesar and Pehowa. From Satrana, the combined river with sufficiently large quantity of water, flowed towards further west in Distt. Ganganagar, Rajasthan, and beyond in Bahawalpur Distt. of Pakistan, then upto Rann of Kachchh. It is now a completely dried up river which does not get any water even during the high floods.

The present exploration of the region under study has a semi-arid monsoon type of climate and lacks sufficient rainfall over large parts. The rainfall is not uniform. The average rainfall in the sub-mountainous rack is above 75 cm while it decreases to less than 30 cms in the south-west.

It particularly reveals a transition between the arid Rajasthan and the moderately humid Ganga Basin.

The exploration was conducted from Sirsa to Ambala along the Ghagghar river basin. An area of about 6000 sq. km covering the Districts of Ambala, Hissar, Kaithal, Jind, Kurukshetra and Sirsa was explored (Fig. 1) to find out the archaeological potentiality and also expansion of the Harappan, Painted Grey Ware Culture and their inter-relations with other cultures in this region. Though 43 sites were discovered, descriptions of 13 sites, some of which showed continued occupation from Harappan times to medieval period, alone have been given here.

1. Malakpur, Tehsil Kaithal, District Kaithal (lat. 29° 53' long. 76° 24' E)

Mound No.1 : Malakpur village is situated around 9 km to the north of Kaithal town and 3 km to the east of Siwan village. The site is one km to the north of village Malakpur and is approched by a *kachcha* road. Most of the area of the site has been levelled up by the villagers for purposes of cultivation; only one acre of land is lying unoccupied and uncultivated. The height of the mound is about 1.5 metre from the surrounding area. The river Saraswati flows 4 km to the north of the site and the river Ghagghar flows 23 km to its north-west. Harappan

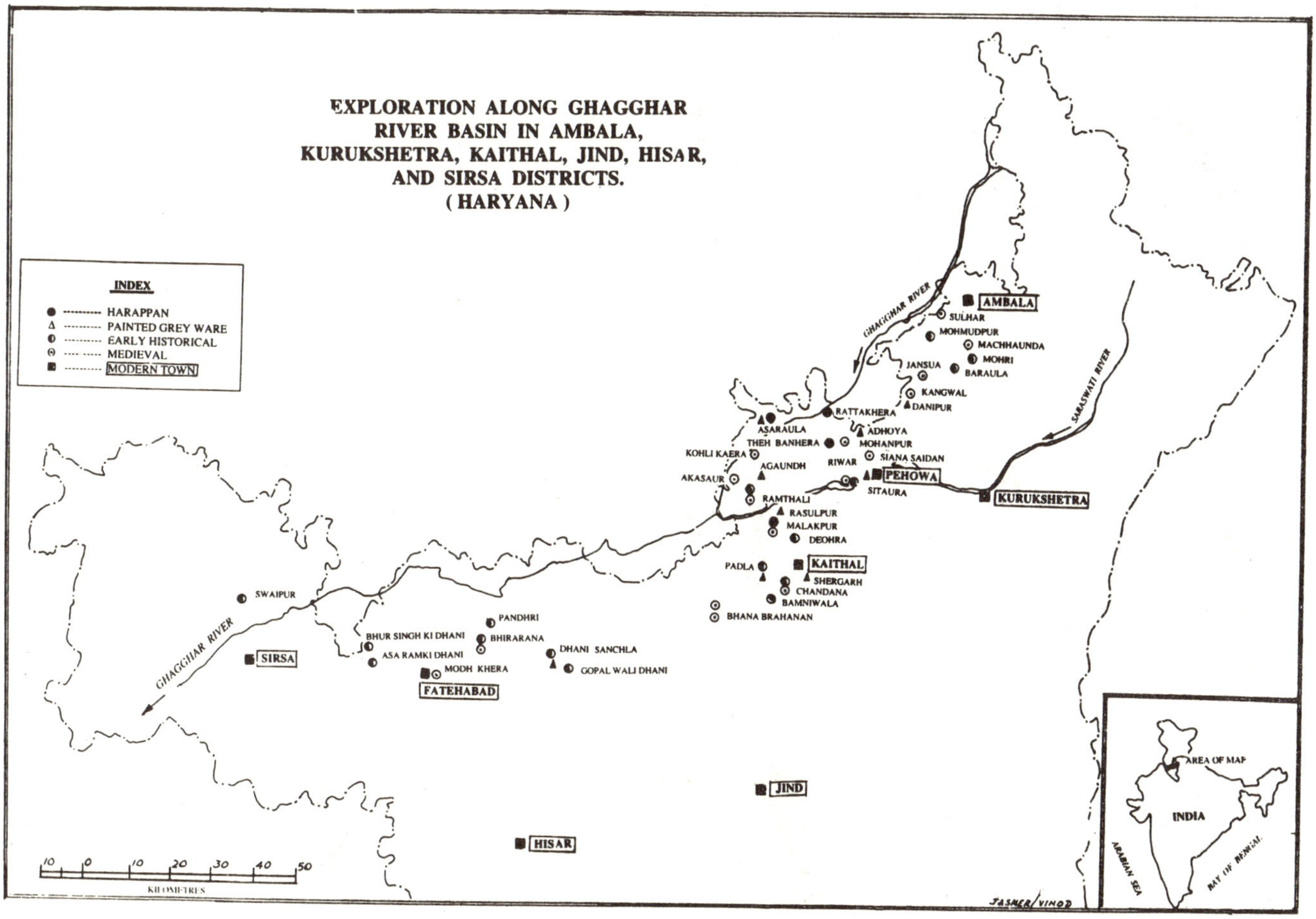

Fig. 1

pottery, in the form of storage jars, vases, dishes-on-stand, and a few decorated fragments bearing incised horizontal and vertical lines and mat designs is found in large quantity. They belong to the early and mature Harappan periods. Terracotta bangles, terracotta cakes, etc. were also collected.

2. Saraula, Thehsil Gula, District Kaithal (Lat. 30° - 06' N, Long. 76° -17' E)

Village Saraula is situated 6 km to the north-west of Chika town and is approachable by a link road from Patiala-Chika road. A *kachcha* path, about 2 km from village Dharmeri, leads to the site which is located on the south-east of the village and on the north bank of the river Ghagghar, the major tributary of the Saraswati. The area is ued for cultivation and it has also been levelled up by the owner, leaving only some parts untouchd. The height of the mound is about 1-2 metres and the area is about 2 acres. The Ghagghar flows 0.5 km to the south of the site.

Late Harappan Ware, Painted Grey Ware, associated red wares and Black slipped ware were collected from the site.

The Late Harappan ceramics includes shapes like storage jars, basins, vases and dishes in thick sturdy red ware. The designs on pottery are notchings, zig-zag lines, horizontal lines,vertical lines and black-on-red (Fig-2) painted motifs. The types in Painted Grey Ware include dishes, bowls, etc. and the painted designs on Painted Grey Ware pot-sherds are dots, horizontal lines, oblique lines, concentric circles,etc. (Fig 3).

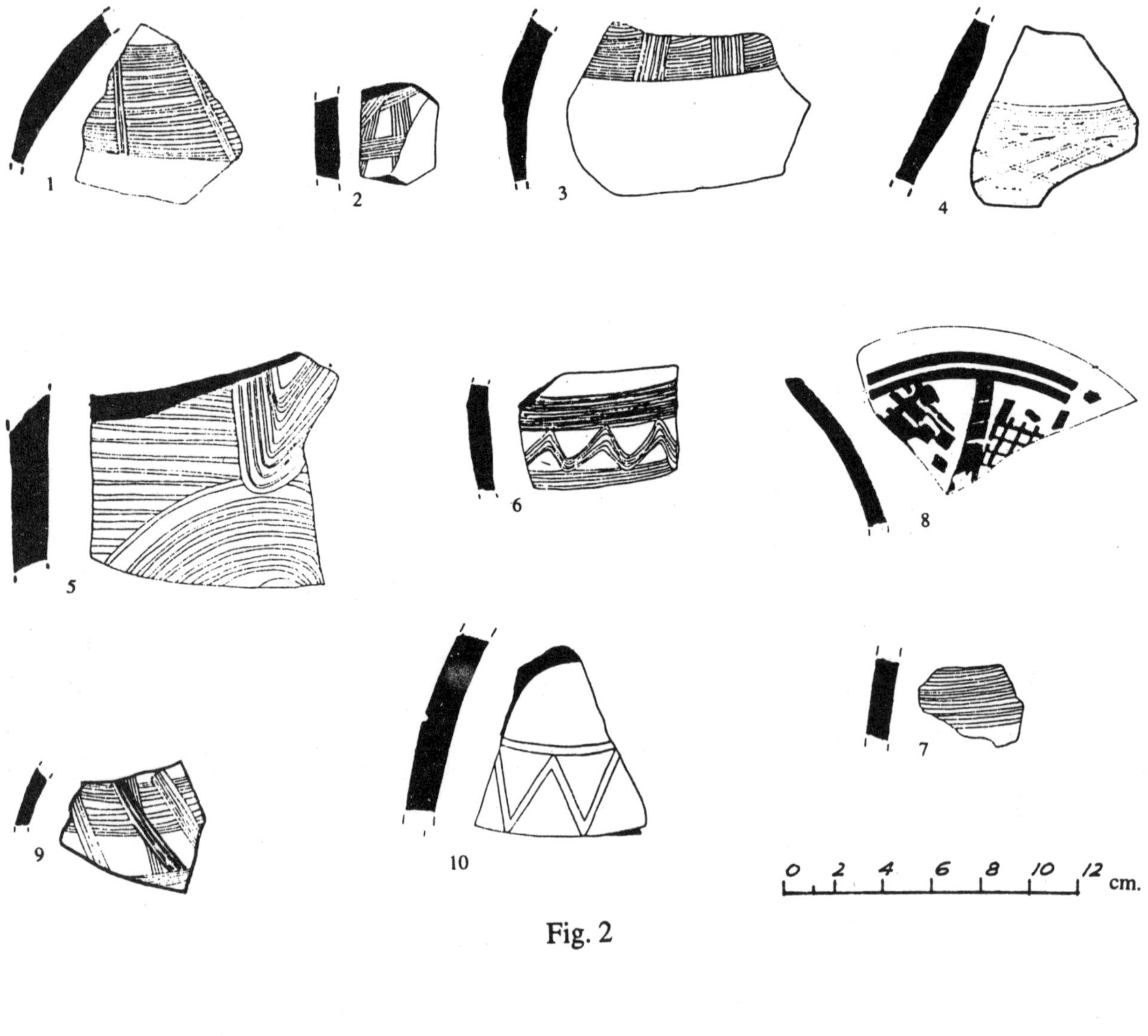

Fig. 2

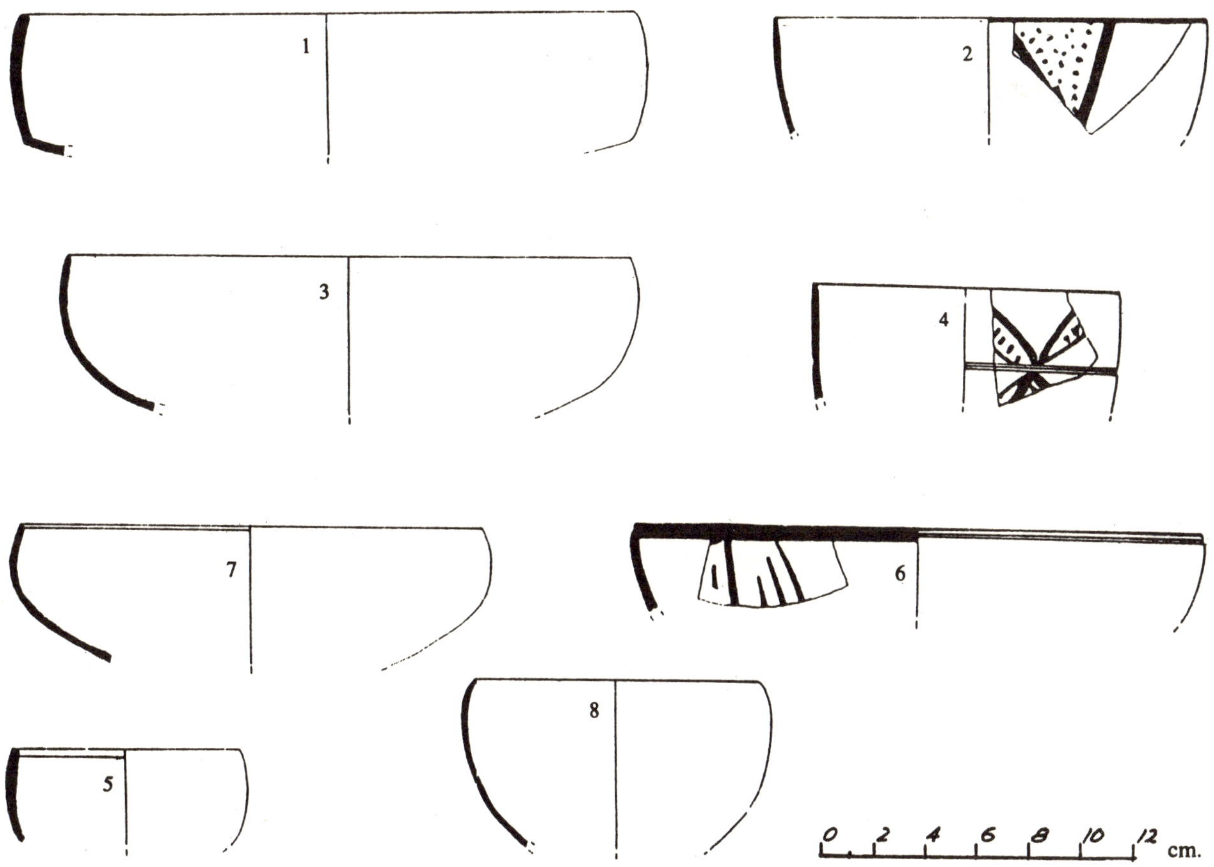

Fig 3.

3. Theh Banhera, Tehsil Gula , District Kaithal, (Lat. 30° 02'N, Long. 76° 25'E)

The village Theh Banhera is situated 5 km to the east of Chika-Kaithal road. It has two approaches, one through link-road from Pidhal-Kaithal road and another link-road from Banhera. The site is on the western side of the village. The height of the mound is 3 metres and the area is about 2 acres; the mound is being used for making cow dung cakes by the local people. The River Ghagghar flows 5 km to the north of the village.

The ceramics is Late Harappan and the shapes included storage jars, dishes-on-stands, vases, basins, and the incised decorations on them include horizontal lines, zig-zig lines, vertical lines and mat designs. Some mud and mud-brick structures are also noticed on the site.

4. Ratta Khera (Kuhram), Tehsil Gula, District Kaithal (Lat. 30° 07'N, Long. 760 26'E).

The village Ratta Khera is situated 8 km to the north of Bhagal town and can be reached through a link road leading to Budhanpur. The ancient site is on the eastern side of the village. The height of the mound is about 2 metres from the general ground level and the area of the site is about 2-3 acres. The Government of Haryana has constructed a school building on it. Close by the locals have built a *dharmashala.* The River Ghagghar flows 0.5 km to the west of the site.

The ceramics include Late Harappan red ware and the shapes include dishes-on-stands, storage jars, vases, and simple pots, while the decorative designs include zig-zig lines.

Among the minor antiquities a piece of faience bangle is noteworthy.

5. Sitaura, Tehsil Pehowa, District Kurukshetra (Lat. 29° 58', Long. 76° 33'E)

Mound No. 2 the village Sitaura is situated 6 km to the west of Pehowa and is approached by a branch road of Pehowa-Bhagal. The mound is located 1.5 km to the west of the village Sitaura on the north bank of the Saraswati river. The hight of the mound is about 2-3 metres and the area covered is about 3 acres.

The Ghagghar flows 12 km. to the north of the site. The mound is very interesting and culturally very significant since it has revealed the presence of the Painted Grey Ware and the Late Harappan pottery *in situ*, in one and the same level. The same evidence is identical to that noticed at Bhagwanpura. This mound is very much disturbed but it may yield many new pieces of evidence to support the evidence of co-existence of the Late Harappan and Painted Grey Ware cultures found at Bhagwanpura.

A very interesting pot found is a globular vessal-on-stand in Grey Ware (fig. 4). The fabric of this is of well levigated clay and its section is thin. It seems to be the product jointly of Late Harappan format with the fabric of the Painted Grey Ware. In the same level dishes-on-stands were also noticed *in situ* on this mound.

The ceramic industry from this site is represented by mixed Late Harappan and Painted Grey Ware cultures. Among the shapes in the Painted Grey Ware are dishes and deep bowls. The paintings in Painted Grey Ware are concentric circles, oblique lines, dots and horizontal lines, etc.

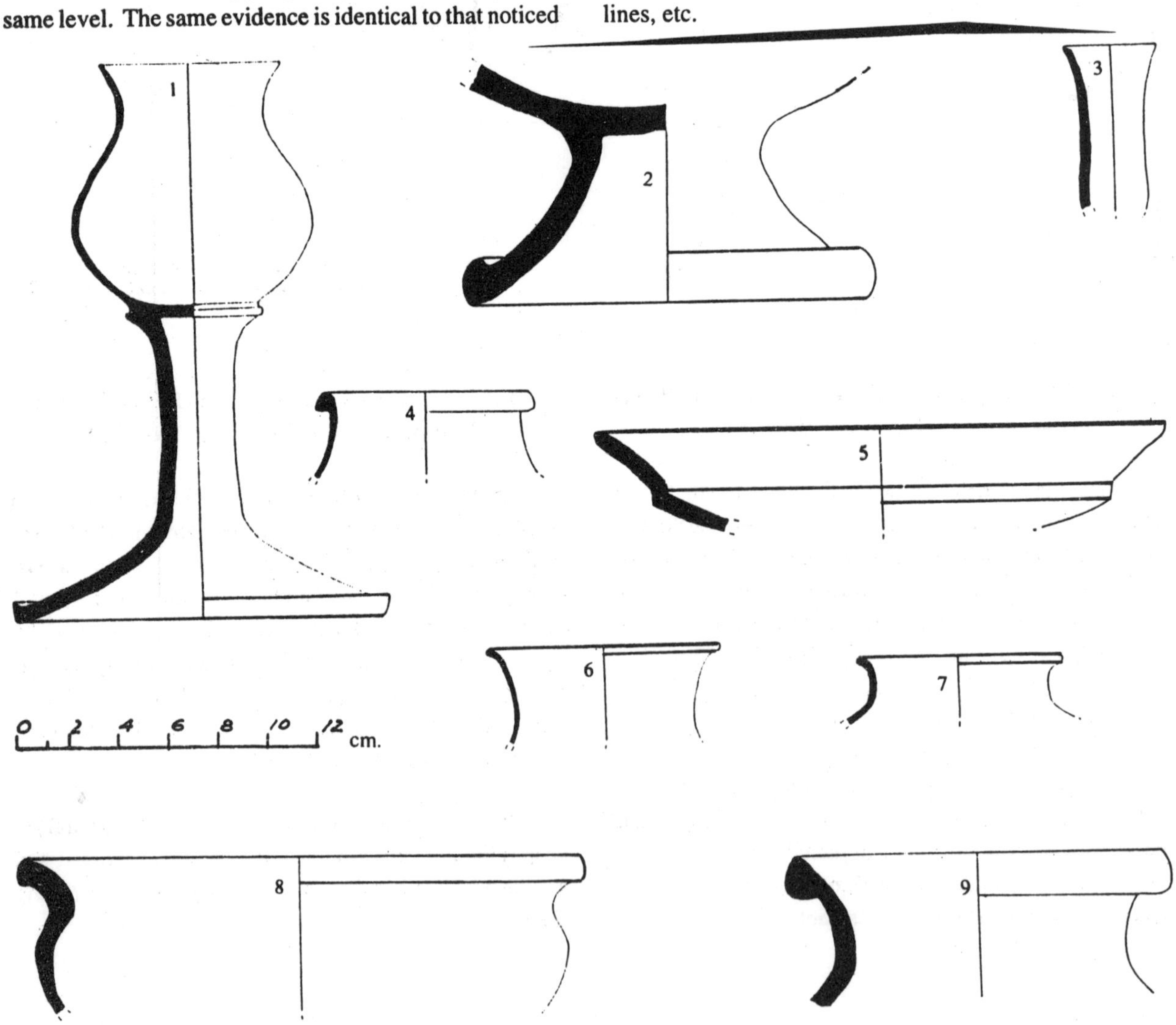

Fig. 4

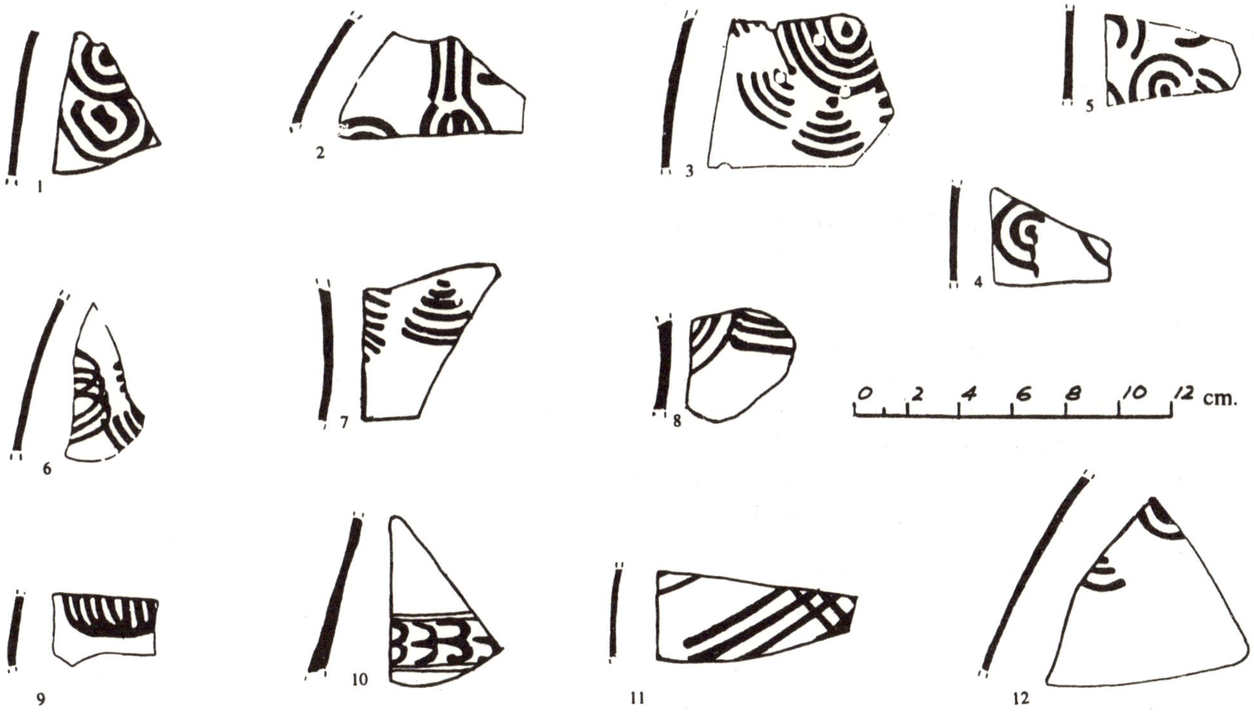

Fig. 5

Among the minor antiquities are included terracotta cakes, bangles and animal figurines.

6. Sitaura, Tehsil Pehowa, Dstrict Kurukshetra (Late. 29° -58' N, Long. 76° -33' E)

Mound No. 1 The village Sitaura is situated 6 km to the west of Pehowa and approached by a road linking Pehowa-Bhagal road. The ancient site is to the south of the village Sitaura and on the north bank of Saraswati river. The height of the mound is about 2 to 3 metres and the area-coverage is about 2 acres. The whole mound is disturbed since a drain has been made on the embankment of the river. The river Ghagghar flows 12 km north of the site.

The ceramics is represented by Painted Grey Ware and the shapes included bowls, dishes, deep bowls, etc. In Red ware the shapes included vases, miniature pots, dishes, basins, etc. The designs in Painted Grey Ware are horizontal lines, oblique lines, concentric circles and dots (Fig.5).

7. Dhani Sanchla, Tehsil Fatehabad, Dist.. Hissar (Lat. 29° -33' N Long. 75° -46' E)

The site is situated on Bhna-Uklana road and 1/2 km north of the main road. It can be approached by a link-road to Dhani Sanchla. The height of the mound is about 3 metres from the surrounding area and the area-coverage is about 6 acres. The river Ghagghar flows about 23 km. north-east of the site.

The site has yielded the ceramic assemblages of Painted Grey Ware, Grey Ware and Black Slipped Ware. In Painted Grey Ware, the shapes included simple bowls, dishes, bowls with incurved rims and deep bowls. In Red Ware the shapes included vases, storage jars, dishes, handis, lids, spouts, etc. Among the minor antiquities a piece of stone with carved moulding, terracotta ball, terracotta bead, shell bangle, etc. are included.

8. Shergarh (Sirkat, Tehsil Kaithal, Distt. Kaithal) (Late. 29° -46' N, Long. 76° - 25' E)

Mound No. 2 The vilage Shergarh is situated 3 km. south-east of the Kaithal township. It is approachable by a link-road from Kaithal-Hissar road and it is about 1.5 km east of the main road. On the northern side of the Mound No.1 there is another small mound. The height of the mound is about 2 metres from the surrounding area. The area is about 3 acres. The ceramics is represented by Painted Grey Ware, Black Slipped Ware and associated red wares, and the shapes included bowls, veses, deep bowls and dishes. In Red Ware, the shapes included dishes, miniature pots, dabbers, incurved bowls, pots with spout, etc. The rest belong to the Painted Grey Ware. It has also yielded a beautiful terracotta round rattle with a holed knob on the top fully opened lotus on one face and a *dampati* seated on an animal, belonging to Sunga-Kushan period.

9. Padla, Tehsil Kaithal, District Kaitha (Lat. 29° 39'N, Long. 76° 19'E)

Mound No. 2 The village Padla is situated 10 km west of Kaithal town. The mound is situated 1.5 km. south-east of the village Padla and approached by a *kachcha* road. The height of the mound is about 1-1.5 metres. The whole area is used for cultivation. The river Ghagghar flows 23 km. north-west of the site and Saraswati is located 1.5 km. north of the site.

The ceramies is represented by Painted Grey Ware, Black slipped ware and red wares. Among the minor antiquities, terracotta beads have been collected from the site. The site belongs to the Painted Grey Ware period.

10. Rasulpur, Tehsil Kaithal, District Kaithal, (Lat. 29° 35'N Long. 76° 25')

Village Rasulpur is 13 km north of Kaithal town and approached by a link-road from Kaithal-Gula road about 4 km east of the main road. The ancient site is on the western side of the village and the eastern portion of the site is being used by the local people for habitation. The height of the mound is about 4 metres from the surrounding area, and the area covered is about 2 acres. River Saraswati flows 2 km north of the site and river Ghagghar is about 22 km west of the site.

The potteries represented here are Painted Grey Ware, Black slipped ware and associated red ware.

11. Kasaur, Tehsil Gula, District Kaithal, (Lat. 29° 58'N, Long. 76° 13'E)

Mound No. 2 The village Kasaur is situated south-est of Gula town and approached by a link road from village Agaundh and about 3 km south-west of village Agaundh. Mound No.2 is situated on north-west of the village and approached by a *kachcha* path about 0.5 km north-east of the village. The height of the mound is about 2-3 metres. The total area is about 3 acres, largely used for cultivation, only some parts lying vacant.

The ceramcs is represented by Painted Grey Ware, Red and Black slipped wares, some belonging to the historical period.

12. Agaundh, Tehsil Gula, District Kaithal (Lat. 30° 00'N, Long. 76° 15'E)

Village Agaundh is situated 7 km south-west of Gula town and the ancient site is on the north of the village. The height of the mound is about 7-8 metres from the surrounding area. The total area is about 20 acres. It is under the possession of the Forest Department of the State Govt. The river Ghagghar flows 7 km north of the site. The mound is lying intact.

The ceramics is represented by Painted Grey Ware, Black Polished and associated red wares.

13. Danipur, Tehsil Ambala, District Ambala,(Lat. 30° 05'N, Long.76° 35'E)

Village Danipur is situated 6 km south-west of Ismailabad. It is approached by a link-road to Jaitpura and Balapur and then Danipur. The ancient site is on the north-west, about 0.5 m. of the village. It can be approached by a *kachcha* path way. The height of the mound is about 2 metres from the general ground level and the area is about 2 acres. It is lying vacant. Ghagghar flows 12 km. north-west of the village Danipur.

The ceramics is represented by red wares and Painted Grey Ware.

CHRONOLOGY

Nearly a dozen sites in Haryana have been excavated so far. They are: Mitathal, District Bhiwani; Siswal, District Hissar. Banawali, District Hissar; Bhagwanpura, District Kurukshetra. Balu, District Jind and Kunal District Hissar. They have established four distinct cultural periods in this region. Harappan, Harappan, Post- Harappan and Painted Grey Ware, upto early historical urban phase.

1. EARLY HARAPPAN CULTURE (3200 B.C.- 2600 B.C.)

The Early Harappan Culture was for the first time recognised in the region at Siswal in 1970 and subsequently this culture was also noticed at Banawali.

2. MATURE HARAPPAN CULTURE (2600 B.C.-1900 B.C.)

The next stage in the growth of culture in Haryana is marked by the advent of urbanisation. Typical Harappan pottery painted in black over red has been discovered from as many sites in the Saraswati, Drishadvati and the Sabi valleys. About half a dozen larger settlements have also been discovered as at Mitathal, Banawali, Rakhigarhi, Balu, Lohat etc.

3. POST-HARAPPAN BRONZE AGE CULTURE (1900-1100B.C.)

The evidence from Mitahal, Balu and Banawali shows a general decline in the urban life of the region during the Late Bronze Age. Of the 145 occupation sites of this phase the bulk is located in the Saraswati, Drisadvati and the Yamuna valleys. The largest of settlements, however, could not attain the size of the larger settlements of the Harappan period.

4. PAINTED GREY WARE CULTURE (1100-600 B.C.)

It is these people who introduced iron technology in India. Painted Grey Ware has been discovered from 258 sites in Haryana and the adjoining territory of Delhi. Of these sites Autha, Daulatpur, Bhagwanpura and Sugh etc. have been excavated in past years. The Painted Grey Ware culture overlaps with Bara culture in the earlier levels and transforms into the Northern Black Polished Ware culture formation about the middle of the first millennium B.C. Carbon-14 date from Painted Grey Ware levels in the Gangetic valley generally ranged between 800 B.C. to 400 B.C. But its advent may be pushed back to circa 1000 B.C. in the Saraswati valley where it happens to be a later contemporary of Post-Harappan.

Acknowledgements

I am grateful to my colleague Dr. P.K. Mishra, Superintending Archaeologist, Archaeological Survey of India, Chandigarh Circle, for his valuable suggestions. My sincere thanks are due to Shri Jasmer Singh, Sr. Surveyor, Shri Vinod Kumar, Draftsman, Shri Baldev Singh, Photographer who helped me in the preparation of the drawings and photographs, respectively.

REFERENCES

Suraj Bhan, *Excavation of Mitathal and other Explorations in the Sutlej-Yamuna Divide,* Kurukshetra

________, "Pre-Vedic and Vedic Cultures of the Saraswati Valley", *Indological Studies,* Davendra Handa(Ed.) pp. 1-11.

_______, Dawn of Civilization in Haryana, *Haryana Studies in History & Culture* (1972) pp. 135-39. Prehistoric Archaeology of the Saraswati and Drisadvati Valleys (Haryana). Unpublished Ph.D.Thesis, (M.S.Univ. Baroda).

O.P. Bhardwaj, *Ganga* to *Ghagghar* with *Valmiki, Vij,* Vol.XVII (1979), pp. 142-167.

Bisht, R.S., Structural Remains and Town Planning of Banawali in *Frontiers of the Indus Civilization* (Eds. B.B.Lal and S.P. Gupta)pp.9-97. Also *Banawali: A lookback into the pre-Indus and Indus Civilization* (Govt.of Haryana Publication).

I.A.R. (*1964-65*) pp. 33-3.

I.A.R. (*1968-69*) pp. 8-9.

Joshi, J.P. "A note on the Excavation at Bhagwanpura", *Puratattva*, No.8, pp. 178-80.

______, Overlap of the Late Harappan Culture and Painted Grey Ware Culture in the light of recent excavations in Haryana, Punjab and Jammu, paper presented in the Seminar on *The Indus Civilizatior: Problems and Issues,* held at the IIAS, Shimla.

Meena, B.R., A note on recent exploration in the Valley of Khari and Mansi rivers, Rajasthan, *Puratattva,* No.16, pp. 17-20.

Phadke, H.A. Haryana: The Landmarks in Historical Growth, in *Indological Studies*, Davendra Ha nda (Ed.) pp. 31-43.

______, *History of Haryana,* pp. 1-15.

S.A, Ex. Br-V,
Archaeological Survey of India,
Vadodara

B.R. Meena

New Megalithic Sites In Chittoor District

Recent explorations in Chittoor district, Andhra Pradesh have resulted in the discovery of altogether thirteen megalithic sites. These monuments exhibit varied and interesting features. Out of the thirteen sites, nine are burial sites, two sites have megalithc paintings and two habitational sites. A list of these new megalithic sites with their general features is given below.

S.No.	Name of the site	Location	Types of monument/ general features
1.	Chikurupalle	78°59'E 13°12'N	Habitation
2.	Durgam	78°53'E 13°07'N	Dolmen
3.	Eguvakantala Cheruvu	78°54'E 13°06'N	Dolmens Dolmenoid-cists, Anthropomorphic figures, slab circles.
4.	Gavibanda Near Dalavaipalle	79°00'E 13°07'N	Paintings
5.	Mallaiahpalle	Near Chandragiri	Dolmen, paintings
6.	Mogili Venkatagiri	78°54'E 13°12'N	Dolmens
7.	Mogili Varipalle	78°51'E 13°11'N	Port-holed dolmens
8.	Mavidimanukunta	78°51'E 13°09'N	Dolmens
9.	Panapakam	79°13'E 13°29'E	Stone cicle
10.	Palam penta	78°52'E 13°12'N	Habitation
11.	Sikkiralladona Near Nagireddipalle	79°01'E 13°06'N	Paintings
12.	Settiboyapalle	78°53'E 13°11'N	Dolmenold-cist
13.	Tekumanda	78°51'E 13°09'N	Dolmen, stone circle

Most of the megalithic monuments reveal chamber character, and most of them are constructed using grey granit slabs or stones. The general features of the monuments and the sites are discussed below.

1. Chikurupalle: Habitational deposit from Neolithic to early-historic, including megalithic phase has been noticed on the top of a small granatoid hillock located about half a kilometre east of the village. The habitational deposit has yielded grey, dull red, buff stamped and black and red wares in profuse quantities both on the plains of the hill-top and also under the rock-selters. Apart from this polshed stone celt, iron slag lumps in good quantity were also noticed.

2. Durgam: Dolmens erected using roughly hewn stone boulders were noticed on top of a high outcrop of the Durgam hill. The dolmens have a thick, roughly shaped capstone which is supported over the boulders. There seems to have been an attempt to form two concentric circles using stone boulders around these dolmens. Though the two monuments are in well preserved condition more seems to have existed here.

The outer diameter of the stonecircle is about 5.95 m. The total height of the dolmen is aout 87 cm.

3. Eguva Kantalacheruvu: A complex of about 40 megalithic monuments with very interesting features has been noticed in and around the village, which is located on elevated plains in a hilly region. Both dolmens and dolmenoid-cists with/without slab circles have been noticed here. The monuments are constructed using thick granite slabs arranged either in clock-wise or anti-clock-wise swastika pattern. Over the orthostats a capstone with uniform thickness is arranged. Some of the monuments contained neatly trimmed floor slab, which fits exactly inside the chamber. Port-holes usually measuring about halfametre, have been noticed on the eastern and south-eastern orthostats. Some of the dolmens and dolmenoid cists are surrounded by flat topped slab circles raising to about half a metre in height. The gap between the orthostats and the slab circle is filled with cairn packing.

One of the monument located very near the Primary school has very interesting features. This monument constructed on the bed rock, has anthropomorphic figures, presently on three sides, but must have had them on its fourth side also. Since the villagers are using the chamber of this monument as a refuse place, they seem to have removed the figure on the fourth side. The eastern orthostat has a port-hole measuring about 55 cm, in front of which a passage is arranged with two slabs. Beyond the passage is an imposing anthropomorphic figure which shows similarity with the ones discovcered earlier at Mottur in Tamil Nadu and Midimalla in Chittoor district, Andhra Pradesh. Very interestingly this anthropomorphic figure is also pierced with a port-hole having a diametre of about 47 cm. There is an attempt to depict trunk and hands, while the head is deliberately avoided. On the western side (back) of the monument another anthropomorphic figure, but assembled in two pieces, has been placed. These two pieces fit in exactly if placed together and constitute a figure similar to the one in the front. On the northern side of the dolmen, a half anthropomorph is placed towards the western half of the orthostat and thus leaving the eastern half of the orthostat uncovered. This probably suggests that on the northern side also there were two pieces of an anthropomorph but now one half is missing. Since the southern orthostat of the monument is removed by the villagers, the figure on this side is also missing. This type of half anthropomorphs have a close parallel from Hire Benkal in Karnataka.

One of the dolmenoid cist, which has been dug up by the villagers some time ago, has revealed thin sectioned high quality Black and Red ware. This suggests that these monuments,though highly evolved, are to be assigned early dates, probably around 5th century B.C. or earlier.

4. Gavibanda: Megalithic paintings were noticed on a rock face inside a rock-shelter known locally as Gavibanda. This rock-shelter is located half a kilometre south of Dalavaipalle village. The paintings are executed in white pigment over the granite rock face. Though five figures could be clearly noticed, there seems to be more which have eroded considerably. Human figures and riders on animals are depicted. These paintings show similarity with the megalithic paintings found on the capstone of a dolmen at Mallaiahpalle in the same district.

5. Mallaiahpalle: A megalithic dolmen was noticed

on an elevated out crop located half-a-kilometre east of Mallaiahpalle village. A huge, thick capstone is elevated by pillars constructed using small stone blocks arranged one over the other. Villagers call this megalithic dolmen as *pandavula banda*. The importance of this monument is that, the inner face of the capstone contains numerous painted figures executed in red and white pigment. Some of the identifiable figures are:

1. Human figures
2. Human figures with weapons in hand.
3. Segmented animals (Arthropods)
4. Riders on animals.
5. Joined human figures.
6. Symbols like plus, sun, rectangles, triangles.
7. Dancing humans.
8. Trident
9. Animals
10. Floral designs

Some of the figures show similarity with the megalithic paintings from Paiyampalle in Tamil Nadu.

6. Mogili Venkatagiri: A megalithic dolmen was noticed on the slope of a hill, located 200 m south-west of Mogili Venkatagiri. Villagers call this monument as *pandavula banda*. The monument is free standing on the bed-rock. A thick roughly shaped capstone is supported by three boulders.

7. Mogili Varipalle: Three megalithic dolmens are noticed on the top of a hill, located three kilometres south of Mogilivaripalle village. All the orhostats of these dolmens are arranged in anti-clock-wise pattern. A floor slab is noticed inside the chamber. The port-holes on these monuments face east, south-eastand north-east, thus showing different orientation. Out of the three dolmens one has a stone-circle and the gap between the dolmen and stone-circle is filled up with cairn packing, probably for giving strength and protection to the monument.

8. Mavidimanukunta: Two megalithic dolmens were noticed on top of a hill located 2 km west of Mavidimanukunta village. Out of the two monuments, one is very large in proportion as it meassures 4.85 m in length and 3.56 m. in width. Villagers call this monument as *Chinnillu banda*.

9. Panapakam: A stone circle was noticed on the western outskirts of the village, just by the side of Chitoor-Tirupati Road. Though the monument is not disturbed, a modern temple has been erected in the middle of this monument.

10. Palampenta: A habitational depoistor is noticed on the foot of a hill located about two-and-a-half kilometres north-west of Palamakulapale village. Though the site yielded Black and Red-and-black burnished wares, not much of deposit is exposed, as the earlier deposit seems to have been covered by the wash from upper levels, due to the slopy nature of the foot-hill.

11. Sikkiralladona: Megalithic paintings were noticed in a rock-shelter, which is located one and a half kilometre south of Nagireddipalle village. Since the site is located in a thicky-forested area it is difficult to approach. The paintings are executed in white pigment. They contained:

1. Human figures.
2. Human figurtes with weapons.
3. Riders on animals.
4. Trident
5. Indeterminant figures, etc.

These paintings show similarity with the paintings of Ubbaramadugu and Gavibanda in all aspects.

12. Settiboyapale: A megalithic dolenoid-cist was noticed amidst the agricultural fields, at a distance of about half-a-kilometer West of Mogili Venkatagiri. The monument was dug up by the villagers some 10 years ago. Now only few pottery pieces could be noticed on the surface. From the narration of the villagers, it could be understood that a dolmenoid-cist existed here.

13. Tekumanda: A megalithic dolmen was noticed 3

km west of the village. The megalithic dolmen is named as *Vaddivadukottina banda*. The under surface of the capstone contained some paintings. The capstone is supported by small stones arranged one over the other in a circular plan.

By the side of this monument another dolmen within a stone-circle is noticed, but the capstone was broken by the villagers some time ago. Four huge boulders arranged at a distance of 80 cm. from each other were place inside the stone-circle. These boulders must have supported a capstone, which is now missing.

BIBLIOGRAPHY

Narasimhaiah, B., 1975 'A Monolithic Anthropomorphic figure at Mottur, Tamil Nadu', *Journal of Oriental Institute,* Vol. XXV (2), pp. 157-159.

Rao, K.P., 1988 *Deccan Megaliths*, p. 21, Pls. 13 & 14. 1987 "Anthropomorphism in Megalithic Culture", *Indological Studies,* (Ed.) Devendra Handa, pp. 13-16.

Sundara, A., 1975, *The Early Chamber Tombs of South India,* Pl.XXI No.2.

Dept. of A.I.H.C. & Archaeology,
S.V. University
Tirupati-517 502

V. Rambrahman

Anthropomorphic Figures And Other Remains At Kumati.

The site (76° 35' 45" E. Long. 14°41' 30 N Lat) from where anthropomorphic figures have been discovered is located 1 km north of the village Kumati, Kundligi Taluk, District Bellary. situated at a distance of 18 km east of the National Highway-13 and is approachable by a motorable road *via* Chikkajogihalli, Gundumunugu, Huralihalu and Olashi. A cart tract deviating from the road between Lashi and Kumati, along the northern periphery of the large tank, leads to the site proper. The site is at a distance of about 500 m west of the confluence point of the stream Peddavanka with the river Chinna Hagari, the main drainage system in the region.

The site proper is at an elevation of about 3 m high from the surrounding area and has a natural gradiant from north to south, draining the rain waters into the large tank situated to the south of the site and north of the village. The area is further characterised by low out-crops susceptible for easy quarrying of sheets and slabs of granite.

The mound, rising only to a height of about 0.30 m from the area immediately surrounding it, is defined by an elliptic alignment of rough medium-sized pebbles and granite flakes. Due to intensive agricultural activity much of the peripheral boulders and cairn packing are disturbed.

Along the north - south oriented longer axis of the ellipse are located three anthropomorphic figures, and some rectangular slabs are located in other orientations. The northernmost figure, which is extant only upto 1.31 m and the broken top edge, has a width of 0.40 m. The thickness of the slab varies from 0.09 m at the centre to 0.65 m at the edges. The figures 1 and 2 are in alignment with north-south axis, whereas the 3rd figure is located 1.26 m west of the main axis.

The second anthropomorphic figure stands 2.28 m south of the first and measures 3.08 m in height and has a maximum width of 1.40 m at the upper levels of the shoulder. The figure has a distinct head, neck, broad shoulders and a broad body further broadening at the ground level. The thickness of the slab varies from a maximum of 0.16 m at the central part to a minimum of 0.08 m at the periphery. The once vertically placed figure is presently slightly leaning to the west forming an angle of about 8 degrees with the vertical. The head slightly broader is roundish and is raised over a comparatively short but well - shaped neck. The left shoulder rises parallel to the ground, the free end pointing to the north and what now remains of the right shoulder as much as half in the width of the former gently points towards the ground and is slightly away from the body. Possibly the right shoulder also pointed towards south and placed horizontally. This figure does not process a distinct waist line but it is present in the third figure.

The third figure represents the last and the southernmost one placed slightly behind, towards west from the north - south alignment and is the most exquisite specimen of the anthropomorphic figures of the group measuring 2.90 m in height and 2.50 m in width. This is slightly shorter than figure 2. Unlike the second specimen this has its both hands fully stretched, away from the body, parallel to the ground, a more pronounced neck and bulbous head with a marked leaning to left. This has also been fashioned in line with the second figure but a clear waist line distinguishes it from the former.

The anthropomorphic figures have developed greyish - yellow patination due to the seasonal growth of lichen and have begun to flake sporadically and are exposed to human vandalism as well.

At a distance of about 2.00 m east of the main axis are the remnants of two rectangular slabs respectively measuring 1.35 m and 1.20 m in width. A third slab is found embedded in the ground at a distance of 1.45 m north-east of figure 1. This slab has east-west orientation. Except figure 1, which is extant to a height of 1.10 m and figures 2 and 3 which are fairly well preserved, the other features are much disturbed and could be traced only in plan.

An irregular-shaped fragment of the upper portion of a figure, probably forming part of anthropomorphic figure 1 is also traced at the site. Further, at a distance of 25 m north - east of figure 1 is part of another menhir - like slab extant to a height of 0.5 m.

The anthropomorphic figures and the other slabs are all fashioned on locally available granite rock. Slabs of large size and of almost uniform thickness have been removed from rocks and the head and limbs are fashioned by the technique of oblique chiselling as evidenced by the sharp peripheral edges of the extant specimens.

The Megalithic Burial

The lone megalithic burial structure that could be associated with the aforesaid anthropomorphic figures is located at about a distance of 2.25 km south of the site where the figures are situated and about 1 km south of the village.

Typologically, this burial belongs to the variety of cairn packed port - holed dolmen enclosed by a slab-circle, and is comparable to the megaliths of Brahmagiri in the neighbouring Chitradurga district and those at Hire Benkal in the adjacent Raichur district. The inner chamber of the megalith is squarish, roughly measuring 175 m north - south and 1.84 m east - west. The orthostat on the eastern side is missing and the others are slanting inwards. The northern orthostat measures 1.95 m in height and 1.85 m in width and has a circular port-hole with a diameter of 0.30 m at the geometric centre of the slab. The western orthostat measures 1.70 m in height and 2.77 m in width, whereas the southern one measures 1.84 m in height and 1.50 m in width. The huge squarish capstone measures 4.10 x 3.10 m with a perimeter of 12.90 m. Since the eastern orthostat is missing the capstone stands at an angle of 60 degrees and rests on the remaining three orthostats.

At an average distance of about 2.70 m from each of the extant orthostats there is a disturbed slab - circle in a roughly squarish pattern.

The extant remains of the slab-circle measures 8.40 m. north-south and 6.50 m east-west. Part of a huge slab (measuring 0.95 m in height and 2.30 m in width) is embedded on the south-eastern side of the megalith. This slab probably formed the eastern orthostat. The space in between the orthostats and the peripheral slabs is filled with cairn packing in the form of flakes of granite, quartz and riverine pebbles. Due to intensive agricultural operations in the field in which the structure is located the slab-circle and the cairn packing are much disturbed.

Prehistoric Kumat

Besides the above unique discovery, an exploration around a square kilometre area to the north of Kumati tank has yielded a fairly large collection of Middle and Upper Palaeolithic artefacts mainly made on opaque quartz, quartzite, milky quartz and chert. Interestingly, a small percentage of the tools is also made on dolorite which is rather an unusual feature in the area.

Typologially, the Middle Palaeolithic assemblage compromises 'tortoise' backed ovates on cores of large medium size, miniature hand-axes on thick leafy flakes, end scrapers on moderately thick flakes, point-*cum*-borers and borer - *cum* - scrapers.

The Upper Palaeolithic tools, mainly on milky quartz flakes of medium thickness, are represented by side-scrapers, end-scrapers and points. This Upper Palaeolithic phase appears to constitute an immediate transitional phase between the Middle Palaeolithic and evolved Upper Palaeolithic in this region.

Suptd. Archaeological Survey of India,
BANGLORE.

K.P. POONACHA

Manikapatna: An Excavation Report

It is a short report on the limited excavations conducted during 1989-90 and 1992-93 in Manikapatna, an ancient seaport of Orissa. The excavation was undertaken by the first author in collaboration with the Orissa Institute of Maritime and South Asian Studies and the Department of Archaeology, Govt. of Orissa.

Location:

Manikapatna (35^0 05' Lat.N and 94^0 05' Long E) is located in Brahmagiri Tehsil, about 45 km away from Puri to its south-west. It is situated on the left bank of a channel which connects the Chilka Lake with the sea (Fig 1). Its position, i.e., being almost on the mouth of the lake, enabled the ships to sail through the channel and anchor safely in the lake.

Origin:

Madala Panji, the chronicle of the Jagannatha Temple at Puri, gives an interesting account as to how the village Manikapatna owes sits name to a pretty milk-maid known as Manika. This account is supported by Kanchi-Kaveri expedition of the Gajapati ruler Purushottamadeva of the mid 15th century A.D.

Purpose of the Excavation

That Orissa had extensive overseas trade is known from literary, archaeological and numismatic sources (Banerji 1930, 1931; Behera 1977, 1993, 1994, 1995; Sahu 1994; Tripathy 1986). The well known seaports were Paloura Dosarin, Konagara, Dantapura, Tamralipti, Simhapura, Kalinganagar, Pithonda, Katikardham, Nanigeina and Manikapatana (Behera 1994).

The goods traded were pearls, fine muslins, silk and mulberry, cotton, bells, conch shells, indigo, jaggery, corn, ivory, peacocks and a variety of spices. In additon diamonds, cats eye, ruby, sapphire, garnet, beryl, topaz and tourmaline were costly export items (Lahiri 1992; Basa 1994),

The goods were sent through boats. There is adequate sculptural evidence in support of the usage of boats in maritime trade. In an example from Deokund (Mayurbhanj Distric), the goddess Ambika is shown seated over the boat. This is significant because of Ambika's association with boat (Patnaik and Tripathy 1992-93). A stone panel carved with a scene showing an elephant being transported on a boat was recovered near Brahmeshwar temple of Bhubaneswar. A boat is carved below the pedestal of a stone image of Mahisasurmardini temple, also found near the same temple. A panel in the *bhogamandapa* of Sri Jagannath temple at Puri depicts a boat. The *jagamohana* of the Sun temple at Konark has a carving on its parapet delineating the Martanda Bhairavas dancing on a boat. Another sculptural piece believed to be from Konark shows a boat being rowed by four persons (Behera 1972, 115-121; Nigam 1990).

The purpose of the excavation was to obtain archaeological evidence with respect to the items of trade, and means of transportation.

Scope

As explained in the purpose of excavation, the scope was restricted to finding items of exports and imports, the type of vessels used and the foreign lands with which Orissa had trade relations. Also to find a dockyard or a warehouse.

Site

The site has a series of mounds of different heights. The highest is crowned by a 13th century temple dedicated to Lord Siva, locally known as Bhavakundleshwar temple closeby and to its east is a tomb dated to 1193 Anno Hejira, i.e. A.D. 1815.

Trenches

Three trial trenches were laid; one on a mound adjacent to the water channel, and two on a mound abutting the embankment of the channel. The trenches were laid in the horizontal plane of the northern side of the mound about one hundred metres from its edges.

Excavation

The excavation revealed a cultural deposit of two periods, Period I(lower) and Period II(upper). The deposit of Period I yielded two celts, probably of Neolithic age, along with pot sherds. The occurrence of celts could have been due to the digging of ring-wells (Plate 1b). Altogether 13 terracotta ring-wells have been exposed. This period may be dated from *circa* 2 nd cent. B.C. upto 5-6th century A.D. With the end of Period I there is a hiatus. The site was probably abandoned and a long time-gap is marked by the sand deposit of two-metre thickness.

The deposit of Period II can be dated from the 9th century to the early part of 19th century. In the lowest strata of this period jade green Chinese Celadon Ware makes its appearance. In the habitation area no complete structures were encountered. However, in one trench a khondolite stone wall, 1.6 m wide, was met with at a depth of 1.10 m. The stones were of different shapes and size. The remains of a circular structure was exposed in the south-western corner of the trench at a depth of 1.2 cm. This appears to have been a storage bin for grains. Adjacent to the Mughal tomb a burial was excavated. This contained the skeletal remains of a woman(Pl.1a.).

The site yielded pottery of various types, both Indian and foreign varieties. The Indian wares include black, red, grey and black red types. The foreign ware unearthed are; Rouletted ware, knobbed ware, glazed egg white and chocolate brown Arabic wares, glazed brown Burmese ware, moulded ware, stamped ware, decorated ware, kaolin ware, celadon ware and Chinese porcelain.

The most important finds were a shard with an inscription in Kharoshti script with legend Dasatradeva and Khida and a Kushan coin. These show that the site of Manikapatna was in continuous occupation from the 1st cent. A.D.

Rouletted Ware

The Rouletted ware unearthed at this site are of fine fabric, of greyish white colour and made from well levigated clay. The pattern is akin to those obtained from Arikamedu.(Gogte, personal communication). This ware is dated to 2nd-1st century B.C., i.e Pre-Augustan in age (Begle 1986). In Orissa, Rouletted ware was reported earlier from the excavations at Sisuplgarh (Lal 1949) in association with NBP.

Knobbed Ware

The knobbed ware found at this site is grey or greyish black polished, black slipped and red and salt glazed. In coastal Orissa knobbed ware. has been reported from Sisupalgarh (Lal 1949), Jamgada(IAR 1956-57), Lalitagiri, Ratnagiri, Udayagiri, Manamunda and Nehana (Brundtner 1994). This ware is dated to the period from 3rd cent. B.C. to 9th-10th cent. A.D.

Moulded Ware

Manikapatna is the only site in the entire east coast of India to yield this ware in large quantities. Here the moulding appears just under the rim of fine textured well levigated black ware and red ware. In some cases the moulding is also seen on neck and body portions of the pots. This particular ware is generally dated between 50 B.C. to A.D 200. (Bay 1994).

Decorated Pottery

The decorative patterns found on pots are: triangles, rhombuses, scroll, linears and criss-cross lines. The decorations on pottery resemble those found at Sisupalgarh(Lal 149. Wheeler. et at 1949).

Stamped Ware

This is grey in colour and generally. floral motifs are stamped on its surface. This ware has been reported from various sites in India and Sri Lanka. The wares from this site matches well with those found at Arikamedu (Wheeler et al 1946). It is dated to the period from 1st cent. B.C. to 1st cent A.D.

Celadon Ware

The Celadon Ware from this site shows considerable variation in quality and raw material. The best quality celadon ware from this site consists mainly of bowls and dishes with ring base. They also bear painted and fluted decorations. A few green jade pieces are characterized by a crystaline glaze. Some carry underglaze relief decorations such as flowers, fish, etc. The poor quality celadon ware may not have come from China proper. Perhaps they come from Southeast Asia. The Celadon Ware from this site may be dated to 13th-14th century, coinciding with the southern Sung Dynasty (A.D. 1127-1279), and the Yuan Dynasty (1271-1368).

Porcelain

The blue and white porcelain, assignable to Yuan and Ming Dynasties (A.D. 1368 to 1644), is close textured, ivory white and transparent. The brown glazed pieces are apparently fragments of big storage jars or pitchers (Behera 19957).

Other finds

Coins: A Ceylonese coin with the legend "Srimad Sahasamalla", two triangular copper coins of Shah Alam, two East India Company copper coins (Pl.IIa, Mughal coins and one Chinese coin were found during digging.

Medal

A British medal(Pl.IIb) was discovered.

Iron objects

A harpoon spear-head, and fishhooks were noteworthy finds.

Beads

Beads of iron, terracotta (arecanut shaped) and bone, and a few of semi-precious stones, were found.

Objects of daily use

Grinder and pestle, and cart wheels were found.

Figures

One small four-armed image of Vishnu made of chlorite, female miniature head, torso made of khondolite stone were noteworthy finds.

Besides the above, a large number of bangles, conches and terracotta lamps with Tantric images were other important finds.

Conclusion

The site is likely to become a victim of expandng urbanism. Large scale excavations are urgently needed to save the site. The short report given here points to the potentiality of the site.

Acknowldgements

The authors are grateful to Prof K.Paddayya and Shri Sylva Kumar for their valuable constructive suggestions.

REFERENCES

Banerji, R.D. 1930 *History of Orissa,* VolI, Calcutta.

______,1931 *History of Orissa,* VolI, Calcutta.

Basa, K. 1994 *Problems and Perspectives in Archaeology of Orissa,* Occasional Papers 4, Bhubaneswar, Dept. of Anthropology, Utkal University.

Begley, V.1986 From Iron age to Early Historical in South Indian Archaeology in *Studies in Archaeology of India and Pakistan,* edited by Jerom Jacobson, New Delhi. American Institute of Indian Studies pp. 297-321.

_______, 1986 Rouletting and Chattering Decoration in Ancient and Present day pottery in India, *Expedition* 28; pp.44-54.

Behera, K.S.1977 Maritime Trade in Ancient Orissa: in *Sidelights on History and Culture of Orissa* edited by M.N.Das, Cuttack,Vidyapur.

_____1993 Ancient Orissa/Kalinga and Indonesia:The Maritime contacts, *Utkal Historical Research: Journal,* 4: pp. 122-182

______, 1994 Maritime contacts of Orissa: Literary and Archaeological Evidence, *Utkal Historitical Research Journal* 5;pp. 55-70

______, 1995 Chinese Ceramic from Coastal Orissa: Indication of Trade and contact with China, *Orissa Review* (January), pp 4-6.

Brandtner, N. 1994 Archaeology of Western Orissa: Finds from Nehama, *South Asian Archaeology*, 1993 Helsinki, Suomalainen tiedeakatemia, Vol I, pp. 101-115

Deccan College, Pune

D. Pradhan
P. Mohanty
J. Mishra

Dantapura, the Capital of Ancient Kalinga

The identification of Dantapura, the capital city of ancient Kalinga is still debatable. The earlier identifications were based upon literary sources. The present paper tries to identify ancient Dantapura on the basis of the archaeological field-work carried out by the authors between 1993 and 1995 aound Radhanagar region.

Literature

The earliest literary source is Daldavamsa, a Buddhist text from Sri Lanka. It narrates the episode of the tooth relic of the Buddha which was taken to Sri Lanka from Dantapura in the 9th regnal year of King Meghavaranabhaya (A.D. 302-330) of Sri Lanka. The Jatakas like *Kurudhamma Jataka, Kumbhakara Jataka, Chula Kalinga Jataka and Kalinga Bodhi Jataka* allude to Dantapura as the capital city of Kalinga (Fourball 1877-97). The *Mahabharatam* (Udyoga and Dronaparva) refer to Dantapura. Another Buddhist text *Dighanikaya* and Jaina text *Uttaradhyana Sutra* (Charpenties 1922) refer to this city. Pliny also mentions it.

Inscriptions and grants of Ganga rulers (M.Rao 1961-63, Subrhamanyam 1955-56) attest to Dantapura as the capital of Kalinga.

Earlier attempts at identification

Several attempts made during the last two centuries have not satisfactorily solved the problem of identification of Dantapura. The table given below summarises these attempts.The authors of this paper have tentatively identified Radhanagar (corrupt form of Raja Nagara, or the King's City) of Dharmasala area in the newly formed district of Jajpur of Orissa. Their identification is based on the accounts furnished in *Dhatavamsa* and intensive archaeological exploration in and around the vicinity of Dharmasala, Kaima-Janakinagar and Radhanagar area. The site, i.e. Radhanagar area, is located not far from the great Mahayana Buddhist establishment of Ratnagiri, across the bank of the river Brahmani. The site lies on the right bank of Keluo river east of the village Ketapur at a distance of 3 km from it. Keluo is a tributary of the river Brahmani.

The site has yielded a hoard of silver punch marked coins, belonging to the period ranging from 5th cent. B.C. to 3rd cent. A.D. Also a number of Puri-Kushan coins, Kushan gold coins (circa 1st - 2nd cent A.D.), the Gupta gold coins of the archer type and lion slayer type of circa 4th to 5th centuries A.D. onwards as well as a large number of typical Early Muslim Mughal, Maratha and

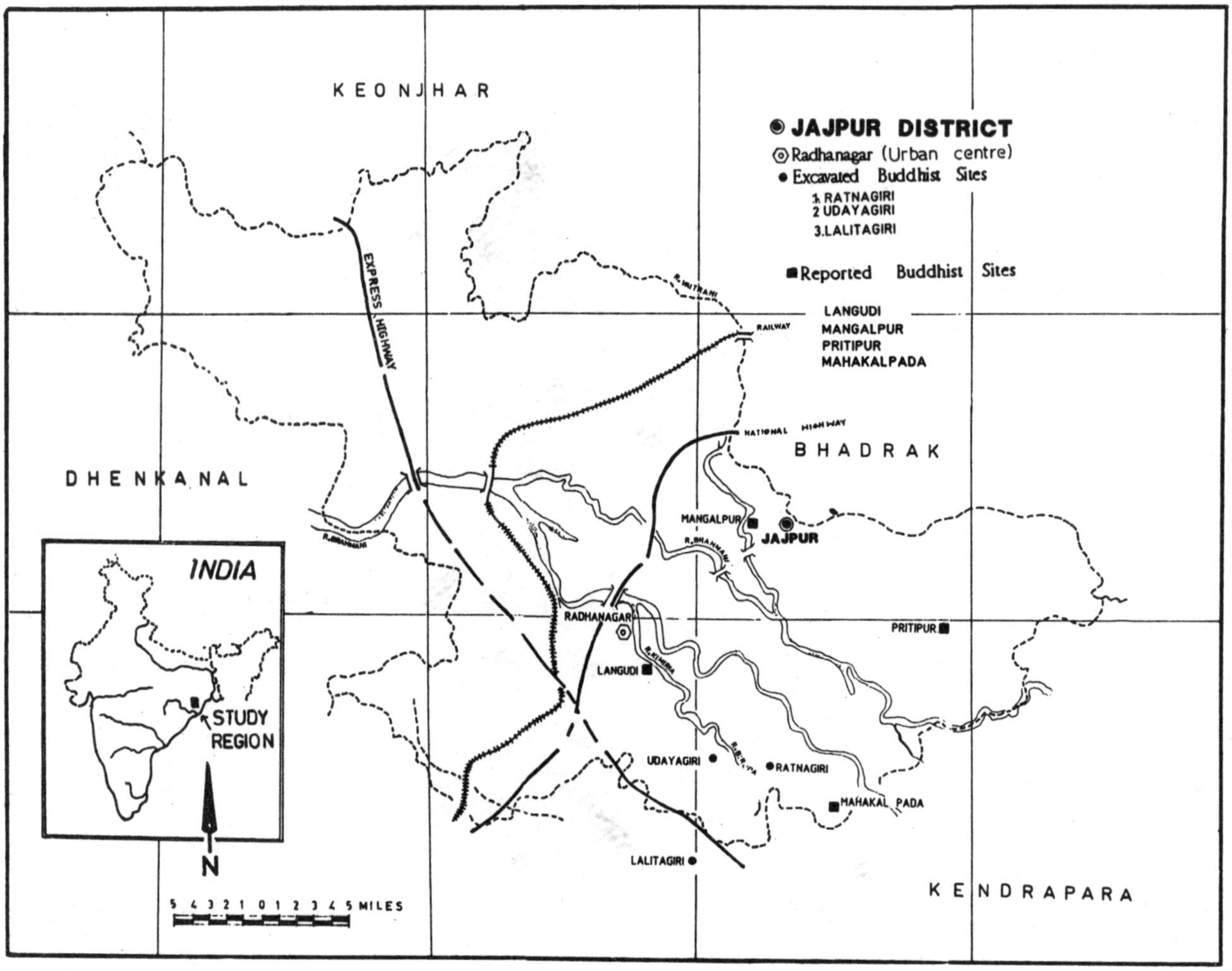

Fig. 1

British coins ranging from circa 12th cent A.D. to 16th to 19th centuries A.D. onwards (Tripathy 1986).

The discovery of hoards of various coins from Radhanagar- Kotapur-Dharmasala area across the right bank of river Keluo numismatically corroborates that Radhanagar was an important international river port and commercial centre.The fact that the river Keluo flows across the recently explored Buddhist sites of Assiah, Majhipara, Chandia, Khandamorei, Ghodka, Kolangiri, Ratnagiri, Langudi, Velayagiri and Lalitgiri and the site is quite close to all these Buddhist sites shows that it was an important Buddhist centre from early centuries B.C. to 3rd century A.D.

The name Kotapura of this site is noteworthy. The name seems to have been derived from the term *kota* meaning fort. This reveals a conclusive connotation of a port or harbour.

Radhanagar has traces of a brick fort enclosing an area of approximately 6 sq. km. and having four imposing gateways facing the cardinal points. The brick walls are 5 m in height. The dimensions of the brick used are: 18 in (L), 12 in (B) and 3.5 inches (thickness). The site plan of the fort resembles that of Sisupalgarh (Lal 1949). The structural remains noticed are: a large number of terracotta wells, monolithic pillars of Khondolite stone and fragments of architectural members.

Table -1

Author	Year in which the attempts were made	Place identified as Dantapura
Cunningham	1871	Rajamahendri [D1]
Hunter	1872	Puri
Levi	1920	Palora of Ptolemry
B.V.Krishna Rao	1929	Amuldalavalsa
Kanungo	1993	Village Danta near Tekkali in Srikakulam

The pottery found on the surface inside the fortified area includes black and red ware, dull red ware, grey ware, fine red ware, etc. (Fig. 2)

As Radhanagar is located in the Dharmasala area of Jaipur district (Orissa), the etymology of the name Dharmasala is of much importance. It will not be erroneous to hypothesize that this name is derived from the Pali 'Dhammasala' meaning the asemblage of Buddghist monks of different sectarian, doctrinal and ideological affilia-

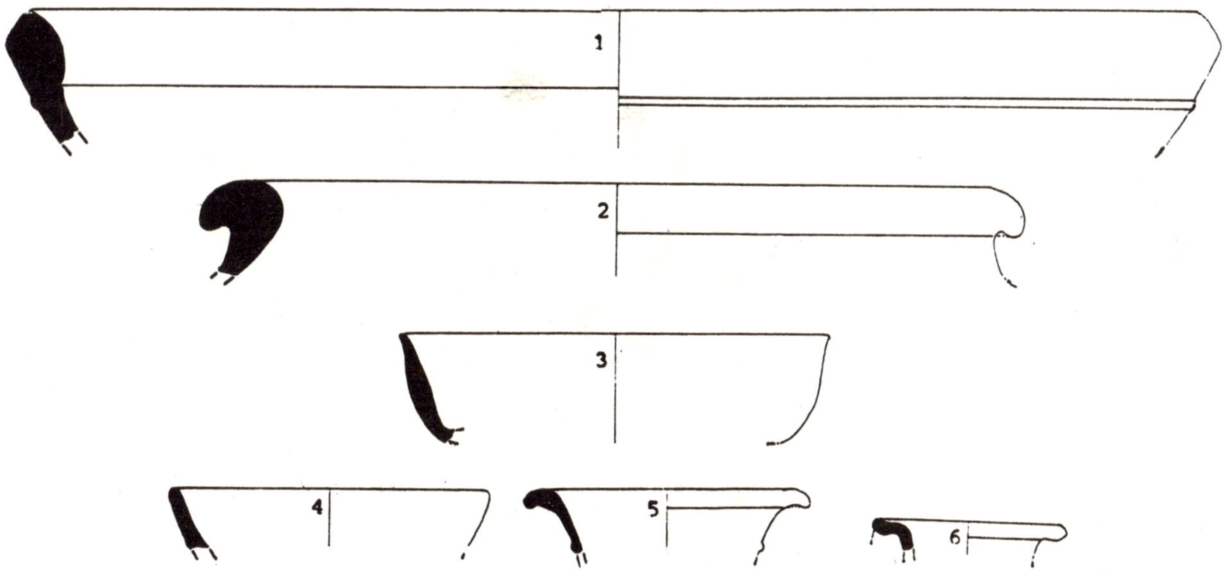

Fig 2.

tion. The Buddhist association with this area is striking. For instance the hamlet called 'Sankha' in this area owes its name to the typical Buddhist word Sangha.

Emperor Asoka is said to have divided the conquered kingdom of Kalinga into two administratve divisions, the southen division with its headquarters at Toshali and the norther division with its headquarters at Radhanagar. Both these cities were embellished with stupas, chaityas, rock-cut elephants and caves.

This fact is borne out by the discovery during reconnaisance in this area of fragments of two railing slabs exquisitly carved with a full lotus medallion in the middle flanked by two half lotus medallions, one at the top and the other at the bottom. These railing pieces resemble the uprights of railings found in the Sanchi and Bharhut stupas. Also an ancient rock-cut elephant of Dhauli prototype was discovered at the foot of Kaima Hills further confirms that Radhanagar was the capital city of the northern half of Kalinga.

In this context the 8th cent. Nagari-Brahmi inscriptions engraved on the back slab of the colossal image of four-armed Jatamukuta Lokesvara at Udayagiri invoking Padmasambabhava, Tara and other Buddhist divinities assume significance. The name Padmasambabhava is believed to be the same as Padmasambhava, the second Dhyaṇi Buddha of Vajrayana cult and the son of Indrabhuti, the king of Udiyana of nothern Orissa. Padmasambhava is believed to have attained perfection or enlightenment at Viraja, identified through epigraphs with present Udayagiri.

On the basis of archaeological findings the Virajamandala can be extended upto Panchakosa, i.e. a radius of 5 kosas or 12 miles to encompass Ratnagiri, Lalitgiri, Udayagiri, Kolangiri, Kaima-Langudigiri, Ghodka, Rangadi , Vajragiri in the south and south-west, Solampur, Khadipada, Tarangsagarpur, Mangalpur, PritipurKapila, Sambala, Erada, Lankadhia, Jahani on the north, with its capital at Radhanagar-Dharmasala.

Radhanagar seems to have been the capital of Bhaumakaras. Jaipur was originally identified with the capital city known as Guhasivapataka, Guhesvarapataka or Guhadevapataka (Mishra 1934, Panigrahi 1981). But this is not satisfactory for the reason that Bhaumakaras being devoted to Buddhism would naturally opt for a site associated with Buddhism and considered sacred. Radhanagar with its assoication with Buddhism was the most suitable choice for them. They chose Radhanagar and made it the capital of their kingdom. They named it after their illustrious predecessor Guhasiva. This is further corroborated by the discovery of copper plate grants of Bhaumakara kings at Neulapur situated close to Radhanagar. The existence of Buddhist and Brahmanical monuments around Radhanagar also lends support to this view.

Conclusion

On the basis of the archaeological evidence the view that Dantapura, the capital of ancient Kalinga, can be tentatively identified with Radhanagar of Dharmasala area in Jajpur District (Orissa). This needs confirmation by extensive archaeological excavation.

Acknowledgement

The many valuable suggestions of Prof K. Paddayya and Dr. K.K. Bara are gratefully acknowledged.

REFERENCES

Charpnties, J. 1922 *Uttaradhyana Sutra* (ed) Uppsala: Appelbergs Boktryekeri Aktiebotag.

Cunningham, A. 1871 *Ancient Geography of India, Buddhist Period*, London: Trubner & Co.

Fourball, V. 1877-97 *The Jataka* (6 vols.) Trubner & Co. London.

Hunter, W.W. 1872 *Orissa*, Vol .1, London.

Kanungo, H. 1933. The Life style of Fishing Communities in Oriya literature (Oriya), in *Sangam Sahitya*, (eds.) K.S.Behera,Cuttack, Dala-rathi Fustakalay.

Krishna Rao, B.V.1929. The identification of Kalinganagara, *Journal of the Bihar and Orissa Research Society,* Vol. XV, pp 105-115.

Lal, B.B. 1949. Sisupalgarh 1948: An Early Historic Fort in Eastern India. *Ancient India,* 5; pp.62-105.

Levis. 1926 *Palor-Dantapura,* translated by Edwards, S.M., Indian Antiquary, Vol. LV, pp.98-99.

Mishra, R. 1934 *Orissa under the Bhauma kara kings,* Calcutta.

Parigrahi, K.C. 1961 *Archaeological Remains at Bhubaneswar,* Calcutta, Orient Longmans.

________, 1981. *History of Orissa,* Cuttack, Kitab Mahal.

Subrahmanyam, R. 1955-56. The Eastern Ganga Grants from Andhavarman, *Epigraphia Indica,* Vol. 31, pp. 202-16

Tripathy, S. 1986. Early and Medieval Coins and Currency system of Orissa, C .300 B.C. to A.D. 1568, Calcutta, Punthi Pustak.

Harish Prusty
Pradeep Mohanty
Jitu Mishra

Deccan College, Pune

Marine Trade in Context of Kushana Settlements of Jammu region

In spite of the fact that no extensive archaeological exploration of Jammu region has been done so far a number of ancient sites here have yielded Kushana pottery. Geographical distribution of such sites is very interesting, as most of them are located along the Chenab river, around the town of Akhnur. The region of Jammu is closely connected with Sialkot, Sakala of the Rigvedic days. And, as shown elsewhere, the Vedic Janas, Indo-Bactrian Greeks and many other people entered the Jammu region through Sakala. Yet the area of Jammu adjoining Sakala has not furnished any evidence suggesting Kushana settlements. Thus, herein an attempt is made to understand the context in which about twentyeight places around Akhnur alone were selected by the Kushanas for habitation.

The Harappan phase of Akhnur is well known and needs no further detail in the present context. The place remained a centre of trade since then. Its fort, whose present structure is of early modern period, was provided with a dockyard keeping in mind the requirement of merchant vessels. The reason is that the River Chenab becomes navigable only at Akhnur after its descent from the hills. Logs, bags containing herbs, etc., are still dropped at the higher ridge and are collected by the agents of traders at this place. It appears that it was this purpose for which the place was popular in early days too. It was an entrepot. Because the reported settlements are very small, these may not have been towns. Most of these are located on high terraces, beyond the flood level of the Chenab. It is, therefore, difficult to imagine that these settlements ever extended beyond their present positions. However, the Kushana rule over the Jammu region is doubtful; it has not yielded so far any Kushana inscription. This suggests that all activities of the Kushana period pertaining to Jammu region are to be understood in relation to trade alone. Even the Valley of Kashmir had witnessed extensive trade during the phase which is conneted with the Kidara Kushana and Gupta rule, because the reported sculptures, etc., from Ushkur, the town connected with Kushanas, are of late Gandharan period, fourth-fifth centuries A.D.

However, when we try to know about the commodity

for which trading settlements were needed then there is reference to only costums whose export to Rome through the port of Barygaza (Broach) is mentioned in the *Periplus of Erythraean sea.* Besides this some early accounts tell about its use by the Hebrew people and the Greeks. At this point one has to take into consideration two factors. In the first place the connection of the Valley of Kashmir with the Silk routes is to be understood properly. Because, if the other goods were carried to the west through that route why costus alone was sent through the sea route. Secondly, we have to take into consideration the quantity of costus, which was exported, to justify many a Kushana *entrepots* of Jammu region. In this regard it is now almost certain that the Central Asian trade route was "first comprehensively described by Marinus of Tyre some two generations later" than the *Periplus of Erythraean Sea.* If so then we have to accept that the early trade of Kashmiri goods was mainly through the sea route *via* River Chenab. Because, as stated above, the export of costus was there since very early days. It was used by the Hebrew priest and Leucus is said to have given in gift one pound of costus to one of his friends. According to Pliny it was treated as very valuable by the Romans; its cost was five *denari* per pound. Thus, we cannot presume that before the popularity of Central Asian trade route the export of costus was not there. Moreover, sea route connection between Western Asia and North-Western India became very popular atleast from the days of Persian occupation of Gandhara region and navigation of the Indus river by a Persian Captain for the purpose of commerce. It was so comfortable and safe that Alexander on his return march had decided to opt only for this one. Further, the belief giving credit to one Hippalus of first century A.D. for the discovery of monsoon winds which gave impetus to Indian ocean trade is now treated as "Roman ethnocentric nonsense." "The people who lived on the shores of northern Indian Ocean knew about monsoon all along, for the same reasons Romans knew about winter and summer. For this part of the Indian ocean, the Monsoonal pattern was more complex than a simple east-west alternation." The export of hill products through the said route is supported from the later accounts also. Accounts of a Muslim author gives a fine description about the system through which Kashmiri goods were sent to Mansura. It says that the peope used to prepare bails of *cast-hundi* (kind of herb). Each bail weighed seven or eight manas. Afterwards the bails were tied with each other and the agents used to float them down sitting on them The journey from foot of he hills to Mansara was completed by such people in about forty days.

Such details lead us to conclude the following :-

(a) The Kushana settlements in Jammu region came into existence mainly due to the marine trade context. They were meant mainly for the collection of small bails of costus from Chenab and their further sail to ports through the Indus river system,etc., for the purpose of export.

(b) The place was in use for the said purpose in early days also. It was perhaps the cost of quality wood costus because of which Persian monarch Darius I had ordered his Captain Scylax of Caryanda to navigate the Indus river system. Interestingly, the said captain is said to have began his voyage from a town of Caspapyara, generally identified with Kashmir. And in the light of this it would not be farfetched to identify the said Kashmiri town with the present day town of Akhnur. The present day people of Akhnur too are mainly of Kashmiri descent. The information again proves that the development of the Akhnur area of Jammu region in early days was mainly because of its importance from the view point of marine trade.

BIBLIOGRAPHY

Curtin, Philip D., 1984, Cultural Trade in World Hisory, *Studies in Comparative World History;* Cambridge Univerity Press, Sydney, p. 97.

Kak R.C., 1923, *Handbook of the Archaeological and Numismatic Sections of the S.P.S. Museum, Srinagar,* Thacher & Spink Co., Calcutta, pp. 131-132.

Indian Archaeology - A Review 1980-81, ASI, pp. 23-26.

Indian Archaeology - A Review 1982-83, ASI, pp. 18-19.

Madhu Bala, 1988 Akhnoor - A Revealing Discovery, *Shiraz,*

Cultural Academy, Vol.1, No.2, Srinagar.

Rapson. E.J.(d) 1962 *The Cambridge History of India,* Vol. 1, S.Chand & Co, Delhi, pp. 335-339.

Singh, Y.B. 1981 From Glory to Glum. The case of Madas Jana, *Journal of Maharaja Gulab Singh Memorial Trust,* Vol. II, No.1, Jammu.

_____, 1990 Silk Route and the Economy of Jammu & Kashmir, *Proceedings of the International Seminar on Kushanas and the Silk Roads,* Kabul, pp. 63-77.

Professor of History,
University of Jammu,
Jammu.

Y.B. SINGH

Vajrasttva

In 1994 the National Museum, New Delhi acquired a small Kashmiri brass relief representing a Tantrik deity (Acc. No.94.12). The exact find spot of the image is not known. However, the image could be dated to 10th-11th Cent. A.D. on stylistic grounds.

The relief shows a four armed male deity seated in *ardhaparyankasana* on a lotus seat supported by two elephants. He holds an arrow in his back right hand, the front right carries a *vajra* against the chest; his back left hand holds a bow and the front left carries a bell resting against his thigh. He wears a lower garment *(dhoti)* and is adorned with a crown and various ornaments, such as, a beaded necklace, armlets, anklets and ear-rings. The eyes and the *tika* on forehead are marked by inlaid silver. Four female deities are shown around the main deity carrying some attributes in their hands which are too indistinct to be identified as the relief is defaced (Pl.1).

As far as the identification of the deity is concerned, the gesture of two hands holding a *vajra* against the chest and a *ghanta* resting on the left thigh of the seated figure suggest that the relief represents Vajrasattva as this gesture and attribute in Indian context is typical of Vajrasattva. The four female divinities around Vajrasattva could be the representation of the four dancing goddesses known as *Lasya, Nritya, Maya and Gita.* In a few other cases these four goddess have been represented around Vajrasattva (Pal 1952 : Fig 52). The form of four-armed Vajrasattva is rare in Indian art. He is usually depicted with two arms. His images have been reported in fairly large number from the various Buddhist sites, viz. Ratnagiri (Mitra, 1981, Vol.I, pl. XCACCXLA), Achchyutrajpur (Mitra, 1981, Fig. 54-58), Nalanda (Saraswati, 1977, Fig. 156-59), Sarnath (Huntington, 1985, p. 460, Fig. 20.13) Salempur (Saraswati, 1977, Fig. 156-59), Sukhbaspur (Bhattasali, Pl. IIIa, p.24) etc. Another known image of four armed Vajrasattva, cast in brass, also comes from Kashmir region (Schroeder, 1981, Fig. 28c, p.153). He is shown as seated in *ardhaparyankasana,* against a flaming aureole, on a lotus throne supported by two lions and a human figure. the attributes and the gesture of hands are shown in similar fashion like the one acquired by the National Museum and discussed above. He wears a *dhoti,* chased ornaments and a crown bearing the effigies of seated Dhyani Buddhas. The eyes and *urna* are marked by inlaid silver. On stylistic grounds the image has been dated to 10th-11th century A.D.

Various forms of Vajrasattva are known from the Tantrik works but they are mostly two-armed. The *Guhyasamaja Tantra* refers to a form ofVajrasattva with two hands bearing an axe and a club (Bhattachaya, 1967, p.103). However, the visual representation of this type has not been found. In Satachakravarti Mandala, Vajrasattva is the central deity and holds a vajra and vajra-ghanta in his hands (Bhattacharya, 1972, p. 79). The Advayavajrasamgraha describes him as two-armed and one-faced. He holds in his two hands the vajra and vajra marked ghanta (Shastri, 1927, p.41). A four armed-form of Vajrasattva is known from the Vajradaka Tantra, but with four faces (Bhattacharya, 1974,p.18). Vajrasattva is also represented in Yab-Yum form (Bhattacharya, 1958, p.74-75) which is kept and worshipped seretely. In this form he is closely associated with his Sakti.

Vajrasattva, the Buddha of supeme intelligence was widely revered deity in Vajrayana phase as evidenced from the number of images reported from Bihar, Bengal Orissa and Kashmir. Vajrasattva, the sixth Dhyani Buddha of the Buddhist pantheon is also cnsidered to be the priest of five Dhyani Buddhas by the Nepalese Buddhists.

Therefore, the brass relief acquired by the National Museum is certainly an invaluable addition to its collection.

REFERENCES

Bhattacharya, B, 1958, *The Indian Buddhist Iconography,* Calcutta, p.75.

_____, (ed.), 1967 *Guhyasamaja Tantra,* Gaikwad's Oriental Series o.53, p. 103.

_____,(ed.), 1972, *Nishapannayogavali of Abhayakargupta* Gakwad's Oriental series No.109, Baroda p. 79.

Bhattacharya, D.C. 1974, *Tantric Buddhist Iconographic Sources,* New Delhi, p.18.

Bhattasali, N.K. , 1972, Iconography of *Buddhist and Brahmanical Sculptures in the Dacca Museum,* Delhi, pl.III.a, p.24.

Huntington, S.L. 1985, Art of *Ancient India,* New York, p.460, fig. 13.

Mitra, D. 1978, *Bronzes from Achutrajpur,* New Delhi, fig. 54,55,55,56,57 & 58.

_____, 1981, *Ratnagiri,* Vol.I, New Delhi, plates XC.A, CCXLA. Pal, P.1978 The *Sensuons Immortals,* Los Angeles, Fig. 52.

Saraswati, S.K. 1977, Tantrayana Art-An Album , Calcutta,Fig.156, 157, 159.

Schroeder, U.V., 1981, Indo-Tibetan Bronze, Hong Kong, Fig. 28. C,p.153.

Shastri, H (ed.), 1927 Advajavajrasamgraha, Gaikwad's Oriental Series No.XL, p.4.

National Museum, Janpath,
New Delhi-110011

JITENDRA NATH

HERITAGE MANAGEMENT
Ancient Monuments, Causes of Decay

What is a monument ? For conservation purposes, it is defined as a public or private building more than one hundred years old which commemorates an historic event, person or represents an archetype of its age. Therefore, it is a cultural heritage and needs to be preserved at all costs

A monument is affected by two causes.

I. Natural II. Man-made.

1. **Natural:** The natural causes can again be subdivided as under:

(i) Earthquakes and floods.

(ii) Lightning.

(iii) Natural wear and tear.

(iv) Growth of vegetation or trees.

(v) Water-logging and erosion of soil.

(vi) Birds' nuisance.

(i) *Earthquakes and floods:* Neither the earthquakes are predictable nor ancient monuments have been constructed with a view to safeguard them from damages of earthquakes. Recent case of Latur in Osmanabad district of Maharashtra state comes to mind where extensive damage was caused to monuments. At times, due to heavy rains, floods cause extensive damage. In the former case, the monuments begin to leak or even fall, some become dilapidaed, while in the latter case the slush and earth etc. get filled in every nook and corner ; foundations sink, parts of monuments bulge/tumble down, develop cracks or even get completely buried.

(ii) *Lightning:* Lightning when it strikes is deadliest in its form. It completely destroys or affects portions of the monument which are in its path.

(iii) *Natural wear and tear:* Nature is also playing its role in causing damage to the monuments in the form of wear and tear. Of the stones, bricks, mortar, wood and paintings, etc. due to hot, wet and cold conditions, the colour of stones/bricks in particular changes, wooden members are attacked by termite, paintings fade and or develop fungi. The monuments which are close to river beds/sea shores, have to bear the brunt of their vagaries. In the case of monuments which are in close vicinity of river beds, heavy winds, particularly during summer months, cause damage by abrasive action of sand.Ultimately it results in disfigurement of sculptures and other architectural members destroying its historical background completely. In the case of monuments situated on sea shore, disfigurement caused by sand and salt ladden winds is enormous. Due to wear and tear of stones, loss of strength in binding materials, development of crevices,result. When it rains, the rain water gets in these crevices and causes gradual damage to the architectural members in it.

(iv) *Growth of vegetation and trees:* Over the years it has been closely observed that two types of trees grow on the monuments, viz. Banyan and Peepal both belonging to Ficus family. On careful study it is seen that innumerable tiny seeds of both these trees are borne by wind and deposited in the cracks and crevices of monuments, where they begin to grow. Now dust, too, plays its own role in giving them protection and on first shower or in the wet weather of coastal area, the seeds germinate and start growing practically at an average length of 1/2 to 1 cm per day, so far as its root is concerned. The roots find their passage by penetrating deep in the crevices growing gradually to colossal sizes, ultimately displacing the members or even engulfing the monument. The trees also grow around the monuments. The growth of vegetation is more during monsoon. This too, if not removed promptly, causes damage to the monument.

(v) *Waterlogging and erosion of soil:* During the months of monsoon, waterlogging around the monuments is quite common, more particularly, when these are situated nearly cultivated fields. For better crops, the farmers prefer water logging and many a times, natural flow of water is diverted to suit individual requirements. This results in flow of water in one direction with great velocity, causing erosion of earth. Apart from this, when there are heavy rains, the earth gets automatically washedoff with the flow of water. Water logging also takes place during floods. Due to these factors, water percolates down below in the foundations causing gradual sinking; bulging takes place and cracks develop particularly in lintels, portions of the monuments which do not get sunlight and as such are apt retain moisture. This results in encrustation of moss, lichen, fungi, algai on the members of the monuments causing disfigurment.

(vi) Bird's, nuisance: the birds, viz. pigeons, bats and owls in particular, find an easy and safe abode in monuments. Their cobwebs, urine in particular, cause disfigurement and damage to the fabric of the materials which have gone in its construction. Apart from this the stinking smell emanating from their urine makes a tourist to walk out of the precints of the monument, howsoever the monument may be rich in architecture.

2. Manmade

(i) Encroachment and disfigurement.

(ii) Industrialisation.

(iii) Dams and canals.

(iv) Mining and quarrying.

(v) Pilferage of architectural masterpieces.

(vi) Lack of public amenities.

(vii) Approach roads and litigation.

(i) *Encroachment and disfigurement:* Today the increase in population has taken toll of land of monuments in the form of encroachment. Law and order authorities are unable to control this for obvious reasons. The result is that the monuments are practically covered from all sides with concrete jungle except its approach path. People have little regard for the heritage of the country. They go on writing/scratching on the walls, damage the architectural masterpieces, even go to the extent of sharpening their axes on plinth and wall stones.

(ii) *Industrialisation:* Due to fast industrialisation in the country, the gases emitted by these industries generate pollution which in turn is taking its toll of world famous Taj Mahal in particular and other monuments situated near industrial areas in each district. Although there are stringent rules for controlling pollution but the rules are hardly implemented.

(iii) *Dams and canals:* Due to increase in population demand for water has increased ,for cultivation purposes in particular. To meet this requirement dams are constructed for storage of water. To irrigate lands, water is supplied through a net work of canals. If the monuments are situated in the catchment area of the dams or in the way of canals, these have either to be transplanted or allowed to be submerged. In case the monuments are situated near the dams/canals, the water table increases resulting in dampness, water-logging, around the monuments, affecting its foundations.

(iv) *Mining and quarrying:* The construction activity in the country is on the increase for residential and shopping complexes, industries, roads, dams and canals. To meet with the requirement of construction materials, heavy mining and quarrying activities are continuing to extricate stones from mother earth. The effects of dynamite for mining and quarrying are having tell-tale effects on the monuments. These activities can also be termed as degenerating process.

(v) *Pilferage of architectural masterpieces:* Due to enormous heritage of the Nation lying unattended in far flung areas, persons have indulged in nefarious activities for petty benefits by taking out masterpieces from monuments for sale/display in drawing rooms of high society. This results in ugly outlook at the monument as no other sculpture can be inserted in its original place.

(vi) *Lack of public amenities:* Today the tourist traffic, local as well as from abroad,is on the increase. There is, by and large complete lack of public amenities,viz.

urinals and toilets near the monuments. Due to non-availability of such facilities, nuisance is created either on the walls of the monument or nearby.

(vii) *Approach roads and litigation:* Many of the monuments do not have any approach road and demarcated boundaries, problems multiply when conservation works are to be undertaken at such monuments as one has to pass through cultivable fields. First and foremost difficulty is faced in transporting tools and plants and materials like stone, bricks, lime, sand, wood etc. Storage becomes another problem in the absence of demarcated boundaries of the monuments as the areas have been encroached in the past. When the proposal is put up for acquisition of land/vacation of encroachment, it takes year to materialise and when it finally materialises, the acquisition of land in particular, is challenged in the Court of Law resulting in stay order. This delays in taking up not only conservation works but also in developing the environment for betterment.

So, in short, conservation of monuments is essential for the preservation of the country's heritage.

Here the question naturally rises - what is conservation? Conservation is not mere preservation where the affected portion is repaired with modern materials. It is something more. The most important fact is the charcter of the monument. The repairs executed should be in the same character or tune so that a person looking it will find it hard to distinguish between what is actually conserved and what is not. this is not necessary in preservation.

Rana Park, Ahmedabad-380061

D. I. Krishnani

Marketing Heritage - Corporate Involvement

The post-Independence scenario in our country is dominated by urbanization, industrialization, emphasis, to a large extent, on science and technology, and now even on informatics; and all this has had a tremendous impact on not just individual values, but on our systems of beliefs and identities as a community. Today with the influx of free-market economy we are entering into yet another era of accelerated economic growth. Nigel Harris, as we all know, has predicted that we are poised to compete even with Singapore.

On this background the question that we need to ask ourselves is whether in our growth-planning are we really conscious that the path we are following will not be deterimental to our national culture? A lot of our neighbours in the Asia-Pacific region are faced with a similar question! Had this been clear, not just to us here, but to the world at large then the UNESCO would not have needed the "World Decade for Cultural Development" to revitalize world over awareness of the role culture has in the entire process of development planning. A report published in 1989 by the Ministry of Environment entitled, "Guidelines for Environmental Impact Assessment of New Towns", mentions, in the context of Bhubaneshwar, how important it is to draw up in advance, guidelines for the promotion of (development) activities without deteriment to the preservation and conservation of cultural heritage. But our experience, of Mumbai city, very often is exactly the opposite. On a number of occasions we announce megaprojects without going into any kind of assessment of the heritage of the region and naturally it leads to avoidable confrontations between authorities and cultural activists.

Our observations, especially on the philosophy of heritage preservation, are intended to provide a backdrop on which the Corporations too could do some introspection.

Culture and Cultural Heritage has a special significance today and world attention is focused on it as we are marching towards the 21st Century. It has been truthfully said that the next century is going to judge us by not what we have preserved but what we have destroyed either negligently or deliberately. On the global scene, the UNESCO has set the mood over a decade back by identifying World Heritage Monuments.

Countries with much lesser heritage than our own are involved with preserving and propagating their antiquity and we, with the longest living tradition are still not firm on our legs.

Heritage in all its connotations is a collective contribution and hence a collective responsibility of a phenomenon we call 'Society'. An understanding of this Society and its societal connotations begins with the very basic question our Upanishadic seers asked

= Who am I ?
= Whether am I going?

Greek philosopher Socrates too asked a somewhat similar question, "How should one live?" Socrates declared that the "unexamined life is not worth living." Going by these diktats, we as society need to examine whether or not we have an IMAGE worth living upto.

Someone else too, Maurice Godeliar, wrote "Human beings in contrast to other social animals do not just live in society, they produce a Society in order to live in".

In an anthropological prespective, therefore, we cannot know ourselves except by knowing ourselves in relation to others. The interactive behaviour of our social life understands "Sociality" as "something people do things with, to, and in respect of each other, using means that we can describe - as "Cultural". In a sense we produce a relationship to live as a Society. This largely creates our identity.

While resolving that, "Every culture represents a unique and irreplaceable body of values since each people's traditions and forms of expression are its most effective means of demonstrating its presence into the world", the UNESCO was echoing the universally accepted principle that man is basically a product of his environment both physical and cultural. And it is this that assigns an identity to the community or a group. This identity of a community is reflected in the legacy it leaves behind in the entire evolutionary process and this evidence is in three distinct forms. These are:

1. Tangible : i.e., in the shape of built-up heritage such as architecture;

2 Intangible : i.e., in the form of traditions, customs and manners.

3. Expressive : i.e., language, music, literature, etc.

All such tangible and intangible relics, which we call heritage serve as tools and sources for an empathic understanding of the past. These remain as points of reference, as data base, as an anchorage of physical and emotional nostalgia in the entire process of cultural evolution. Herein we seek our identity, in a sense a historic continuity which helps maintain a balance between changing metaphors and static values Preservation of this heritage in all its connotations is, today, a significant aspect of a well thought out "Culture Management Policy".

Mary Zurbachen of Indonesia, at the recently concluded symposium in Tokyo on "Culture in Development and Globalization" said, " To conclude, I think that we are actually on the way to new and insightful understanding of culture's role in development in the Asia-Pacific Regions. In the next century, developmentalists will need to acknowledge traditional belief-systems as reflecting valid systems of knowledge. Traditional adaptations to the environment will be examined for their wisdom and understood as alternative solutions to professionals seeking to enhance international and inter-cultural cooperation, perhaps we can help culture to be viewed more as an asset than as a hindrance in the development process by national Governments. This is a most worthy goal".

It is an opportunity to participate in this activity of reaching the goal Mary is talking about, that the Corporations need to consider stepping-in in a big way.

Maslows theory of the hierarchy of needs propagates

that the highest state is that of self-actualization, i.e. the need of an individual *to be socially acceptable.* This, the authors maintained, can easily be applied to corporates since all professionally managed organizations wish to significantly establish their presence in the market, and hence it is essential for them to recognize their duty to the Society in which they operate.

Generally it is the "User-pays" that suggests marketing. Before, however, we take off from here it may be relevant to paraphrase the different elements of the heritage movement.

We the enlightened citizens, ungrudgingly accept that all forms of heritage need to be preserved/conserved as essential facets of our personality or the personality of our community - our country. The objectives of any conservation movement are in four stages :

1. Establish standards for historic preservation;

2. Identification and documentation of significant historic resources;

3. Education of general public about the value of preservation; and

4. Assist in historic preservation efforts by providing assistance to public and or private preservation agencies.

Neverheless, the movement is also beset with obstacles. The main obstacles are:-

1. Ignorance of the cultural, emotional, historic and exclusive value of the resource;

2. Overrated commercial value, more out of self interest;

3. Lack of proper legislation; and

4. Inadequate appreciation of the discipline of conservation both from the architectural as well as restoration point of view.

5. And can we overlook the political considerations?

But besides these obstacles, there are other factors which have adversely affected heritage -

1. Absence of patronage and consequent dwindling of interest in pursuing and/or documenting various expressions of heriage, e.g. today the number of reciters of the Vedas has dwindled to such an extent that the entire process would die out if care to train more people is not taken or even to record what exists.

2. Physical destruction due to neglect especially of built-up heritage.

3. Alteration of the property's environmental setting, and

4. Introduction of visual, audible or atmospheric elements which are incongruent.

There is a massive ignorance about what heritage resource means today. The Heritage Conservation Committee at the Bombay Municipal Corporation receives several proposals in respect of heritage districts which are not only inconsistent with the concept of Cultural Heritage but demonstrate a phenomenal misunderstanding of the entire exercise.

Sometimes, the mode of presentation of these Corporate representatives reminds me of a statement made by Bertrand Russel almost six decades ago :

"Men in the past were often parochial in space, but the dominant men of our age are parochial in time. They feel for the past a contempt that it does not deserve and for the present, a respect that it deserves still less".

This was primarily the reason for my remark that the philosophy of heritage preservation needs to be re-stated for a clearer understanding of the problem.

Sponsorship per-seis an age old concept and has been practised by all societies all over the world. In our own country the innumerable monuments were often sponsored by corporate bodies, e.g. a Sanchi *Torana* is the donation of the guild of ivory-carvers. Patronage of the arts and culture has left permanent impressions of personalities in history like Vikramaditya for his patronage of Kalidasa, or Akbar for his *karkhanas* of art. This idea has been consistently practised in our country and in our own city by several Corporations. Then, if sponsorship is in existence what is it that we mean by 'Marketing' heritage?

In our area of Museum and Heritage the term has gained hesitant acceptance during the past two decades.

In a pioneering book published in 1975, its author Philip Kotier said.

"Marketing is the analysis, planning, implementation, and control of carefully formulated programmes designed to bring about voluntary exchange of values with target markets for the purpose of achieving organizational objectives".

This adequately explains the basis of the assumption that corporate involvement would accelerate a widespread and sustainable interest as against a 'top-down' central agency control. In other words what we need today is a proactive involvement which would mean.

1. A motivated and conscious activity;

2. Planning a forward looking strategy to achieve a "desired- goal", and

3. Involving and mobilizing others with similar visions into significant realities.

All these strategies imply that we are talking a lot more about heritage than mere passive "preservation". Even the UNESCO through all its three conventions, one Declaration and twelve recommendations has sharply focused on two aspects:

1. Preservation of a country's heritage; and

2. Linking it with tourism to benefit the country's economy.

Tourism, today is included in the list of thirty-six priority industrial sectors which are likely to be influenced by the economic liberalisation which is expected to induce new technological expertise and innovative ideas. Yet, the term Cultural Tourism still remains to be adequately defined. All I am reminded today is the remark my friend Robertson Collins made at a US/ ICOMOS Conference. He said, "Highly professional scholars and genial dedicated amateurs have strong views about the potential of Tourism, the threat of Tourism, the cost of Tourism and the profits to be derived from Tourism. Everyone seems to have an opinion on how it should be praised, damned, managed, changed, channeled or eliminated". Having spent three long decades at the Museum, I for one cannot think of Tourism as an activity sans heritage. In fact tourism is both, our PR and Marketing agency.

UNESCO's launching of the World Decade of Cultural Development in 1988 was also intended to evaluate "Effects of Tourism on Culture and Environment" in nine countries of the Asia-Pacific region. We are awaiting the report. Tourism has today branched off into Eco-Tourism, Sustainable Tourism and now into Endemic Tourism.

These and several other Heritage areas anticipate Corporate involvement in various ways. But despite their involvement, there are some prevailing misconceptions in their mind about either the need or the extent of their involvement.

Those commonly quoted are that business must alienate from society and that the additional costs would make business unprofitable.

Yet, the opinions collected by the Great Britain based, 'Association for Business Sponsorship of the Arts' succinctly summarizes the present trends. We will hear just two opinions:

".......We do not believe that the future development of sponsorship rests upon the "Good citizenship approach". It has to be part of a company's marketing or public affairs strategy."

Or

".....every bit of publicity that my company receives through the medium of its arts sponsorship is valuable to us in enhancing our reputation."

Commentators have analyzed Corporations in three Categories which reflect their outlook:

1. Economic Isolation : A self-centered outlook inclined towards profit maximization instead of wealth-maximization.

2. Social Altruism : Considers impact of business policies on Society it serves - contributor to stability - strength-harmony.

3. Trusteeship : A mid-way concept balancing both, besides generating wealth and paying taxes, it should aim at wider social contribution in a planned manner by weighing the pros and Cons.

The objective of today's marketing strategy is not just restricted to making funds available. It needs to involve :-

Personnel,

Technology,

Training;and

Academic facilities and much more.

Corporations all over the world are being involved in major cultural events. But while doing so Paul Elickes, SCM's President's comments still stand out as he says : "I have heard more than one company say that concern for the arts as such is the guiding force behind its contributions. You won't hear that from us. We have not sponsored the Treasures of early Irish Art at the Metropolitian or any of the other eight major exhibitions over the past four years out of the goodness of our hearts. We do it because it is good for the Arts, it's good for the millions who get pleasure viewing great works of Arts and not least it's good for the SCM Corporation". As against this we have often been confronted by the

"*Manastambha* syndrome. Instead of being just the 'pillar of glory' it tends to become "pillar of my glory".

Paradoxically, globalisation has introduced excessive exteriorisation leading to the problem of "existential vacuum". Simultaneously, with "skill orientation" there is need to infuse "value orientation". Even the two reports of UNESCO on global education showed shift of emphasis from "Learning to do" (1962) to "Learning to be" (1982).

It is accepted that those Corporations which are committed to a social cause alone can project an image of being a professionally well managed body. Corporations too need an "IMAGE" of their own and for this reason they need to balance their own business and their societal responsibility.

The influx of foreign based Corporation with their understanding of a Corporate image is bound to make the locals look small unless they make timely attempt to elevate their own social status.

A series of symposia held recently in Nangkhai, Hanoi and Tokyo on "Culture in Development and Globalisation" clearly suggest that we are neither the first nor alone in holding a dialogue on this topic. That we have finally begun is in itself a good sign.

Our Development planners have adopted the concept of ecologically sustainable development. I hope we will be able to pursuade the planners to add the concept of "Heritologically Sustainable Development".

Former Director
Prince of Wales Museum, Bombay

SADASHIV GORAKSHKAR

BOOK REVIEWS

S.P. Gupta, *The Indus-Saraswati Civilization : Origins, Problems and Issues,* Pratibha Prakashan, Delhi, 1996, pp. xiv + 204; Figs 49, Plates 23, Price : Rs.750/-.

Here is yet another book on the Harappan Civilization. But this time by an author who is known for his insight into the subject of Harappan Studies. This publication is in many ways much different from others available in the market.

The very title, the Indus-Saraswati, is distinct since it emphasises the fact that the Harappan Civilization was the gift of not one river alone, the Indus, but of two rivers, the Indus and the Saraswati. And this is now amply clear from not only the discovery of larger number of sites in the Saraswati basin than in the Indus basin. The available data show that the basins of the rivers of the Saraswati System, which includes the old beds of the Sutluj, Ghaggar, Drishadvati, Yamuna, etc., had around 700 sites while the basins of the rivers of the Indus System account only around 200 sites. The author is, therefore, fully justified in using a term which reflects the ground realities. Moreover, quite a few of the Saraswati basin sites embody the remains of earlier than the Mature phase of the Harappan Civilization, for example, Kalibangan and Banawali. The recent-most discovery of Kunal, a site in Distt. Hissar, about 15 km from Banawali on the Saraswati, has yielded the remains of materials going back to the 4th millennium B.C. The present work has given details of this epoch-making discovery.

The book also gives the details of the results of the ongoing excavations conducted by R.S. Bisht at Dholavira, the most prominent Harappan site in Rann of Kachchh, Gujarat. Here also there is a huge deposit of the so-called Pre-or Early Harappan Culture which too goes back to the 4th millennium B.C.

Dr. Gupta has done a great service to the Harappan archaeology by bringing together at one place the details of Kunal and Dholavira, not only because these are new discoveries but because these discoveries prove beyond doubt that the roots of the Harappan Civilization go back to the 4th millennium. Fortunately, the recent excavations conducted at Harappa by R.H. Meadow and Mark Kenoyer have proved exactly the same—the beginning of Harappan township goes back to the 4th millennium. The excavators of Harappa have now brought to light around 4 m of deposit below the so-called Early Harappan or Kot Dijian levels; the deposit is marked by various levels of mud and mud-brick houses, hand-made black on red ware and copper objects. We may recall that the early Harappan deposit at Harappa had given us several dates ranging between 3300 B.C. and 3100 B.C. We will not be surprised if the Ravi Culture, the name given by the excavators to the pre-Early Harappan or pre-Kot Dijian deposits at Harappa, goes back to the fifth millennium. G.F. Dales's excavations at Bala Kot had also indicated that the early levels go back to the 4th millennium. Dr. Gupta, therefore, rightly maintains that the antiquity of the Harappan Civilization is as old as the Mesopotamian Civilization.

Dr. Gupta has also highlighted the so far dimly appreciated phase of the Harrapan Civilization called 'Transition from the Early Harappan to the Mature Harappan'. The excavations of Dholavira has revealed the existence of this phase in Stage III of R.S. Bisht's excavations at the site. It is to be given around 200 years. Jim Shaffer, G.L. Possehl and a few others were not prepared to give more than 100 years for this phase. One must note that it is from this phase that we have typical pictographic Harappan seals but without writing. Weights and measures also appear in this phase. Graffiti similar to Harappan characters appear in large numbers and at various sites, e.g. Rehman Dheri.

These are not the only contributions of this book. The book deals with several problems and issues of Harappan archaeology, including the most debatable issue of Harappan and Vedic commonality. For this he quotes extensively from the writings of Bhagwan Singh, the author of the famous and most authentic book entitled *The Vedic Harappans* (Aditya Prakashan, New Delhi, 1995). He also quotes R.S. Bisht in this regard. It is now more than clear that the Vedic people were not the primitive nomadic pastoralists, as once Max Muller thought, they were in fact fully aware of the craft specialisations of the urban culture. Since there is no other pre-600 B.C. urban culture in India except the Harappan, there is no way out but to accept the proposition that the Harappan and the Vedic were neither two different culture-complexes nor the earlier preceded the latter. The Myth of Aryan Invasion of the Harappan towns has also been dealt with so also many other controversial issues, such as the presence of true domesticated horse at several Harappan sites including Mohenjodaro; Kalibangan, Ropar, etc.

The author then deals with the problem of origins of the Indus-Saraswati Civilization. He rightly observes that the birth of no civilization lies in any single place or single factor because civilization is a process and not an event. He then identifies various sites from Baluchistan through Haryana, each one of which evolved some thing or the other in terms of craft specialisation which was gainfully used by the emerging civilization. It took around 1000 years to integrate all these cultural elements into an urban process the components of which were villages and townships interacting with each other and supporting the growth of Harappan Civilization. The author rightly observes that the effective long-distance trade with West Asia was the out come of urbanization of India and not vice-versa. In this context the author has discussed in details the views of various authors based upon new discoveries on the subject of long distance trade between India, the Persian Gulf countries and Mesopotamia. The author has pointedly discussed the problems of Indian colonies in Mesopotamia and the integration of Indian and Mesopotamian people.

Dr. Gupta is a leading archaeologist of the Harappan studies and the present work certainly proves beyond doubt the penetrating eye with which God has endowed him. The plates are beautifully printed but the text-paper should have been better. In any case, the book is a tribute to the scholarship of Dr.Gupta. Everyone is bound to benefit from it.

V.N. Misra

Gregory. L. Possehl, *The Indus Age: The Writing System,* Oxford & IBM Publishing Co., New Delhi, 1996 pp. xvi + 244 Price : Not mentioned.

The book is the latest publication on a very special subject of the Indus studies by a well known scholar and authority on the Indus-Saraswati Civilization—Gregory Possehl. It deals with a subject about which the less said the better: the Indus script. Till date there are around thirty known claims of having this script deciphered and many of them are so opposed to each other—Indo-Aryan *vis-a-vis* Dravidian, numerals *vis-a-vis* astronomical signs that to the reviewer all these claims are suspect. Possehl has, therefore, at the very outset said that "all of them have to be judged to be failures, at least insofar as can be proved by independent tests. This book is not an another attempt at decipherment." Then why this book ? The author says "It is in-depth survey of the nature of Indus writing and a comprehensive review of the most prominent decipherent attempts". He is right. Not that others had not given historigraphy and critical appraisal of the attempts to decipher the Indus script, for example, B.B. Lal had done exactly the same in an article published in *India's Contribution to World Thought and Culture* (1972) edited by Lokesh Chandra et. al. Asko Parpola had done it in *"Recent Developments in the study of the Indus Script in Sind through the centuries"*, 1981 (Ed. Hamid Khuhro), but undoubtedly the present work is not only 'the most comprehensive' one but also the one which takes into account the latest attempts as well as the latest opinions of those who are in a position to guide the scholars engaged in this effort, for example those of Kamil V.Zvelebil. Even, on so many other counts this book is a welcome addition to those who have interest in the study of the Indus-Saraswati Civilization as a whole.

Ashwani Asthana

Dilip K.Chakrabarti and Nayanjot Lahiri, *Copper and its Alloys in Ancient India,* Munshiram Manoharlal Publishers Pvt. Ltd., New Delhi 1996, pp. 228, 30 figures, 4 maps, numerous charts, Price: Rs.475/-.

The present book *"Copper and its Alloys in Ancient India"* offers a "synthesis of available geological, archaeological, literary and ethnographic data "of the metal copper and its alloys under consideration in a cogent manner.

The authors are very well aware of the pitfalls in ore-artefact correlation in the absence of sufficient data that is required under various parameters for a plausible conclusion in this regard. The authors did well to avoid it.

Introducing the subject the authors recount the achievements and publications of previous researchers - R.B. Foote, V.A. Smith, E.Mackey, John Marshall, P.Neogi, M.Sanaullah, B.B. Lal, K.T.M. Hegde and others besides drawing heavily on the publications of the Geological Survey of India. They conduct us from protohistoric to pre-Industrial India. Thus they rely on the long "tradition of academic research".

In the chapter "The Geographical Distribution of ores and old workings" types of ores, their distribution in the subcontinent and its adjacent countries are highlighted. In the matter of alloying materials with copper, tin, lead, zinc and arsenic appear to be the minerals in general. Their provenance, mining and extracting methods are discussed.

By far the longest chapter is the one dealing with archaeological data with a map, forty one charts and thirty figures covers more than one hundred pages. The subject is dealt with under convenient sub-headings, viz. pre-Indus phase, Indus Civilization, Late Harappan, Neolithic - Chalcolithic times, Copper Hoards, Protohistoric Iron Age, Historical sites and miscellaneous objects. Pre-Indus phase is represented in India by Ganeshwar period dating to 4th mellinnium B.C.

Textual evidences for the copper and copper alloys is gathered from the *Sruti,* i.e. Vedas, and *Smriti* literature: *Rig* and *Atharva Vedas* being of the first category *Grhya* and *Srauta sutras*, *Manu* and *Vishnu smritis, jatakas etc.*

For later times Kautilya's *Arthasastra,* alchemic literature such as *Charaka samhita* and *Silpasastras* come handy. In this chapter terminology and techniques for copper and copper alloys are discussed. Metallurgical details and religious usages of copper objects as evidenced from literature throw much desired light on the subject.

The Section "The Pre-industrial Tradition" 'analyses the different metal working traditions, their geographical distribution, artisanal communities, the primary and secondary manufacturing zones, the traditional manufacturing techniques of some specific artefacts.' This caste - based tradition is helpful in many respects for the proper understanding of the archaeological data of copper and copper alloys. Here aspects of the primary smelting manufacture of artefacts, furnaces, image making traditions and ethnographic survey are all discussed in detail.

Concluding, the authors do accept that they are "not in a position to offer any stage wise and evolutionary delineation of the growth of copper metallurgy in the Indian subcontinent." They also aver that "the archaeological picture is too complex to be reduced to a clear-cut generalities .... the diversity which runs through the main spectrum of archaeological data and the pre-Industrial craft practices and yet sets up the subcontinent as a great and independent centre of copper-based metallurgical traditions."

It is significant to note from the authors that India did not import copper from outside. Copper had been worked in many mines from different parts of India excepting perhaps Tamilnadu which does not seem to produce any copper. The authors feel that it is not possible to postulate a "simplified evolutionry picture of the use of copper and copper alloys in India".

Those who have been following the writings of Chakrabarti as well as of Lahiri will find it an extension of their previous writings and approaches, particularly *The Archaeology of Indian Trade Routes* by Lahiri.

The book is well produced and moderately priced.

K.S. Ramachandran

Baldeo Sahai, *Indian Shipping: A Historical Survey,* Publications Division, Ministry of Information and Broadcasting, Government of India, 1996, pp. 372, Price: Rs.175.00

India has a very long coastline, nearly 6300 km, exclusive of the islands Lakshadweep and Andaman and Nicobar. The economic zone of India spreads over 2.2 million square km. From ancient times India, as its history shows, has been a nation of seafaring people. From the Indus-Saraswati period (3000 B.C.) we have masted ships sailing to Dilmun in the west, carrying long-distance trade, down to modern times when steam and diesel driven mammoth leviathans of iron carry merchandise to far off lands. Unfortunately, not many books have been published on this subject. However, two books are to mentioned : one R.K. Mookerji's *The History of Indian Shipping* and Rear Admiral Sridharan's *A Maritime History of India.* Now Baldeo Sahai has joined the elites by presenting a comprehensive history of Indian shipping from the earliest to modern times with an excellent foreword by Sir C.P. Srivastava, Secretary General Emeritues, International Maritime Organisation, U.N.

The book is divided into nine chapters. The first chapter deals with background such as geographical and topographical, the role of monsoonal winds, and shipping in the protohistoric period of the Indus-Saraswati Civilization; here the major port being Lothal in Gujarat. In the second chapter we hear of the relationship with the Akkadians, particularly Sargon of Akkad, and the Semites. We also know about the ports on the Mediterranean coast. Here Sahai equates Phoenicians with Panis of ancient India. The ships from this region reached Barbaricon at the mouth of the Indus, Barygaza (Bharuch) in Gujarat and Tyndis and Muziris on the west coast of India. Chapter III gives us a glimpse of the maritime activities during the Mauryan and post-Mauryan periods. The data are mainly based on Kautilya's *Arthasastra.* In this period we come to know of maritime ventures from the ports of Bengal, Orissa and south India from where ships sailed to the Far East spreading the message of the Buddha besides trade. Sahai also mentions the double-masted Satavahana ships sailing the seas to distant countries carrying articles of trade. The coins of the Satavahanas bear the figure of these sea-going ships.

During the succeeding periods, chaotic conditions prevailed and it was left to the Guptas and the Cholas to revive the maritime glory of India. Guptas maintained a powerful navy. So also the Cholas. The Great Raja Raja I fought many naval battles as evidenced by his titles *Kandalur Salai Kalamaruttarulia* (victorious at the naval battle at Kandalur Salai) *alai kadal naduvil pala kalam chelutiya* (who had sailed several ships on the high seas). Raja Raja subdued the Sailendras of Srivijaya in the Far East with the help of his powerful navy. His son RajendraI conquered Kadaram *(Kadaram Kondan),* the modern Keddah.

In the successive three chapters, V to VII, Sahai tells us about the coming of the Europeans, the Portugese domination of the western sea and their conflict with the Marathas. After them came the Dutch, French and the English. He deals in detail the Indian naval decline and the western domination of the seas.

Chapter VIII informs us all about the ship-building, instruments, materials, etc. used in the ships for navigation right from the Vedic to modern times. The final chapter is about the status of ships and ship-building after Independence.

This is an exhaustive study of Indian shipping in all its aspects. The author has been meticulous in gathering information and presenting the same in a cogent manner and in a readable style.

Baldeo Sahai's book is a welcome addition to this aspect of History of Indian Science and Technology.

K.S. Ramachandran

A.K. Sharma, *Emergence of Early Culture in North-East India,* Aryan Books International, pp. 95, plates LV, Price: Rs.800/-

Garo Hills, part of present day Meghalaya, has yielded numerous Stone Age artefacts, particularly of the Neolithic affiliation. Post-Independence years have added much information to the meagre pre-Independence findings. However, the major work of the British period was anthropological-social and cultural mainly dealing with customs and manners and life style of the tribes. Only after 1947, especially after the setting up of archaeological departments and museums in the north-eastern region, in Assam, Manipur, etc. archaeological investigations started in right earnest ; and in this Assam led the way.

In Meghalaya (western Garo-hills region) about which the present book deals, excepting for sporadic finds of stray pottery, terracotta and sculptures by enthusiastic amateurs, no regular exploration or excavations were conducted, till Sharma excavated in 1992, the site of Vadagkugiri (Bhaitbari) situated on the river Jinjirama, flowing on an old bed of Brahmaputra and 8 km west of Phulbari on the Phulbari - Tura road. The results of this excavation have been projected back to formulate the cultural beginnings of the entire Meghalaya.

Bhaitbari is a fortified town of about 20 sq. km. in area. The fortification is an irregular polygon following the natural contours and is made up of earth with brick revetment on the outer face. A deep moat surrounded the fort. A road ran along the fort walls on the inner side. The fort itself was repaired and its height raised three times (three periods); correspondingly the brick revetment too was raised. The road also was relaid over the existing ones in these periods. A gateway was found on the southern side. No datable evidence was obtained from the cuttings across the rampart.

Inside the rampart notable discovery was a *stupa* and several tanks and temples. Several mounds remain unexcavated. Of the notable excavated remains are the *stupa* and an octogonal Siva Temple, all of them of medieval times. The Siva temple is interesting with eight *garbhagrihas* in eight directions with attached *mandapas* and a later addition of a platform on the exterior of each of the *mandapa.* Digging beneath the *stupa* revealed habitational deposits yielding handmade grey ware pottery mostly of kaolin and decorated with stamped ornamental design, red and grey wares the whole deposit divisible into three periods. Middle level shapes in red ware were vases and bowls besides grey and buff wares. Lower level shapes were *lotas,* bowls, cups-on-stand, etc. Some seals and lids were also found. No writings was found on the seals. Of the other finds included a number of terracotta sculptured plaques which on stylistic grounds belong to the Pala-Sena period and beads of semiprecious stones.

The book carries an important chapter on conservation besides the usual ones to be found in an excavation report.

As this is the first ever report on a first ever excavation conducted in Meghalaya, the author deserves commendation. The book has been beautifully produced is well illustrated with photographs and a few line drawings. but the price is also comparatively very high.

K.S. Ramachandran

P.K. Trivedi, *Art Traditions of the Paramaras of Vagada,* Publication Scheme, Jaipur, 1995 pp. xxxiv + 340, Plates 156; Figures 20, Price: Rs :1800/-.

On the eve of the Muslim rule in Delhi and during the last phase of Buddhism in Gujarat, U.P., Madhya Pradesh, i.e. during the 11th and 12th centuries, northern India was practically littered with Hindu temples under the Imperial Paramaras of Dhar, the Chandellas of Khajuraho, the Gahadavalas of Kannauj, the Solankis of Gujarat, etc. They developed the *Nagara* style of temple architecture to great heights. In this context, what is significant to note is the fact that it was not the imperial rulers themselves who always financed the construction of these temples, their subordinates, including the collaterals, supported activities to a great extent. The Paramaras of Vagada, located on the borders of Malwa and Gujarat, with a dynasty of seven local rulers, did exactly the same - they supported the erection of some two dozen Saiva, Vaishnava and Jain temples, including one for the 64 Yoginis, at Arthuna, Baroda, Panaheda and Talwara. The most elaborately carved ones are Madalesvara of Panaheda and Nilkantha Mahadeva, both belonging to the 11th century. The former (A.D 1059) is the earliest dated *Nagara* style temple with *Bhumija* Sikhara in India, similar in design to the more widely known one, called Udayesvara, of this style erected by the Imperial Paramar ruler Udayaditya.

The book is the most detailed work on a group of very important templs so far generally neglected by scholars. With hundreds of photographs and line drawings it has been visually enriched, although the photographs needed better art paper and printing.

The book's greatest asset is the full use of correct terminology for icons and temple architecture contained in *Silpa* texts. The book has for the first time identified particular *devakanyas, surasundaris,* etc. which profusely embellish the surface of the temples. Anyone interested in deep and detailed study of early medieval north Indian temples at micro level will find this a most useful book.

S.P. Gupta

Devangana Desai, *The Religious Imagery of Khajuraho,* Franco-Indian Research Pvt. Ltd., 20, Dr. E.Moses Road, Mumbai - 400 011, Foreword by Michel Postel, pp xxx + 269, 18 figures 224 photographs 18 drawings and one map

This volume by Dr. Devangana Desai, one of the foremost and authoritative exponents of Khajuraho art, architecture and symbolism, is indeed the pick among art books of the decade; for it is not only visually and aesthetically pleasing but supremely satisfying on account of its perceptive insights in the profound religious symbolism of the temple-art which had, so far, attracted all and sundry by the erotica it contained.

Writing about architecture in his book '*Significance of Indian Art*', the scholar-saint, Sri Aurobindo had mentioned (page 33) "Indian temple, to whatever godhead it may be built, is in its innermost reality an altar raised to the divine Self, a house of Cosmic Spirit, an appeal and aspiration to the Infinite. As that and in the light of that seeing and conception it must in the first place be understood, and everything else must be seen in that setting and that light, and then only can there be any understanding". With a thorough going approach, the author has studied indepth the architecture, iconology, iconography and art of Khajuraho together with *vastusastra* norms, and relevant religious cults, history, chronology, patronage, religious currents, and parallels from other centres of temple art. The secret and sacred meaning of the Khajuraho temple art is brought out here clearly and in a lucid manner so that both the scholar and the average intelligent reader will derive an inner delight which he had missed so far.

The volume does not deal with the entire range of temples of Khajuraho, the author has selected for indepth study, the Lakshmana temple (A.D. 950-970), dedicated to Vishnu-Vaikuntha and the Kandaria Mahadeva (A.D. 1030), dedicated to Siva which together constitute, by far, the finest achievement of the Khajuraho architect demonstrating the superb harmony of architecture and sculpture with a unique sense of rhythm in their architecture-profile enlivened with a sculptural scheme in which the author has perceived a deeper significance. Earlier in 1995, in her first book, '*Erotic sculpture of India - A Socio-cultural Study*', her approach was essentially sociological. In 1981 when she was preparing her paper for the symposium 'Discourses on Siva', she was struck by the planned and well integrated placement of the images, the erotic motifs placed on the *kapili* wall portion joining the hall and the *sanctum* of the Lakshmana temple to convey metaphorically something beyond the erotic. The erotic sculptures were, according to her, meant to convey puns and double meaning and in order to explain this further there is a separate chapter dealing with "Puns and Enigmatic language in sculpture". In this, she refers to the drama *Prabodhachandrodaya* of Krishna Mishra staged to celebrate the victory of the Chandella King, Kirtivarman, over his Chedi rival in about A.D. 1065. This theme, among others, is liable to interpretation at different levels and allegorically refers to the combat between the forces of the Chedi ruler, who is likened to Delusion, and the Chandella General, who fought him is called Discrimination (Viveka). Attention of readers is drawn to other literary works like the Jain novel *Upamitibhava prapanchakatha* which helps explain the significance of the name of the temple town, Khajuraho. The author explains that *Kharjura-vahaka,* the ancient name has double meaning, carrier *(Vahaka)* of date-palm *(Kharjura tree). Kharjura* also means a scorpion and *Kharjura-vahaka* would thus mean "Scorpion bearer". The latter interpretation is derived from the description contained in *Aparajitaprichha* (212 :15) and the *Rupamandana* (IV, 6) and thus *Kharjura-vahaka* would mean Siva in his Aghora (fierce) aspect. Many *surasundari* images on the temple walls of Khajuraho with scorpion on their legs exposing themselves on the pretext of removing the scorpion also become *Kharjura-vahaka* in a way. The author also explains the pun on Adinatha ,the first tirthankara of the Jains, appearing apparently without any reason, on Devi Jagadamba temple as suggesting 'Siva-Digambara'. The author further refers to two images of Sadasiva (frontispiece and Plates 6 and 57) having six visible heads topped by linga, twelve arms and four legs - *Chatushpadas,* the last mentioned feature signifying the fourfold *padas* viz. *Jnana-pada, Charya pada, Kriya-pada* and *Yoga-pada.* This is thus a pun on the *pada* which has the double meaning of feet and divisions.

This sumptuous volume *"The Religious Imagery of Khajuraho"* is thus remarkable in many ways and I can only describe it as a very extraordinary and thought-provoking work for understanding the inner significance of India's sacred art which had been misunderstood and misinterpreted, so far, by many Indian and foreign scholars.

The book has been copiously and tastefully illustrated with coloured illustrations and is an intellectual, aesthetic and delightful treat. The printing and format also are impeccable and deserve unstinted praise.

M.N. Deshpande

Michel Danino and Sujata Nahar, *The Invasion that Never Was* Mira Aditi Centre, Mysore, 1996, pp. 128. Price : Not mentioned.

This small book - just 128 pages - divided into two parts, is a repetition of the Biblical story of slaying the mighty Goliath by the puny David; for the theory of Aryan Invasion advanced by the redoubtable Max Mueller and fostered by Griffith, Monier Williams, Keith, Wilson and a host of others is indeed hard to kill: it is still found in our text books. Michel Danino has killed the giant with his mathematically precise lucid arguments based not only on the views of renowned persons like Swami Dayanand, Swami Vivekananda, Sri Aurobindo but also from the concrete and irrefutable archaeological evidence. The author has given charitably not only a decent burial to this theory, but also laid its ghost to rest once and for all. The book is most readable, enjoyable and thought provoking Sir Mortimer had declared - Indra stands accused; Danino has proved that Indra was after all a native and innocent of any crime.

The second part of the book is an exposition of the well known *Gayatri Mantra* in the most eloquent way possible. A reading of her beautiful, clear and brief explanation of this famous *mantra* at once brings forth the full import and potency of Vedic hymns.

S.Ganesh Rao

N.L. Batra, *Heritage Conservation: Preservation and Restoraion of Monuments,* Aryan Books International, New Delhi, 1996, pp.267, Figures 40, Plates 24, Price: 1600/-

The book, which was a long felt need, is an attempt at dealing with different problems of conservation. The principles of conservation followed by the Archaeological Survey of India (A.S.I.) are based on the *Conservation Manual* of John Marshall (1922) which outlines the principles of conserving monuments from decay and saving them for posterity. The Science Branch of the A.S.I. equally helps in preserving them with the aid of suitable chemicals and also suggests measure for air pollution control.

Divided into eleven chapters with a bibliography and an index specific problems of conservation in Indian context have been discussed in this book. Chapter I deals with the history of conservation, whereas chapter II the concept of conservation, embodies two Venice International charters (1964) and the Burra charter. The third chapter tells us about salvaging, transplantation and reconstruction of ancient structures . Besides it also includes problems of environmental developments in the urban areas. In the next chapter, a methodological study of monuments with sixteen appendices on the development of monuments of the Ajanta - Ellora, monuments in Gwalior regions, in Bilaspur District, Dhamner caves, District Mandsaur, Khajurho temples, Amarkantak temples, Udaigiri caves, Saru-Maru monastic complex, Mandu monuments, Bagh caves, Sanchi, Satdhara all have been discussed. Chapter V deals with types of buildings, whereas chapter VI discusses the causes of decay and techniques of conservation. The next chapter deals with mortars used in ancient buildings. Chapters VIII, IX and X are concerned with the foundation of ancient structures, preservation of excavated sites and remains and technical terms used in conservation. The final chapter is devoted to the problems of estimating and assesing cost involved in carrying out a specific work.

Though the author has tried to give a detailed treatment of problem he is silent on the execution part. It is hoped that in the next edition he will include a few other examples of works from different parts of the country so that an overall picture of works done is presented. The book on the whole is informative, useful to all archaeological conservationists in India.

K.N.Dikshit

Arundhati Banerji, *Early Indian Terracotta Art: Northern and Western India (2000 B.C. - 300 B.C.),* Harman Publishing House, New Delhi; 1994, pp. xxx + 244. Plates 102, Figs XXI. Price: Rs.800/-.

The book deals with a very difficult subject because the material is scattered over hundreds of publications; some of them dating back to more than 100 years. Moreover, scholars in the past generally dealt with it sometimes very casually or at great length. At times the subject was deemed as pottery as if these are archaeological specimens the sole purpose of which was to date the strata. On some occassions this was seen as works of art to be appreciated primarily for their aesthetic quality.

Dr. Banerji, however, rightly felt that we have to combine both the approaches in order to evaluate the art of protohistoric terracotta. It is this framework which has made this work outstanding.

Chapter I of the book deals with not only the basic issues involved in the study but also the position of the art of terracotta figurines, largely of the 'mother gddesses', from Mehrgarh, Quetta, Amri, Kulli, etc. which were of pre-Harappan and Harappan times. She has also taken into acount the human and animal figurines from the Mature Harappan sites of Harappa, Mohenjodaro, Kalibangan, Lothal, etc. However, her main concern has been the art of terracotta of the post-Harappan Chalcolithic Cultures and the early Iron Age cultures. Therefore, Chapters 2,3 and 4 deal with the terracottas found at the archaeological sites of Loebanr, Pirak, Sibri, Mahorana, Hulas, Lal Qila, Prakash, Dangwada, Kayatha, Nagda, Nevasa, Ahar, Daimabad, Inamgaon, Aligrama, Bhagwanpura, Atranjikhera, Jakhera, Hastinapura, Rajghat, Mathura, Kausambi, Ayodhya, etc.

The author has been able to show whether these are male figures or female figures or the figures of animals and birds, there are definite patterns belonging to different periods, and the patterns are based upon basic concepts of male and female principles as well as the styles and idioms. There are, however, regional variations as also site preferences. Thus, northern Baluchistan, southern Baluchistan, Punjab and Haryana, Uttar Pradesh, and Madhya Pradesh do exhibit, throughout history, their individual characteristics in terms of regionalism. Styles and idioms also change but largely along the lines of material cultures. There are many other facets of her study.

We recommend this work for all archaeologists and art historians although, as in many examples, the publisher has used poor quality of art paper, virtually killing the aesthetic aspect of the beautiful works of art.

S.P. Gupta

Wahengbam Yumjao Singh,. *Archaic Meitei or Early Manipuri,* W. Gourchandra Singh, Imphal, 1985; pp. XIV + 112; Price:Rs.120/-.

Many books see the light of day as soon as they are written; some take a long time. A few take not only a long time but also have the distinction of being published posthumously. This book belongs to the last category. It owes much to the indefatigable efforts and perseverance of the author's son, W.Gourchandra Singh.

Embarking on a book of grammar of a language in use is a hazardous task; more so when the language is archaic like early Manipuri. Undaunted, the author has dealt with the subject, displaying consummate mastery over it. The presence of economy and precision and total absence of prolixity and pedantry is praiseworthy. The book is in four chapters and is complete in 112 pages.

Passing from its history he takes on to grammar. How pleasant it is to learn that the parts of speech are only five: noun, pronoun and adjective, verb and adverb - no gerund and no participiple and hence nothing to confound and confuse the reader! He gives an entire chapter of examples to serve as guides to the parts of speech. Further, the fourth and last chapter enriches the reader with vocabulary.

We close the book with a feeling of sorrow; that such a lovely and melodious language is not much in vogue.

At a price of Rs.120/- the book is a good buy; those who have a taste and gift for languages, especially early ones, shall find it most absorbing.

S.Ganesh Rao

INDIAN ARCHAEOLOGICAL SOCIETY

INCOME AND EXPENDITURE ACCOUNT FOR THE YEAR ENDED 31.03.1995

Expenditue	Amount	Income	Amount
To Honorarium	51,675.00	By Grant in aid received from I.C.H.R.	14,250.00
To Ground Rent paid to D.D.A.	23,000.00	By Institutional Fees	2,500.00
To Puratattva	37,786.00	By Membership Fees	890.00
To Travelling Expenses	3,088.00	By Delegation Fees	3,900.00
To Electricity & Water charges	3,357.00	By Sale of Publication	10,820.00
To Conveyance charges	14,592.10	By Service Charges	2,500.00
To Conference Expenses	8,900.00	By Bank Interest	1,02,714.00
To Audit Fees	5,750.00	By Excess of Expenditure over Income	1,28,212.45
To Printing & Stationery	11,423.15		
To Municipal Taxes	66,687.00		
To World Archaeology Conference	9,000.00		
To Awards	22,000.00		
To Refreshment	558.90		
To Freight & Cartage	120.00		
To Bank Charges	123.00		
To Postage	3,148.50		
To Misc. Expenses	2,386.00		
To Accounting Charges	300.00		
To Books & Periodicals	1,341.80		
To Professional Charges	550.00		
Total	2,65,786.45	Total	2,65,786.45

GENERAL SECRETARY

TREASURER

For Rajan Sharma & Co.
Chartered Accountants

Sd/-

Place : New Delhi
Dated : 06.09.1995

(RAJAN KUMAR SHARMA)
Proprietor

OFFICE BEARERS OF THE INDIAN ARCHAEOLOGICAL SOCIETY

Headquarters:
INDIAN ARCHAEOLOGICAL SOCIETY
B-17, Institutional Area, Mehrauli, New Delhi-110 016
Office: 6960654
Tel: S.P. Gupta/Shashi Asthana-3388067
K.N. Diskhit-6948971

Plate-I. Sankisa: A 1, QD. 4 – Floor with post-holes NBPW period (B.R. Mani).

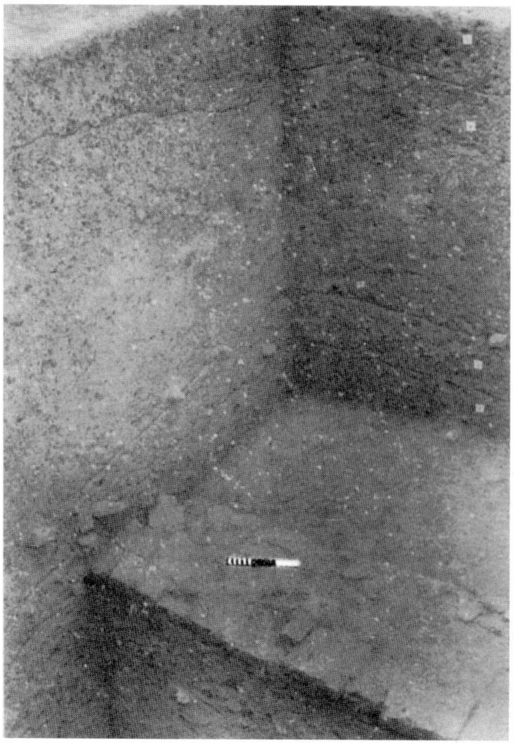

Plate-II. Sankisa: E 10, QD. 3 – Kushan Brick wall (B.R. Mani).

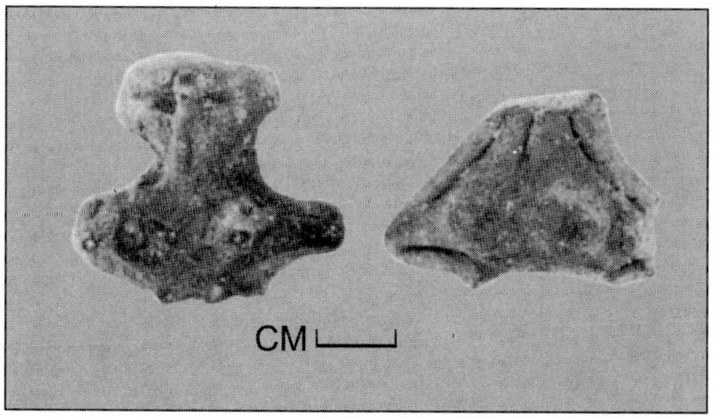

Plate-III. Sankisa: Terracotta female figurines from PGW levels (B.R. Mani).

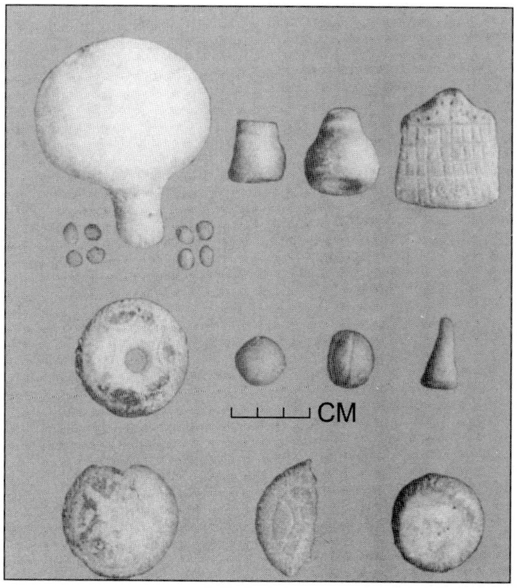

Plate-IV. Sankisa: Terracotta objects from PGW levels (B.R. Mani).

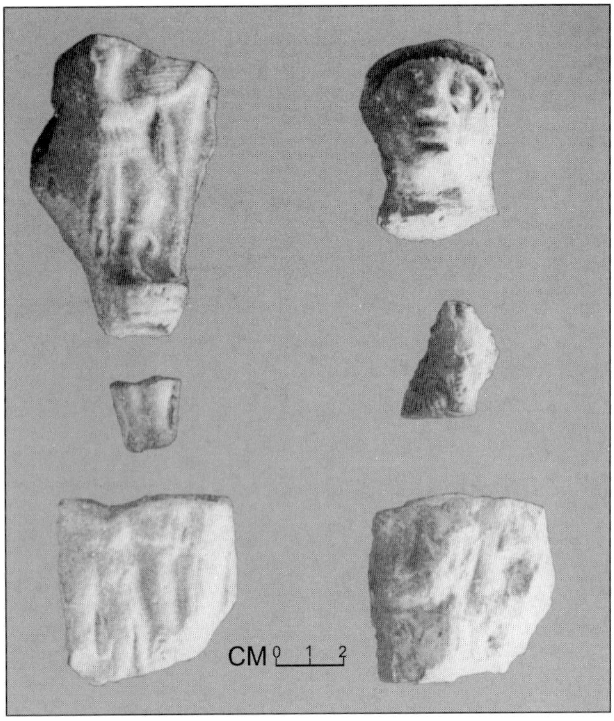

Plate-V. Sankisa: Terracotta human figurines, Suṅga period (B.R. Mani).

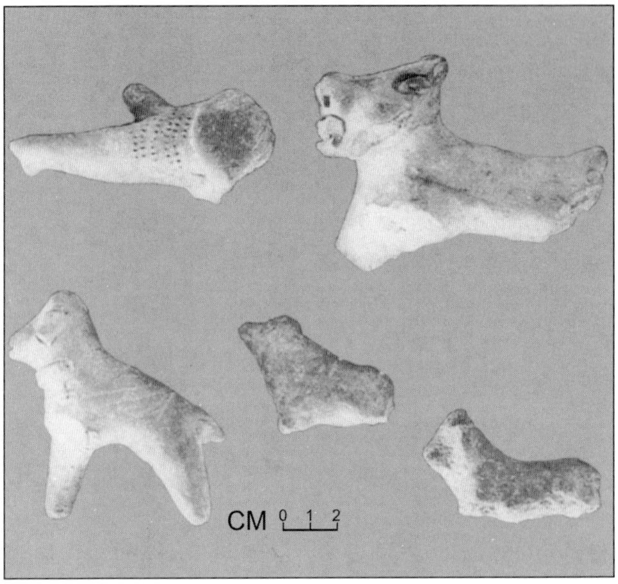

Plate-VI. Sankisa: Terracotta animal figurines, NBPW and Suṅga-kuṣāṇa levels (B.R. Mani).

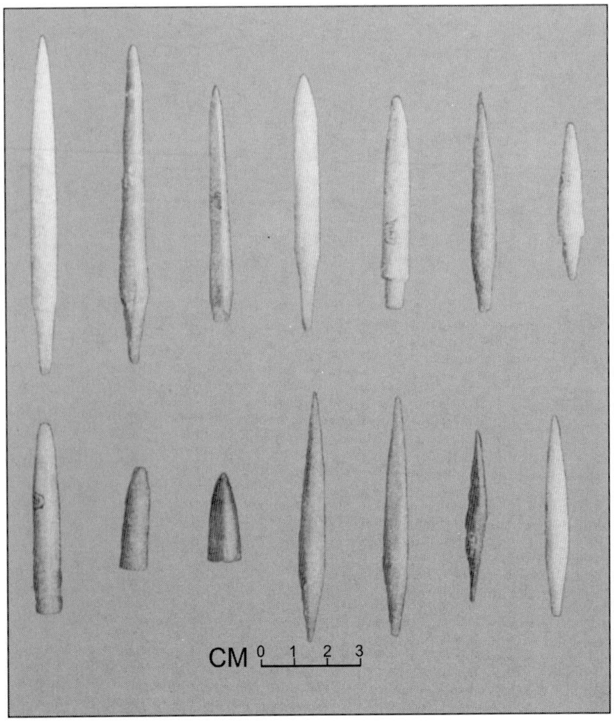

Plate-VII. Sankisa: Bone points and arrowheads, NBPW period (B.R. Mani).

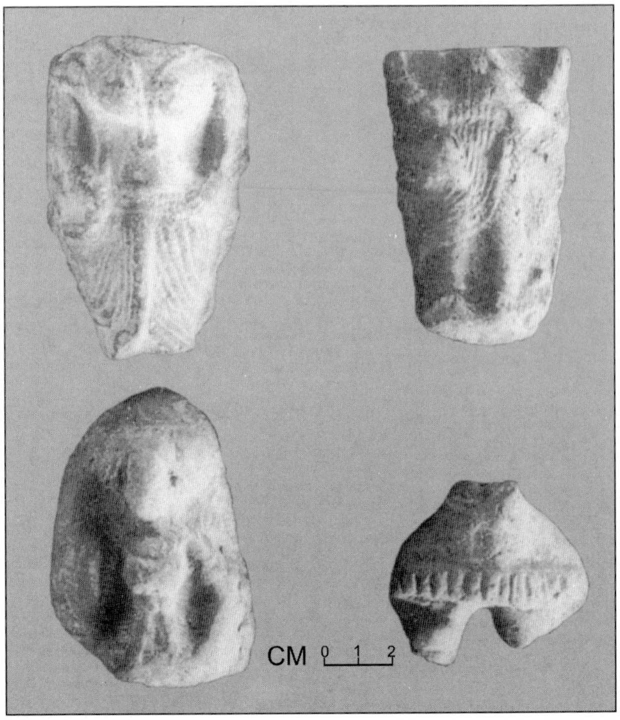

Plate-VIII. Sankisa: Terracotta female figurines, Maurya-Suṅga period (B.R. Mani).

Plate-IX. Sankisa: Terracotta human figurines, Suṅga period (B.R. Mani).

Plate-X. Sankisa: Terracotta female figurines, Suṅga period (B.R. Mani).

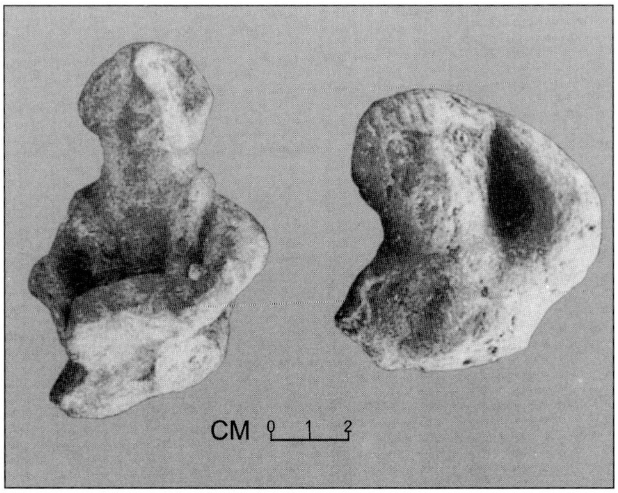

Plate-XI. Sankisa: Terracotta figurines, Kuṣāṇa period (B.R. Mani).

Plate-I. Taj Mahal : Marble facing of Dome (P.B.S. Sengar).

Plate-II. Taj Mahal : Trial pits along the outer wall (P.B.S. Sengar).

Plate-III. Taj Mahal : A series of foundation wells supporting the weight of Mausoleum (P.B.S. Sengar).

Plate-IV. Taj Mahal : Two spurs were constructed to deflect the River (P.B.S. Sengar).

Plate-I. Stone Tools : Tansa Valley (A.K. Sharma).

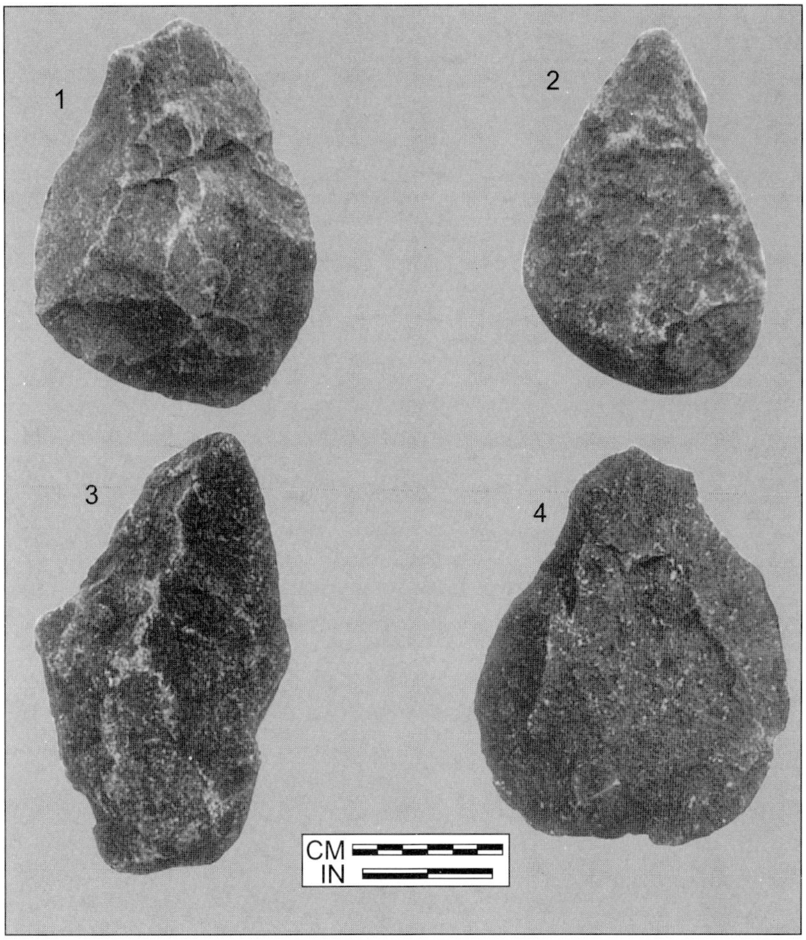

Plate-II. Hand Axes : Tansa Valley (A.K. Sharma).

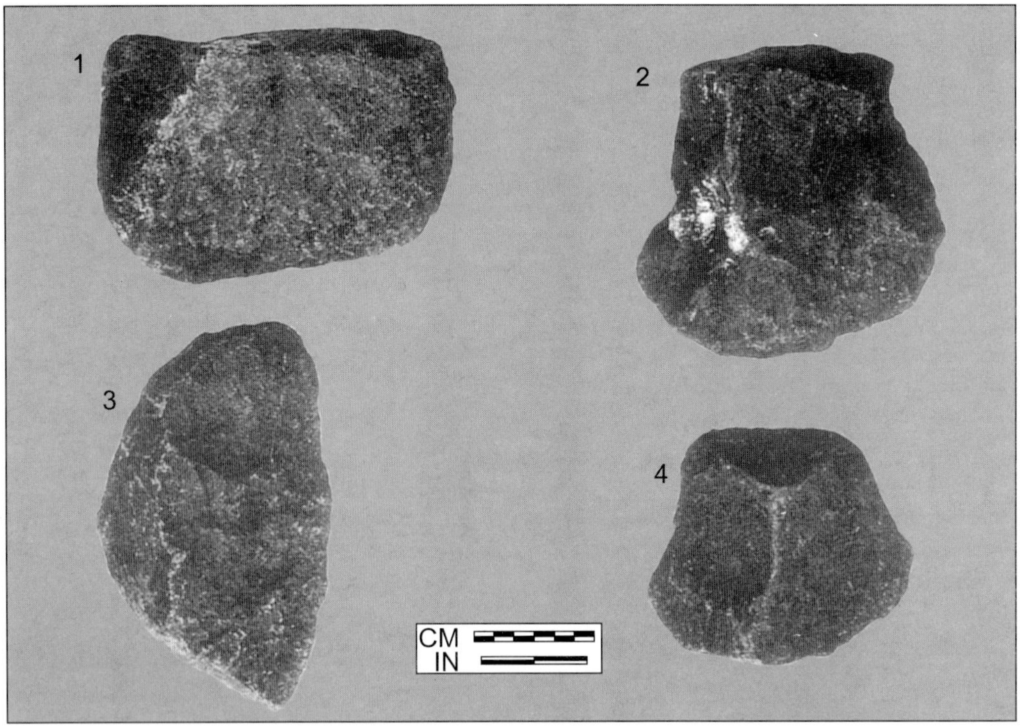

Plate-III. Cleavers and Scraper Tansa Valley (A.K. Sharma).

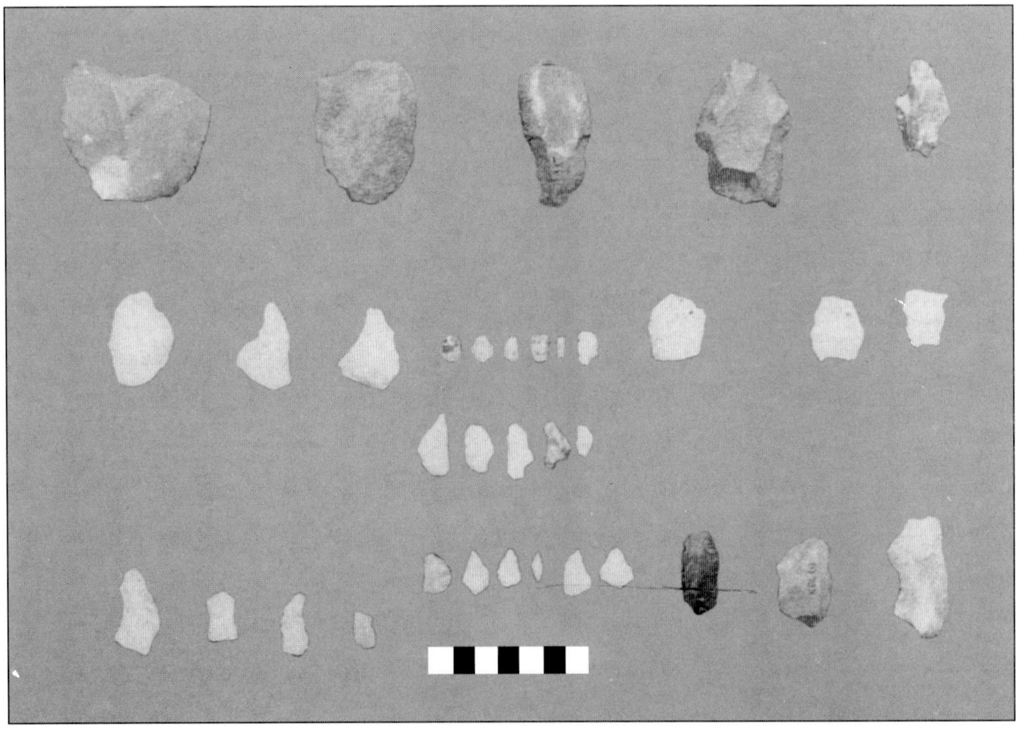

Fig. 2. Microliths from Kirandul : Upper Ros Tools on Iron ore (Alok Rath)

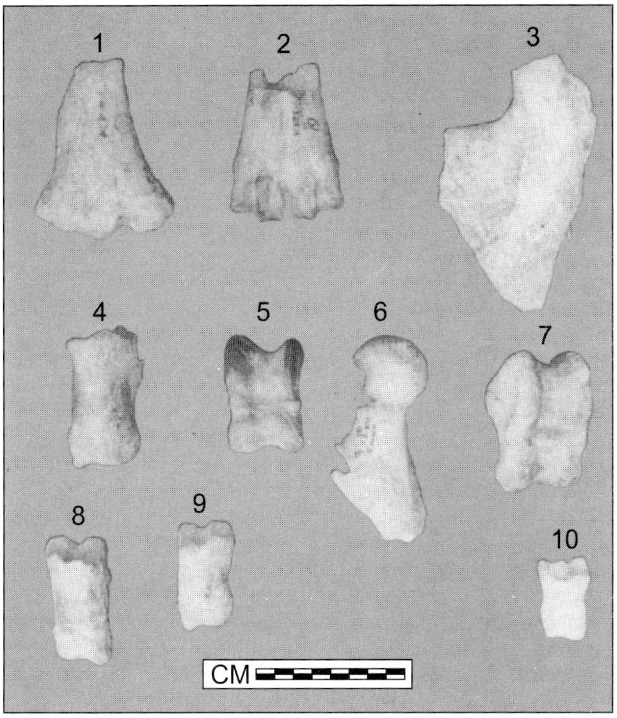

Plate-I. Bones of Cattle-
Period I - 1, 2, 8 and 9
Period II - 3, 4, 7 and 10
Period III - 5 and 6 (A.K. Sharma).

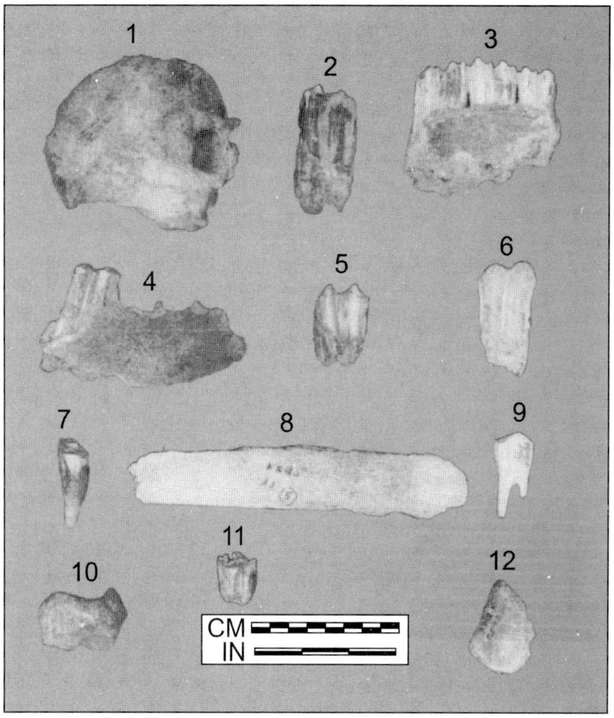

Plate-II. Bones of Cattle-
Period I - 3, 7, 8 and 11
Period II - 5, 6, 9 and 10
Period III - 1, 2, 4 and 12 (A.K. Sharma).

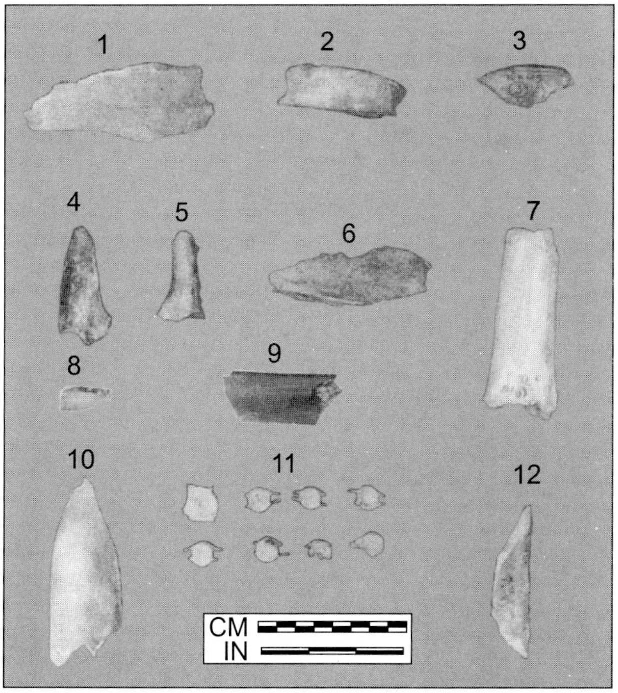

Plate-III. Cut marks and tools-1-10 and 12
Fish Vertebrae-11 (A.K. Sharma).

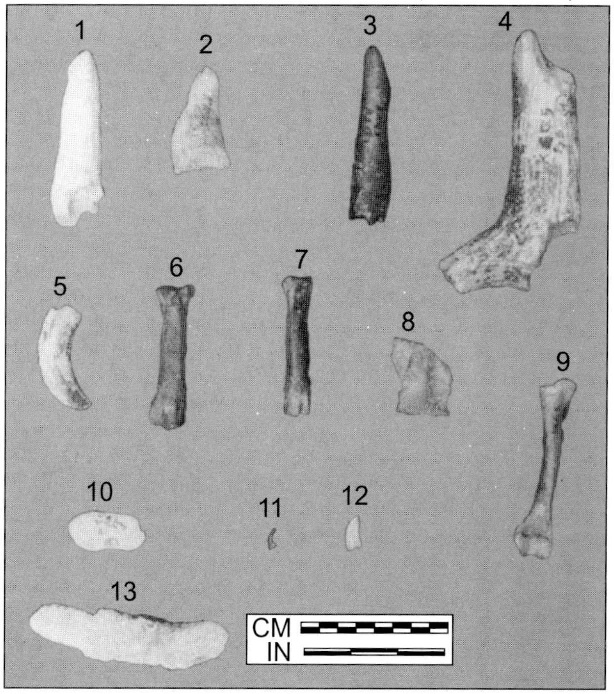

Plate-IV. Period I-Deer-3, Sheep and Goat-2, Equus-5, 6, 7 and 8, Rodents-11 and 12, Pig-13, Dog-9, Period II. Deer-1 and 4, Fresh water muscle-10 (A.K. Sharma).

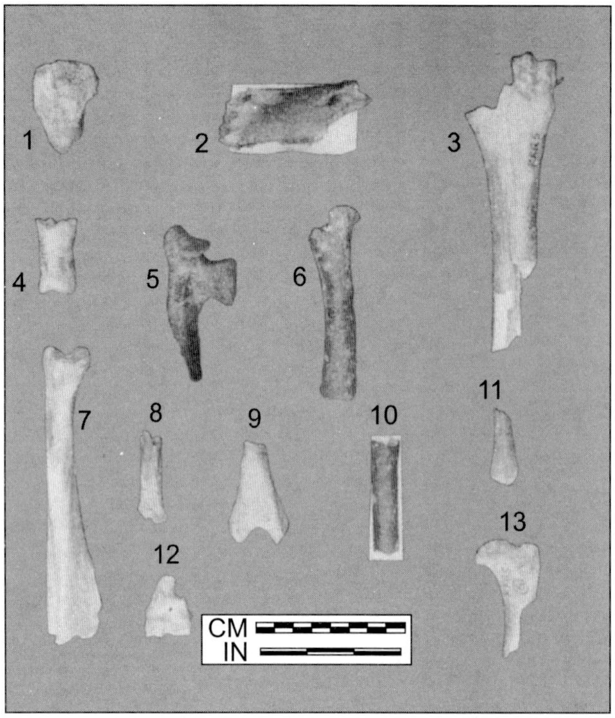

Plate-V. Period I - Deer - 1,2,3,4,5 and 6
Sheep and Goat - 8 and 11
Period II. Sheep and Goat - 9, Dog - 12
Charred shaf with teeth marks - 10
(A.K. Sharma).

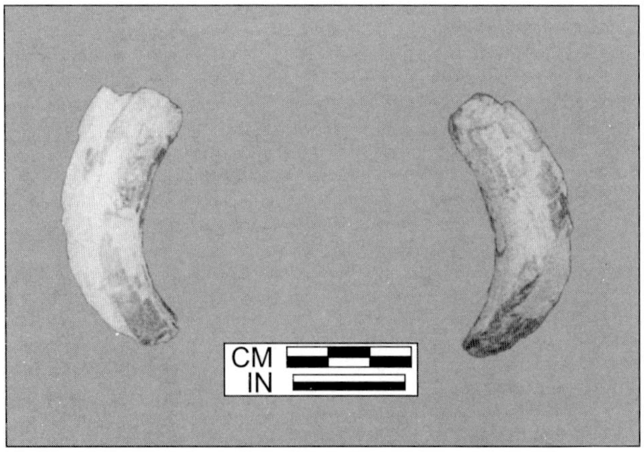

Plate-VI. Equus Canine from Period I - Charred with rubbing marks (A.K. Sharma).

Vajrasattra Kashmir, 10th-11th century A.D. (Jitendra Nath).

New Megalithic in Chittor District (Jitendra Nath).

No I. Anthropomaorphic figures Kumati; Tk: Kudligi, Dist: Bellary, Karnataka.General view from North-East (K.P. Poonacha).

No II. Anthropomorphic figure Kumati, Tk: Kudligi, Dist: Bellary, Karnataka close up from East (K.P. Poonacha).